Social Working

Exercises in Generalist Practice

Second Edition

Social Working

Exercises in Generalist Practice
Second Edition

Phyllis J. Day

Sandra M. Shelly
Indiana University

Harry J. Macy
Ball State University

Allyn and Bacon
Boston • London • Toronto • Sydney • Toyko • Singapore

Senior Series Editor: Judy Fifer
Editor-in-Chief, Social Sciences: Karen Hanson
Series Editorial Assistant: Julianna M. Cancio
Marketing Manager: Jackie Aaron
Electronic Composition: Modern Graphics, Inc.
Manufacturing Buyer: Julie McNeill
Cover Administrator: Jenny Hart
Composition and Prepress Buyer: Linda Cox
Editorial-Production Service: Modern Graphics, Inc.

Library of Congress Cataloging-in-Publication Data

Day, Phyllis J.
    Social working : exercises in generalist practice / Phyllis J. Day, Sandra M. Shelly.-- 2nd ed.
        p. cm.
    Includes bibliographical references and index.
    ISBN 0-205-29131-7
    1. Social work education.   2. Social case work--Moral and ethical aspects.   I. Shelly, Sandra M. II. Title.

HV11 .D384 1999
361.3--dc21

                                                                                99-046797

Printed in the United States of America

10 9 8 7 6 5 4 3 2 1   04 03 02 01 00 99

*To all our students,
from whom we have learned so much*

Contents

Preface   xi

Section ONE   **Introduction to Social Working**   **1**

Chapter ONE   **Problem Solving and Generalist Practice**   **3**

Purpose and Objectives   **3**
The Guided Problem Solving Method: Demystifying the Jargon   **4**
Problem Identification   **6**
Exercise 1.1 Pick a Problem   *6*
Exercise 1.2 Who Are the Clients?   *7*
Exercise 1.3 Behavioral Specification   *9*
Exercise 1.4 Partializing the Problem   *10*
Guided Problem Solving   **11**
Exercise 1.5 For Fun: Writing Limericks for Fun, Profit, and Better Grades   *13*
Exercise 1.6 For Real: Learning Guided Problem Solving   *19*
Portfolio Building   **25**
Summary   **26**

Chapter TWO   **Theoretical Perspectives for Generalist Practice**   **27**

The Strengths/Empowerment/Social Justice Perspective   **27**
Exercise 2.1 How We Look at Clients   *28*
Exercise 2.2 Looking at the Strengths/Empowerment Perspective   *30*
Exercise 2.3 The Empowerment Process   *32*
Exercise 2.4 Action for Social Justice   *32*
The Ecological/Systems Perspective   **42**
Exercise 2.5 Your Own Dyadic System   *43*
Exercise 2.6 Walking Through Your Agency's Systems   *46*
Exercise 2.7 Newcomers   *48*
Portfolio Building   **50**
Summary   **51**

Chapter THREE   **The Internal Process of Problem Solving: Values and Ethics**   **52**

The Importance of Values   **52**
Societal Values and Latent Functions   **52**
Exercise 3.1 American Values   *53*
Exercise 3.2 The Latent Functions of "Isms"   *54*

Exercise 3.3 Pick a Problem   56
Values Awareness   57
Exercise 3.4 We Are Heterosexist Because . . .   57
Exercise 3.5 But My Folks Told Me That . . .   57
Values Conflict in Social Work   60
Exercise 3.6 The Other Side of Battering   60
Exercise 3.7 Helping Clients Help Themselves   61
The Social Control Issue   62
Exercise 3.8 Losing Power   62
Exercise 3.9 Advocacy against Values   63
Exercise 3.10 If I Woke Up Gay Tomorrow   66
Exercise 3.11 The Teenage Pregnancy   67
Exercise 3.12 Values in "The Teenage Pregnancy"   79
Exercise 3.13 Ethical Dilemas and Issues in General   79
Exercise 3.14 Who Makes the Decision?   80
NASW's Code of Ethics and Empowerment Practice   82
Exercise 3.15 Definitions of Core Values   82
Exercise 3.16 The Dirty Home   83
Exercise 3.17 Coin of Payment   84
Portfolio Building   85

Chapter FOUR   Levels of Generalist Practice   86

Simultaneous Practice across Levels   86
Exercise 4.1 Now What Do I Do?   88
Exercise 4.2 Working across Levels   89
Exercise 4.3 The Abused Spouse   90
Problem Solving and Practice Levels   101
Exercise 4.4 Relevant Constituencies   101
Exercise 4.5 Hoop Dreams   102
Looking at the Levels   106
Portfolio Building   106

Section TWO   Micro Practice with Individuals, Groups, and Families   107

Chapter FIVE   Working with the Individual Client   109

Exercise 5.1 Who Can We Trust?   109
Exercise 5.2 Who Can We Tell?   110
Relational Skills   111
Exercise 5.3 Kicked Out by the Computer   112
Exercise 5.4 The Roommate Problem   113
Exercise 5.5 The Vanishing Lover   114
Cognitive Skills   114
Exercise 5.6 Cognitive Exercises   116
Social Diagnosis: The Art of Social Assessment   117
Exercise 5.7 Intake Interview Scenario: Introducing Don Duguid   118
Exercise 5.8 Cognitive Tasks and Goals   131
Exercise 5.9 Writing the Social Assessment   140
Portfolio Building   144
Looking Ahead   145

Chapter SIX   Social Work with Small Groups   146

What Is Small Group Practice?   146

Dynamics of the Treatment Group   **147**
Phases of the Group   **148**
Exercise 6.1 Writing a Pre-Planning Design   *149*
Exercise 6.2 Pre-Planning: Families with a Future   *151*
Exercise 6.3 Planning a Growth Group   *152*
Exercise 6.4 Planning an Independent Living Program   *154*
Exercise 6.5 Why Me? Mothers with HIV/AIDS: Group Formation   *155*
Leadership Processes   **156**
Exercise 6.6 The Work Phase in Group Work: A Role Play—Not with My Daughter . . .   *157*
Exercise 6.7 Out of the Nest: Terminating a Treatment Group   *158*
Exercise 6.8 Role Play: A Celebration of Life   *158*
Exercise 6.9 Facilitating the Sloan House Independent Living Program   *159*
Dynamics of the Task Group   **168**
Exercise 6.10 My Own Task Groups   *168*
Exercise 6.11 Planning a Task Group   *169*
Leadership in the Task Group   **171**
Exercise 6.12 Lay Persons Developing Client Programs   *171*
Exercise 6.13 Leadership in Conflict   *172*
Exercise 6.14 Evaluating the Sloan House ILP   *172*
Portfolio Building   **182**
Looking Ahead   **183**

Section THREE   Mezzo and Macro Practice Levels   185

Chapter SEVEN   Working in Organizations   187

The Social Work Organization   **187**
Exercise 7.1 Commitment to Children   *188*
Exercise 7.2 Know Your Organization   *190*
Organizational Structure, Processes, and Culture   **192**
Exercise 7.3 Your Organization's Structure   *192*
Exercise 7.4 The Organization's Timeline   *192*
Exercise 7.5 Your Agency's Culture   *193*
Exercise 7.6 Money Is Power   *194*
Exercise 7.7 The Hierarchical Element   *194*
Exercise 7.8 The Organizational Theory Game Show   *194*
The Worker in the Organization   **196**
Exercise 7.9 The Dying Patient   *196*
Exercise 7.10 Establishing a Training Program on Death and Dying   *206*
The Power of Communication   **208**
Exercise 7.11 The Program Proposal   *210*
Exercise 7.12 Writing a Memo   *211*
Exercise 7.13 Why Did She Answer "It's Harry's Fault" When I Asked If She Liked Blueberry Pie?   *211*
Exercise 7.14 Classroom as Organization: The Executive Search   *224*
Exercise 7.15 Classroom as Organization: The Audit   *224*
Portfolio Building   **226**
Moving On Up: What's Next?   **227**

Chapter EIGHT   Mobilizing Resources: The Community   229

Community Practice   **229**
What Is Community?   **229**

Exercise 8.1 The Functions of Community *230*
Exercise 8.2 The Ecology of Public Assistance *232*
Exercise 8.3 Your Field Agency Network *233*
Exercise 8.4 Coordination of Resources *233*
Needs Assessments **234**
Exercise 8.5 Assessing Client Needs in Your Community *235*
Exercise 8.6 Preparing a Needs Assessment: Why Another Program? *236*
Fund Raising **238**
Exercise 8.7 Funding Sources *238*
Exercise 8.8 The Search for Funds *240*
Mobilizing Community Resources **250**
Exercise 8.9 Identifying Mobilization Roles *250*
Exercise 8.10 Group Mobilization *251*
Exercise 8.11 Developing a Community Service: Food for the City *253*
Grass Roots Organizing **256**
Exercise 8.12 Mobilizing for Advocacy *257*
Portfolio Building **261**
Looking Ahead **262**

Chapter NINE **Exercises in Social Policy** **264**

Concepts and Definitions **264**
Exercise 9.1 Following the Policy Continuum *267*
Identifying Problems for Policy Practice **268**
Exercise 9.2 Specifying the Problems *268*
Identifying Policies for Policy Practice **269**
Exercise 9.3 Stating a Policy *270*
Exercise 9.4 Reformulating a Policy *271*
Policies and Politics **272**
Exercise 9.5 Mothers' Wages *273*
Why Social Welfare Policy? **275**
Exercise 9.6 The Context of Policy Development *276*
Exercise 9.7 The Policy Formulation Process *277*
Policy as Practice **279**
Exercise 9.8 Permanent Housing *279*
Social Working Synthesis **282**
Exercise 9.9 Serendipity, Incorporated *282*
Portfolio Building **297**
Concluding Remarks **298**

Glossary 299

Preface

Excellence in social work practice requires us, as students, to incorporate both the skills, values, and knowledge of ethical practice and a personal growth process moving us into professionalism. Our workbook promotes generalist practice competence from a strengths perspective through structured learning exercises across all levels, from interpersonal through macropractice. Simulated problems help us look at practice techniques while examining our values concerning clients, their strengths and resources, and dilemmas.

Guided problem solving underlies the major exercises, demonstrating how to use the problem-solving method in steps guided by the instructor's knowledge for critical thinking, and real practice situations exemplify the cross-level context of generalist practice at its best. Problem solving, the essence of social work practice, is integrated into our traditional and new theoretical and professional bases.

We decided to revise the workbook for several reasons, among them the need to unite service delivery with policy, new ideas concerning the strengths and social justice perspectives, and the realization that, though problem solving is perhaps our most useful tool across practice levels, we need to be reminded of its utility and the simultaneous nature of cross-level considerations.

While exercises in the first edition are still useful, we wanted to update those and to add more that related to problems today. Our students have field-tested the exercises, and colleagues have added situations and successful solutions from their own courses. Although we still touch some areas only lightly, we believe that we have "fleshed out" the scope of the book considerably. *Social Working* is organized into nine chapters, each including basic descriptions of theoretical information for tasks in problem solving and exercises in varying lengths and complexity. Each chapter includes a section on portfolio building for students' self-assessment as they proceed across the social work curriculum. Briefly, the chapters cover the following.

Chapter 1, Problem Solving and Generalist Practice, introduces problem solving and the guided design method, while Chapter 2, Theoretical Perspectives for Generalist Practice, speaks to some of the theories underpinning practice, including the strengths/empowerment/social justice perspective and ecological and systems frameworks.

Chapter 3, The Internal Process of Problem Solving: Values and Ethics, focuses on the value base and ethical standards for professional social work practice and assesses the relationship between personal and professional values in contemporary practice dilemmas.

Chapter 4, Levels of Generalist Practice, includes exercises that stress how social workers can work with problems at one level while planning for interventions at other levels. Chapter 4 also introduces students to the simultaneous nature of practice across levels.

Chapter 5, Working with the Individual Client, looks at both the relational and cognitive skills necessary for competent social work practice. It provides an in-depth look at a micro-practice situation and the problems faced by a social worker new to the field. We include exercises on how the social worker writes a social diagnosis while dealing with his own values and lack of knowledge.

Chapter 6, Social Work with Small Groups, has exercises for developing and working with both treatment and task groups, dealing with leadership in both types of groups, and the place of nonprofessionals (boards) in extending or developing new programs.

Chapter 7, Working in Organizations, considers organizational theory, the worker in the organization, and communications in organizations. It provides practical exercises in writing proposals and memos and identifying both formal and informal communication networks.

Chapter 8, Mobilizing Resources: The Community, speaks to understanding communities, the importance of needs assessments, fund raising, and mobilizing for action, while Chapter 9, Exercises in Social Policy, presents exercises for you to explore social policy from agency work to synthesis across levels.

Phyllis J. Day, MSW, Ph.D.
Sandra M. Shelly, ACSW
Harry J. Macy, MSW, Ph.D.

Acknowledgment

We would like to thank all those people who have helped make this book a reality. Our students deserve the most thanks, because they continually bring new questions to us and test the way we answer them. Our exercises are based on both their questions and the ways in which we try to evoke practice principles in answering them. We are also grateful to our colleagues: Our first edition, coauthored by Professors Harry Macy and Gene Jackson, was our starting point, and contributing colleagues for this edition include, again, Professor Harry Macy of Ball State University, and Professors Lisa McGuire and Valerie Nash Chang of Indiana University. Special thanks are due to the reviewers of this edition: Eric Albers, University of Nevada, Reno; Bruce Friedman, Michigan State University; and Suzanne McDevitt, University of Northern Iowa; your comments were both helpful and encouraging. Our thanks also go to the editorial staff of Allyn & Bacon, especially to Judy Fifer, who kept us on track, and her assistant Julie Cancio. We hope you all will enjoy the exercises and that they will be useful to you and to students at all levels of learning.

Phyllis J. Day, MSW, Ph.D.
Sandra M. Shelly, ACSW
Harry J. Macy, MSW, Ph.D.

Section ONE

Introduction to Social Working

ChapterONE

Problem Solving and Generalist Practice

Purpose and Objectives

Generalist practice is, according to Dubois and Miley,

> [B]oth a way of thinking and a way of doing. Social workers, as generalists, view problems through a wide-angle lens rather than a microscope . . . [to plan] multifaceted interventions that address both the individual and societal dimensions of any given problem.[1]

As generalist social workers, we work across a broad range of helping tasks. We are involved in such interpersonal work as interviewing and communication, using support and empathic skills, and serving individual clients by developing resource systems or advocating for clients' needs within the community. We may also work on community (or wider system) levels to insure that whole groups of clients receive benefits to which they are entitled, or we may be engaged in developing new benefits for clients who have unmet needs. Very often—perhaps most often—generalist social workers are involved simultaneously in all such tasks, from single, interpersonal work to work with many people on behalf of whole groups of clients.

Our purpose in this workbook is to provide exercises for social work students so that they may apply theoretical classroom concepts in simulated practice sessions. The exercises range from those of primarily interpersonal practice to the development of policy issues. Some exercises are very brief, taking only a few minutes. A few are extensive and show in greater detail the extent of influence of even very small tasks. Throughout the exercises, the clarification of students' personal values in relation to social work ethics is a major theme, as is the "client strengths" perspective.

Our educational objectives for the workbook include the following:

1. To teach future generalist social workers problem-solving technique;
2. To demonstrate that problem-solving skills can be used at any level and in any situation, from individual casework to policy as practice;
3. To provide examples and models of problem-solving activities across all levels of practice;
4. To teach students to interpret problems from both personal and political perspectives;
5. To teach skills in moving problems from the personal to the political;
6. To inculcate major practice principles—ways of thinking, doing, and being—that underlie the profession of social work into the problem-solving model.

We emphasize that this is a workbook, not a text, and that its basis is the problem solving model. Although some conceptual materials in terms of appropriate generalist practice are developed, the book relies primarily on the many fine theoretic texts already available, and it may be used across the curriculum with any practice text.

One concept is particularly important for this book: when we say "problem solving," we mean solving the problems clients have—clients with problems are not themselves the "problems" or "cases." Rather, problem solving means a specifically detailed plan of action toward a goal determined feasible by the client system. Beyond the problem-solving method, the book has several theoretical facets, the first of which is the *strengths/empowerment perspective*. In this, both the system and the dynamic process of problem solving constitute a lens through which we view clients not as victims but as working partners in the social work process. Instead of focusing on deficiencies, we look at clients' assets and capacities to move toward goals, realizing that their strengths come from life experiences from the very personal through the cultural to the societal. Second, we work within the *ecological systems* perspective, which we see as a series of "pictures" of relationships moving across time within their environmental context. Individuals and their environments are inseparable, mutually influence one another, and must be considered jointly. Third, this book concerns *levels of generalist practice*, stressing the necessity of practitioners to work across all levels, from the individual to the societal. We will discuss each of these concepts later.

The Guided Problem-Solving Method: Demystifying the Jargon

Problem solving is a *model* by which we logically proceed from *problems* through *alternatives* to the most feasible *solution* for dysfunctions in the system. An important addition to the traditional problem-solving model for generalist social workers is that, in the information-gathering step, issues of social justice and client strengths are considered important sources of information. Every walk of life, from farming to physics, has its own variations in and jargon for the problem-solving method; however, problem solving is in fact a very simple process common to all living creatures. In simple language, *problem solving is the logical process by which individuals (human and otherwise) realize they need something and look for ways to find it*. It is some variation of the process shown in Figure 1.1. This common process has many names and a few adaptations, depending on the field in which it is used, but, basically, the problem solving that works for cats also works for human beings.

Naturally, in dealing with people and their problems, complications arise. Human affairs are fraught with emotions—fear, anger, love, grief—and with social and cultural values about work, morality, money, and social status. We have a great deal of difficulty sorting out problems in human interaction and, therefore, in choosing feasible solutions or plans. Moreover, most human problems have an economic basis; that is, those who have money have power and establish laws, rules, and regulations for those who do not. To determine who wins and who loses in any problem situation, therefore, we try to see who benefits if the problem continues and who loses if the problem is solved.

For example, in the United States people are hungry, but we don't solve the problem of hunger by eating grubs and snakes, although they are easy to find and catch, have nutritional value, and are food sources in other societies. As a nation we have also decided through the new Temporary Assistance to Needy Families (TANF, 1996) legislation that if people do not work, they will not be fed, despite our position as the world's wealthiest nation. What appears shameful to some nations is, to us, a major societal value.

Problem solving as a social work technique lets us cut through emotions and values to clarify what really is the problem. Take any social problem—juvenile delinquency, for example—and you find that the *contexts* in time, place, or era with its social beliefs define the "problem" differently. For example, in the 1880s "delinquents" included street children who stole for food because they could not find work, while from 1911 on, children, both

FIGURE 1.1 *Looking at Problem Solving*

Step	Description	Human	Cat
1. Identify problem	Felt need	Job for subsistence	Hunger
2. Name and set goal	Goal	Find job	Find food
3. Gather information	Job finding?	Job bureau, papers, friends, networks	Smell mouse holes; hear electric can opener; smell table scraps
4. Weigh alternatives	What works?	Brainstorming	
5. Select	Choice	Job bureau	Scraps don't run
6. Implement	Do It	Go to job bureau; follow leads	Up on the table
7. Evaluate success	Feedback?	Got the job?	Still hungry?
8. Use feedback	Yes	Go to work	Yes: walk on sleeping owner's face
	No	Back to 4	No: go to sleep
9. If negative feedback, repeat steps 4 to 8.			

those who committed criminal acts and those who were "status offenders," such as runaways or truants, became labeled as delinquents.

The following exercise starts you out with the most difficult task in problem solving, which is not to develop a solution but to identify the problem itself.

Problem Identification

Without clearly identifying the problem's real nature, we may miss the mark on what clients are really telling us they need. At the beginning of every intervention, we undertake three steps: *identify* the client systems, *specify* each problem or part thereof in *behavioral terms,* and *partialize* the problems clients bring us. Once we have completed these three steps, we move forward through each situation logically and in a timely fashion.

The whole class should participate in the following exercise, with the instructor leading the discussion. Each person should write his or her answers in the spaces provided and then share them with the class.

Exercise 1.1 Pick a Problem

In the class as a whole, choose any social problem and use the problem-solving process:

1. Identify, in clear and concise terms, why this is a problem.

2. Identify the problem in behaviorally specific terms (describe the actions, not the offense).

3. To whom is this a problem? List at least three entities.

(1)

(2)

(3)

4. What is the problem's economic basis? Who benefits, or "cui bono?"

Identifying the Client Systems

Every problem situation has a potential multitude of clients, ranging from individuals who express the problem to society itself. While we are usually accustomed to thinking only of individuals as clients, we may in fact have as our clients wider systems: families, organizations that need our services, and even whole populations at risk. Being aware of the many client systems in any problem situation is essential to unified practice, particularly when our profession's goals are empowerment and social justice for individuals and groups who have been denied citizen and civil rights.

Exercise 1.2 Who Are the Clients?

In small groups discuss the following case: You are an intake worker in an emergency psychiatric unit. Mrs. Jones, an extremely thin and weak African American woman, was just admitted on a court order requesting attention to her emotional disturbance, which has manifested itself in extreme neglect of her seven children. Her family history shows that, before her admission, Mrs. Jones resided with her husband and children in a small, deteriorated apartment in a ghetto neighborhood. Though Mr. Jones works, the family's income provides only basic necessities, so the children are ill-clothed and look malnourished. Mrs. Jones is emaciated, and though there seems to be no physical basis, she claims that "voices" tell her that all her food is poisoned. She has both visual and auditory hallucinations. She is essentially nonverbal; she nods and gestures and occasionally grunts or moans. She does not appear to see her children, nor does she touch or speak to them. She seems to be afraid of Mr. Jones and of other adults.

When Mr. Jones admitted his wife, he said she would not care for her children, cook or keep house, or perform her "wifely" duties. He mentioned that he had left her once but came back "just for a place to live." He says he is not sure the children are even his and will take no part in rearing them. The children range in age from two to twelve. The oldest, a daughter, has taken charge of caring for the family, as much as she can. There are four school-age children, whose attendance at school is erratic, with learning difficulties and behavior problems in class. The oldest girl is usually truant. One of her sisters (age ten) remains at home, is severely retarded, and is unable to dress herself or tend to her sanitary needs.

Discuss and list all the possible clients in this case. Explain why each is the client.

Client 1. _____ Why?

Client 2. _____ Why?

Client 3. _____ Why?

Client 4. _____ Why?

Client 5. _____ Why?

Client 6. _____ Why?

Others? _____ Why?

Who is the primary client? On what bases did you decide? Why did you choose *this* client? Discuss this and list your reasons.

Behavioral Specification

To find the focus of our work before we begin it, we need to clearly state, in behavioral rather than general terms, each problem element. If we neglect this, we may waste time, jump to conclusions and solutions that do not deal fully with each problem aspect, and deny our worker–client partnership the benefit of knowledge and skills in the helping process. *Behavioral specification* means we look at actions rather than assumptions. For example, in a wife-battering situation, we talk about numbers of times per week a woman is battered; we discuss the baseline of battering and the increasing brutality; we note that battering occurs most often on weekends, when the batterer is drunk, or when the abused spouse goes to visit friends. Being able to specify a problem in behavioral terms and then to identify why and to whom it is a problem gives direction to the helping process and sets time for action toward our goals.

A behavioral specification has two parts. The first is a statement of what the difficulty is (identifying the problem) using *behavior* as criteria rather than more theoretical terms. In other words, use *actions and behavior* of the client, the *number of times* something occurs, or the physical or emotional *response* of clients to certain stimuli, without diagnosis or theory. For example, in the Jones case above, in identifying the problems of the child who is developmentally disabled, one would not identify the problem as "the child is developmentally disabled." That may be true, but there is no solution to that—there is no way to make the child not disabled. Proper problem identification would be that (1) the child cannot dress or feed herself, (2) she will not speak to others, and (3) she is not toilet trained. Having identified behaviors and partialized them, we can then propose solutions that will modify the behaviors.

The second part of behavioral specification is a statement of why this is a problem and to whom. If the fact that the child soils herself bothers nobody and does not give her medical or other problems, it may not be a problem. If a social worker perceives it as a problem, stated in behavioral terms, the situation would be that "the child soils herself, and this is a problem to the social worker because the idea of an eight-year-old who soils herself is offensive." The person whose problem it is, then, is not the child but the social worker. Of course that is too simplistic: we would probably identify the problem as "the child soils herself and this creates medical and social problems for her in relating to the rest of the family," or "she soils herself and this causes extra work and distress for Mrs. Jones."

Exercise 1.3 Behavioral Specification

Using the Jones case history, behaviorally specify the problem(s) of each of the potential clients. For each client, be sure that you identify the problem with behaviors and state why it is a problem and to whom.

Partializing the Problem

To partialize means two things. First, clients are likely to bring a whole complex of problems at once, because they have not learned to partialize either. As partners in the intervention, we learn how to pick the problem(s) apart and prioritize it (them) by listing the most pressing first, then the next, and so on. Second, to partialize means to look at the tasks that must be done to solve each problem or part thereof according to the priorities we have listed. Although several tasks can be worked on at once, clearly separating out goals and tasks for each helps to cut through the complexity. Usually the presenting problem—the problem for which the client asks for help—is the first priority, although there are exceptions, such as when there is clear and present danger to the client or others.

Client	Behavioral Specification	Whose Problem?	Why?
1.			
2.			
3.			
4.			
5.			
6.			
7.			

Exercise 1.4 Partializing the Problem

Using the Jones case

A. Separate out (partialize) Mrs. Jones's problems and list them in descending order of importance (prioritize them in terms of need for immediate attention).

B. What is your rationale for this prioritizing?

	Problem	Goal	Tasks
Priority 1			
Priority 2			
Priority 3			

Partialization allows us to separate out problem elements so that we can work with specifics rather than trying to find our way through an amorphous mass of trouble. Prioritizing allows us to put the most pressing problem first.

Guided Problem Solving

In general, the structure of our longer exercises follows the "guided problem-solving technique" based on the work of Charles Wales and Robert Stager.[2] The model provides immediate feedback from instructors at each step of the process as they demonstrate how professional social workers would handle particular problem situations. When the exercises are finished, you will have experience not only in working with particular social work problems but in the process of problem solving itself. Moreover, you will learn problem solving by "practice" rather than by rote in a "safe" educational and reality-based situation.

The study guide in Figure 1.2 is the general model, which can be modified to some extent depending on the problem. (It is also an excellent format for writing papers and professional documents.)

FIGURE 1.2   *Study Guide for the Problem-Solving Model*

---

1. *Identify the problem.* The *problem* is the basic situation that your work will solve. Be sure you know specifically with what you are dealing. It is too easy to make quick assumptions and then go off on a tangent, wasting time and energy. Look beyond the symptoms to find the problem, and state it clearly and unambiguously: Who, what, where, why, and when?

2. *State the goal(s) of your work in clear and objective terms.* The *goal* is a statement of what would be the problem's solution. Don't confuse the *problem* with the *goal* of your work. That goal will dictate the *means* to the solution. Consider both the major goal and specific objectives that lead to the goal. The goal statement focuses your thoughts on the real problem to be solved. It should be a statement broad enough so that no possible reasonable solution is eliminated, yet specific enough so as not to be merely idealistic.

3. *Gather information.* Gathering information actually occurs throughout the problem-solving process, rather than only as "Step 3." The first part is deciding what information you need to have about the problem and then where you might find the information. You must specify exactly what you need to know before you can begin working toward your goal. Part of your information can come from your own experiences, knowledge, and backgrounds, from relevant others, community resources, books, printed matter, experts, experimental work, and so on. Your instructor is a major resource.

   Remember that this model includes the strengths perspective and social justice. While you gather information, identify clients' strengths and rely on their ability both to identify and act upon them. As for social justice, be aware of the societal implications of problems of individuals and look at parallel populations-at-risk (those who might also have the same troubles), policy decisions, societal values, and the historic time context of both organizational and societal reactions to problems and relevant clients.

4. *State constraints, assumptions, and facts.* This step can narrow the alternatives considerably and often points to logical and feasible solutions. *Constraints* limit the outcome of the project and cannot be changed. *Assumptions* can be changed to simplify the problem and make it solvable. *Facts* are known truths—not values but reality.

5. *Generate possible solutions.* Now is the time for creative thinking. Don't judge ideas as they are generated; get all the different thoughts you can. Remember that solutions lie not only on the personal but also on the political level, and try to work at both levels in your solutioning. Prioritize your list on the basis of *how well the solution will solve the problem.*

FIGURE 1.2 *Continued*

6. *Preliminary evaluation and choice of alternatives.* Determine which possible solution is most likely to solve the problem in terms of probability (will it really do the job you want?) and feasibility (is it possible?). Make note of how the solution can be applied at all levels of generalist practice.

7. *Analysis.* Having made a choice, consider the components or elements of the plan. Separate (partialize) the pieces to determine how to deal with them. Determine what further information you need to develop each element and find it.

8. *Synthesis.* This is your action and implementation plan. Combine all your previous work in the exercise to create a detailed solution, and write the solution in clear and unambiguous terms.

9. *Implement your solution.* Discuss factors such as values, latent and manifest functions, roadblocks to success, people or organizations who might be involved—in other words, what it will take to get your solution implemented.

10. *Evaluation.* Plan this often omitted step before leaving the problem solving process. Set up mechanisms to provide feedback so you can see how the process is working, revise your plan, and get rid of problems that keep it from working as you intended. Feedback should also alert you to unanticipated consequences, the plan's effectiveness and efficiency, and how the plan has changed during implementation. At this point you will also evaluate whether the plan actually satisfies the basic goal of the work, and if it is feasible, practical, economical, safe, legal, and moral.

11. *Report the results and make recommendations* (optional). Prepare a report that describes what you have done and decided. Think about the information needs of the person(s) who will read the report. Don't write what is not necessary.

STOP! Do not proceed to the next page until your instructor has evaluated your work on this step.

Exercise 1.5 For Fun: Writing Limericks for Fun, Profit, and Better Grades

General Instructions

Divide into groups of four or five. The instructor will inform you what a limerick is. Do not proceed to the next step until your instructor has looked at your work and given you feedback.

Instruction 1.5.A   Identify the Problem

You have a problem. In order to pass your English course, you need an A on this project in creative writing. Your instructor, however, says that excellence in composition is often not enough for a good mark—a sense of humor is needed for this assignment. Your instructor has been known to give an A just on the basis that a composition has been amusing. *State your problem in the space below.*

STOP! Do not proceed until your instructor has looked at your work.

Feedback 1.5.A

You have not yet reached the point at which you can decide what to do to tickle your instructor's fancy. Your problem is that you need an A for this project and must figure a way to get it.

Instruction 1.5.B State Your Goal

You have heard, from former students, that one sure way to get a good mark from this instructor is to write up projects in limerick form. You don't know much about limericks, but you decide to learn enough so that you can write one. *The limerick, then, is the means by which you intend to solve your problem. What, then, is your goal?*

STOP! Do not proceed until your instructor has looked at your work.

Feedback 1.5.B

Your goal is to write a limerick to fulfill this project, so that you can get an A and pass this course.

Instruction 1.5.C   Preliminary Analysis

Unfortunately, you do not even know what a limerick is. In fact, you need to know several things about limericks before you can begin. *What do you need to know? Where can you get the information?* Write your ideas below.

Information Needed   *Source of Information*

STOP! Do not proceed until the instructor has considered your work.

Feedback 1.5.C

Things you need to know are:

1. What is a limerick?

2. Structure: What is the structure of a limerick?

3. Content: What content is most appropriate to the limerick form?

You have two sources of information: your instructor and yourselves.

Instruction 1.5.D   Gather Information

First, see if anyone in your group has information on limericks. *What do they think a limerick is? How would they write one? What can your instructor offer?*

STOP! Do not proceed until the instructor has evaluated your work.

Feedback 1.5.D

1. A limerick is a form of verse developed in the eighteenth and nineteenth centuries in English-speaking countries.

2. Its structure consists of five lines, usually, the rhythm is anapestic, and the first, second, and fifth lines have three measures each and rhyme. The third and fourth lines have two measures each and rhyme with each other. An anapestic measure has three syllables, with the third syllable accented. An example: "There's a HORSE in the BATHroom aBOVE us." Try a few anapestic measures yourself.

3. A limerick's content is *always* humorous, often ribald (ask your instructor).

Instruction 1.5.E   Brainstorm Solutions

At this point, you need to begin to work on form and content. Decide on the topic, begin rhyming, throw out the words, rhyme, and rhythms that do not work. *Write a rhythmic scan for your limerick,* using your ideas and rhymes.

STOP! Do not proceed until the instructor has evaluated your work.

Feedback 1.5.E

A rhythmic scan shows the rhythm of your limerick and how it will rhyme. In this case, it should be

> *Da da DIT da da DIT da da RHYME a,*
> *Da da DIT da da DIT da da RHYME a,*
> *Da da DIT da da RHYME b,*
> *Da da DIT da da RHYME b,*
> *Da da DIT da da DIT da da RHYME a.*

The first, second, and fifth lines can also have one or two hanging syllables (da da). Try it with "There's a HORSE in the BATHroom aBOVE us, (oh well)."

Instruction 1.5.F Synthesis

At this point you are ready to write your limerick. Decide on your topic, be sure the structure is correct, and make the limerick humorous. Put together your best effort. *What is your limerick? Write it below.*

STOP! Do not proceed until the instructor has approved your work.

Feedback 1.5.F

Ask your instructor for an initial evaluation of the work.

Instruction 1.5.G   Evaluation

Does your limerick fit all the necessary requirements? Is it in verse, rhyming at the appropriate places? Does it have anapestic measures? Is it funny? Do you get an A? Read your limericks to the class.

Exercise 1.6 For Real: Learning Guided Problem Solving

This exercise will give you experience in learning problem solving by doing it. We repeat the study guide steps with some modification. To make sure you are on the right track, go one step at a time. When you are sure you have the answer, ask the instructor, who will review what you have done and give you feedback. Remember, your instructor is your best resource. Ask for help when you get stuck.

Problem Situation

You are social work students in a program that uses guided problem solving as a major teaching tool. You know nothing about it, and there is a test on it tomorrow. You have to learn it now, because you want to make a good impression on your instructor.

Instruction 1.6.A   Problem Identification

Identifying the problem is one of the most difficult tasks in problem solving. Yet if you don't know how to specify it, you may start out on the wrong track and end up solving some other problem. Often, this step is confused with goal setting, that is, making plans for solving a problem before examining it. One way to differentiate between problem identification and goal specification is that the problem *asks the question* and the goal statement *tells you what you need to do to answer it*. Now, with this in mind, *how will you identify the problem specified above?* Use the space below to write the exact problem, then call your instructor for verification and feedback.

STOP! Do not proceed until the instructor has evaluated your work.

Feedback 1.6.A

The problem is that you know nothing about guided problem solving but want to make a good impression on a test tomorrow.

Instruction 1.6.B   Goal Identification

Now that you know what the problem is, *how will you solve the problem?* What is your end goal?

STOP! Do not proceed until the instructor has evaluated your work.

Feedback 1.6.B

Your goal is to learn about guided problem solving quickly and thoroughly enough to make a good grade on the test tomorrow.

Instruction 1.6.C State Constraints, Assumptions, and Facts

What problems will keep you from reaching your goal? Do you think you can find the right materials? What facts do you have about the problem? Assumptions? Constraints? List them below. *What are your strengths in this?*

List them after constraints, assumptions, and facts.

Constraints   **Assumptions**   **Facts**

Our group strengths are:

STOP! Do not proceed until the instructor has evaluated your work.

Feedback 1.6.C

Constraints are your lack of time and your lack of information.

Assumptions you make are that the information is available and that you can find it, and that this is a worthwhile use of your time and energy.

Facts are that it is essential to understand guided problem solving and to get a good grade on the test.

Strengths: Remember, when you are problem solving with a client, you must gather information related to strengths, those assets and resources the client brings to the situation at hand.

Instruction 1.6.D   Gather Information

At this point you should have a good idea of what guided problem solving is and be able to find references that explain it more fully. Your instructor has already informed you that the process is taken from problem-solving models, and you feel it would be a good idea to find some examples. Your instructor may agree that you should go to the library to find appropriate texts, including

Gilbert, Neil, and Paul Terrell (1998). *Dimensions of Social Welfare Policy,* 4th ed. Needham Heights, Mass.: Allyn & Bacon

McGinnis-Dittrich, Kathleen. (1994) *Integrating Social Welfare Policy and Social Work Practice.* Pacific Grove, CA: Brooks/Cole Publishing.

Ginsberg, Leon, ed. (1996) *Understanding Social Problems, Policies, and Programs.* Columbia, SC: University of South Carolina Press.

Now *list the general steps in problem solving.*

STOP! Do not proceed until the instructor has evaluated your work.

Feedback 1.6.D

Your instructor is your best source to explain the problem-solving steps. They are

1. Identify problem
2. Gather information
3. Set basic goals
4. Note constraints, assumptions, facts
5. Generate solutions
6. Evaluate solutions and their consequences
7. Choose the most reasonable alternative
8. Analyze choice for feasibility
9. Synthesize and evaluate alternatives
10. Establish and implement plan
11. Evaluate and modify through feedback

Instruction 1.6.E   Preliminary Analysis

You have found several different models that have basically the same format. *Chart the basic similarities and differences* among the general models you have found.

Model Name	*Similar Steps*	*Differences*

STOP! Do not proceed until the instructor has evaluated your work.

Feedback 1.6.E

Your instructor will write on the board the major differences and similarities you have found. Discuss them in class.

Instruction 1.6.F   Analysis and Synthesis

You now understand the modeled problem-solving process in general, but *what is the difference between the general process and the process used in generalist social work?*

STOP! Do not proceed until the instructor has evaluated your work.

Feedback 1.6.F

The process of guided problem solving alone does not include an assessment of client strengths, nor does it take into consideration values and ethics. Although problem solving is perhaps the most useful tool social workers can use, regardless of level of practice, we must always use a client strengths analysis, an empowerment basis, and a social justice perspective for populations at risk as part of our information gathering process. In addition, we always consider values and ethics in formulating goals, choosing feasible solutions, and implementing plans.

Instruction 1.6.G   Evaluation

Have you reached your goal? Do you now understand the process of guided problem solving in social work well enough to pass a test on it? The elements, of course, include the format, the problem-solving model (i.e., what are the steps), and the group process. In addition, we consider client strengths, empowerment, and a social justice perspective. If you know all this, congratulations! You have learned the problem-solving model.

Portfolio Building

1. What have you learned about generalist practice from the exercises in the chapter?

2. What do you now know about the problem-solving model?

3. How is the problem-solving model used in generalist practice?

4. What new strengths do you have in problem solving?

5. What more do you need to know (what are your limitations) about problem solving?

Summary

In this chapter, we have introduced some of the essential elements of problem solving, and how the problem-solving model applies to generalist practice. The model is actually a step-by-step device for planning, whether that be interventions in partnership with clients in their problems or methods to accomplish tasks at higher levels all the way to the development and implementation of policy. However, we have done nothing apart from the essentials of a theoretical underpinning in problem solving.

Notes

1. Dubois, Brenda, and Karla Krogsrud Miley (1992). *Social Work: An Empowering Profession*. Boston: Allyn and Bacon, p. 7.
2. Wales, Charles, and Robert Stager (1977). *Guided Design: Conference Procedures*. Morgantown, W.V.: West Virginia University.

ChapterTWO

Theoretical Perspectives for Generalist Practice

The Strengths/Empowerment/Social Justice Perspective

In addition to using the problem-solving model as the chosen method of intervention, we stress empowerment within social work interventions. Social work is a partnership activity, with workers and clients as partners in problem solving. As Haley says,

> Shifting one's thinking from the individual unit to a social unit . . . has certain consequences . . . not only must the therapist [read practitioner] think on different [terms] about human dilemmas but he or she must consider himself or herself as a member of the social unit that contains the problem.[1]

The goal of generalist practice is empowerment on the personal level and social justice at the societal level. Empowerment begins with an awakening to self and pushes toward strengths and resources to recognize the resiliency of the human spirit in the face of personal, social, and institutional barriers. Moreover, partnership practice mitigates our tendency to judge people on the basis of society's definitions rather than personal reality. According to Saleeby,

> To recognize the strengths in people and their situation implies that we give credence to the way clients experience and construct their social realities.[2]

Some practitioners believe that the problem-solving framework is a "deficit model" antithetical to a strengths/empowerment perspective. We disagree on at least two counts. First, the framework is just that—a *framework* to hang ideas on as we progress through a logical, goal-directed thought process, value-free unless we inject it with negative or positive perceptions. Historically, the process was dubbed "problem solving" rather than "solution generating," and we see no reason to change the nomenclature. People problems do exist and do need solutions. Through a strengths perspective we do not discount client problems but require an assessment and evaluation of the sources and remnants of client troubles, difficulties, pains, and disorders, along with how they have managed to survive so far and what strengths have sustained them.[3]

Second, blaming that nomenclature for our historic lack of concern with clients' strengths begs the question. Until only recently, social work accepted society's definitions of clients' deviance and dysfunctions. Our realization of society's power to oppress was long in coming, as was recognition of clients' strengths to survive—and thrive—against oppression. Our perception of clients' strengths applied to their problems produces empowerment at the personal level and social justice at the societal level.

> The strengths perspective anchors itself in the belief that a problem does not constitute all of a person's life. Whether the name of the problem is schizophrenia, addiction, child abuse, or troubled family relations, a person is always more than his or her problem.[4]

Traditionally, in fact, social workers have used a deficit perspective in assessment of client problems, even to the point of "blaming the victim." Assessing client strengths, however, emphasizes the strengths inherent in the social worker–client partnership and resources available in both organization and community. These factors fits easily and beneficially into the problem-solving model in the step called "gathering information." This part of the model, of course, is used throughout the problem-solving process itself: we should be looking for new information as we work our way toward feasible solutions.

Exercise 2.1 How We Look at Clients

In many social work settings, workers use the medical model of "diagnosing" the problem. The client becomes an "unperson," a case or label. This is a deficit approach as opposed to a

	Deficit Definitions	*Strengths Perspective*
1. Poverty	a.	a.
	b.	b.
	c.	c.
2. Homelessness	a.	a.
	b.	b.
	c.	c.

3. Gay life style	a.	a.
	b.	b.
	c.	c.

4. Wife abuse	a.	a.
	b.	b.
	c.	c.

5. Inner city crime	a.	a.
	b.	b.
	c.	c.

6. Mental illness	a.	a.
	b.	b.
	c.	c.

strengths-based perspective. Our next exercise is intended to replace deficit client definitions with positive ones in situations social workers deal with every day.

For each situation or problem, list adjectives that indicate a deficit perspective. Follow this with a list of strengths clients bring to their problem situation.

Discuss the strengths in each situation with the full class.

Understanding client strengths and working toward people's self-fulfilling goals is basic to social work practice, and assessment of client strengths and their use in client empowerment are logical bases for problem-solving (or solution-based) practice. Assessment means that in the information gathering stage and before we begin looking at alternative solutions, we learn

> . . . what people have learned about themselves, others, and their world as they have struggled, coped with, and battled abuse, trauma, illness, confusion, oppression, and even their own fallibility; . . . their personal qualities, traits, talents, and virtues; . . . their knowledge of the world around them, both educationally and through their life experiences; . . . their cultural and personal stories and lore; . . . pride; and . . . their communities.[5]

According to Saleeby, some empowerment intervention strategies include basing helping relationships on collaboration, trust, and shared power; accepting clients; definitions of the problem; identifying and building on clients' strengths; actively involving clients in the change process; helping clients experience a sense of personal power within the helping relationship; and mobilizing resources or advocating for clients.[6]

Exercise 2.2 Looking at the Strengths/Empowerment Perspective

In small groups, consider the following problem situation. You are a social worker in a halfway house for people who are developmentally disabled. One of your residents, John, an eighteen-year-old with Down Syndrome, was recently moved to the residence by his older siblings. His parents, who had cared for him at home, were recently killed in an automobile accident. While his five adult siblings love him, they have family responsibilities of their own and cannot take him in.

In your initial assessment, you find John to be a reasonably happy person with enough skills so that he does not require assistance with any of his personal needs. In addition, he can prepare his own meals and often helped his parents with cooking and cleaning chores. They kept him virtually isolated at home, however, believing that if they gave him any outside responsibilities, such as going to the store or riding the bus, he would become confused, lost, or hurt. Therefore, he has very little knowledge of anything outside the home. In addition, he has never attended school and, therefore, cannot read, write, or do arithmetic at all.

You believe that he could be empowered to live outside the residence, given help with the areas his parents did not address. You need to demonstrate this with a strengths assessment. For this exercise, pattern the agency and community resources after similar resources in your own town.

A. Discuss and list strengths/resources for

   1. John

   2. John's siblings

   3. Agency Resources

   4. Community resources

B. Decide what actions you will take to involve John in steps toward independent living and what resources you would use.

Steps to Independent Living	*Resource to be Used*
1.	
2.	
3.	
4.	
5.	

The Power Element

Empowerment focuses on changing the distribution of power and eliminating oppression to increase personal, interpersonal, or political power so that client systems can take action to improve their situations. While in the past social work has tried to adapt the individual to the environment, empowerment practice focuses on modifying the environment to better serve the individual.[7] Fisher and Karger[8] lay out some of the requirements for an empowerment model, and on their concepts we lay out, in Figure 2.1, a useful way to visualize the strengths/empowerment/social justice model.

The client comes to us with a crisis, say domestic violence. We intervene and engage the client in the helping process, that is, for crisis intervention and appropriate referral. When her situation stabilizes, that is, when the immediate crisis ends, she will go back to the problem situation. At this point, agency services ordinarily cease (**STOP**). Fisher and Karger suggest that this is not true empowerment unless we have linked our client to an action group in the community (e.g., battered women's support group), which enables her and others to mobilize for social action at the political level.

Often, once people reach some stability through the social work relationship, they leave. Once helped, they move on, and we cannot mobilize them to work against institutional factors contributing to their problems. Individual problems almost *always* have social and political implications, and if we intend to truly empower people for a better society, we have to find ways to work with them at all levels of practice. A special problem

---

FIGURE 2.1   *The Empowerment Process*

Micro ————————>		Mezzo ————————>			Macro
Person in need is served	↔	Process of helping through strengths	↔	Stabilizes	S ↔ Link to ↔ Link to
					T collective political
					O
					P

exists today with managed care: it often ends payment for social work interventions once the initial crisis is past, further complicating the empowerment/social justice process.

Exercise 2.3 The Empowerment Process

Take a client at the point of diagnosis (or any other client at a point of crisis) and follow him or her through the empowerment process as laid out in Figure 2.1.

Micro-Practice			*Mezzo-Practice*	*Macro-Practice*
Client ⟷ Process ⟷ Stablilizes	S T O P		⟷ Collective Link	⟷ Policy Link

The Social Justice Element

Fisher and Karger speak about "contextualizing social work practice," taking it out of the privatized context and

> . . . knowing and understanding the connection between daily social work practice and the structural dynamics of society—its history, economy, politics, and social and cultural dimensions. . . . At the heart of a critical contextualization is an analysis of power and inequality and a social change ideology that translates this critical analysis into action.[9]

For example, the Americans with Disabilities Act (ADA), passed during the Bush Administration, was a hard-won structural change. Though this fight for social justice was won, there was no rush to carry out its mandates. Changes came one by one as those affected protested ADA violations. In the following modified guided problem-solving exercise, you should look at the policies of your own school, as most colleges and universities have the same regulations regarding the ADA.

Exercise 2.4 Action for Social Justice

Problem Situation

At a large eastern university, a major problem for people in wheelchairs was that, although there were eating places in almost every building, the counters were too high for them to order food without help, and the tables were too low to accommodate wheelchairs. In your social work policy class, two of your classmates use wheelchairs and have brought the problem to the class as a practical exercise in social justice.

Instruction 2.4.A   *Problem Identification*

State the problem in clear behavioral and objective terms.

STOP! Do not proceed until the instructor has looked at your work.

Feedback 2.4.A

The problem is that persons using wheelchairs for mobility have limited access to campus eating establishments because the counters are too high for ordering food and the tables are so low that wheelchairs cannot fit under them for comfortable eating.

Instruction 2.4.B   State the Goal

State the goal in behavioral terms. Be sure it is to the point and specific.

STOP! Do not proceed until the instructor has looked at your work.

Feedback 2.4.B

The goal is to advocate for students with physical disabilities so that they have equal access to eating establishments.

Instruction 2.4.C   Gather Information

What information do you need to work on the problem? *Where can you find it?*

STOP! Do not proceed until the instructor has looked at your work.

Feedback 2.4.C

Your instructor is your best source to help you locate materials that will be helpful. You will want to become familiar with the basic tenets of the ADA. Because you should understand the university's responsibility to students with disabilities, you may contact the office on campus that assists students with disabilities to reasonable accommodations. The State Department of Human Resources also has a specialist available to answer questions about the ADA and its implications for college campuses. Likewise, your state's vocational rehabilitation office often helps students with disabilities confront barriers that impede completion of their training or retraining and may have pertinent information to share.

You need to know just how much difficulty the students with disabilities are facing, and, if possible, how many students are affected. You should understand the problem from their perspective and learn what efforts they have made toward alleviating the problem. You should find out what the administration's understanding of the problem is and if they have made any attempt to alleviate the problem. How will you determine this?

What else do you need to know?

Instruction 2.4.D   Discover Relevant Constituencies

What are your *relevant* constituencies, and how will you *mobilize* them?

STOP! Do not proceed until the instructor has looked at your work.

Feedback 2.4.D

In supporting any population through advocacy, you must remember that you are NOT the expert. In this case, the experts are people using wheelchairs who cannot order food nor eat food in most buildings on campus. Your job is not to solve the problem but to facilitate the work of the individuals who are affected by the situation in finding and implementing a solution.

One important component of social justice or advocacy work is knowing who to involve. Your relevant constituencies are people who will support you as well as those who might act against your planned social action. Your primary constituency is students at this university who use a wheelchair and who eat on campus. Who else might be involved in this case? Who will help you plan and convince others to at least not fight against you? Who will help you form persuasive arguments to neutralize opposing arguments? Among possible constituencies, look at

Other politically active groups on campus;

Able-bodied students who support their challenged colleagues;

Other students with disabilities who do not use wheelchairs;

University personnel who work with students with disabilities;

Groups who advocate for persons with disabilities in the community or with the government;

Other social work students who are committed to social justice causes.

There are many other groups. Now, how will you mobilize them? In this situation, to mobilize means to activate and engage others toward accomplishing an end. Remember, the social worker is not the expert, the constituencies are the experts. How will you inspire and support them in the change process? You might

1. Educate them in community organizing techniques;

2. Facilitate a discussion on various change strategies;

3. Assist them in formulating an action plan by using the guided decision-making model.

Instruction 2.4.E   *Identify Action Target*

The action target is the system that your action coalition targets to make the changes you want. It is the system with power over the specific client system and, therefore, has power to make changes in that system's situation. *Name your action target.*

STOP! Do not proceed until the instructor has looked at your work.

Feedback 2.4.E

The action target is the group that must be approached for change to occur. The food service management may be the target, or the university's administration may be the target. You will need to do your homework to discover who has the power to make a decision on this issue. If you can obtain a chart of the department that is responsible for services to the disabled, it would be helpful.

Instruction 2.4.F   Develop and Prioritize Solutions

List possible plans for action.

Action Plan   *Priority*

1.

2.

3.

4.

5.

6.

STOP! Do not proceed until the instructor has looked at your work.

Feedback 2.4.F

Remember that you are helping those with the problem generate the solutions. Some possible solutions might be the following:

1. Hosting a sit-in at various eating places
2. Meeting with the powers-that-be to discuss the problem, and demanding immediate access to *all* eating places on campus.
3. Holding a press conference to alert the media and, thereby, the community-at-large to the problem
4. Meeting with the administration to outline the problem and propose a solution (perhaps such as asking for access in the most centrally located eating sites)
5. Contacting the state's regulatory offices, and asking for an ADA inspection of the campus facilities
6. Working with Legal Services, or a sympathetic law firm, to file a class action lawsuit
7. What others have you brainstormed?

When a group prioritizes solutions, social workers must be skilled in interpersonal methods of group work. The group must discuss each option and rank it according to their capacity to face the personal, social, and institutional barriers each poses.

Instruction 2.4.G   *Choose the Most Feasible Solution*

State the most feasible alternative as your *action plan*. What *compromises* are you willing to make to get your plan implemented?

STOP! Do not proceed until the instructor has looked at your work.

Feedback 2.4.G

The most feasible plan is the one that threatens the university the least. That would probably be meeting with Student Services to have them put the issue before the administration. They might even be able to enact a solution at that level. The general rule is to start with the least intrusive plan and escalate the action as resistance to change escalates. When you meet with those in charge, outline the problem and propose a solution. This lays the basis for your action plan.

Instruction 2.4.H   Implementation

List the steps that must be taken to implement the plan.

1.

2.

3.

4.

5.

STOP! Do not proceed until the instructor has looked at your work.

Feedback 2.4.H

Steps to implement the action plan.

1. Propose a policy change to allow construction for new accessibility.
2. Set time table for completion of work.
3. Arrange budget to pay for work; insist on a priority of accessibility according to ADA guidelines.
4. Evaluate process to insure it is timely: if timely, take no action; if delayed, begin process of action again.
5. Others?

Instruction 2.4.I   Feedback and Evaluation

How will you know your plan is working? What time frame do you have for completion? What mechanisms will insure you that the plan is in place?

STOP! Do not proceed until the instructor has looked at your work.

Feedback 2.4.1

You will know the plan is working if accessibility construction is completed in a timely manner (according to the time schedule agreed by the administration). You will set up intervals at which to check the progress of the construction, and use that feedback to evaluate progress.

The Ecological/Systems Perspective

The strengths/empowerment/social justice perspective gives us, through the dynamic process of problem solving, a lens through which we may view clients not as victims but as working partners. Rather than focusing on deficiencies, we looked at clients' assets and capacities to move toward goals, realizing that their strengths come from life experiences, from the very personal through the cultural to the societal. The ecological/systems perspective, in which persons and their environments are inseparable, mutually influence one another, and must be considered jointly, provides another basis of generalist social work practice. In it, we use systems concepts integrated with an ecological model to picture relationships and interactions in generalist social work.

Major assumptions include a holistic awareness of different system levels with emphasis on transactions between people and their environments and on stresses and balances within and among systems. To develop competence, people need successful transactions with their environments, and an ecological/systems model helps us visualize how the environment supports or suppresses clients' competence. In addition, ecological theories give us strategies to help mitigate clients' problems by examining the contexts of the cultural environments; that is, family, economic situation, ethnicity, religion, gender, and so on. While the systems framework emphasizes *systems'* abilities to change and develop, the ecological perspective focuses on *people's* ability to negotiate with their environments.[10]

In the systems framework, a system is any structured relationship in which a number of units (social units in our case) interact within a given boundary over a defined period of time. Getting rid of the jargon, that means that we all interact with our environments over time, whether they are family, cultural, geographical, or other environments, and that we understand the limits (boundaries) of our activities within them. Systems can be any size: an atom is a system with interacting parts; a universe is a system with interacting galaxies; a person is a system with interacting organs bounded by skin; a family is a system with interacting people bounded by its relationships. Smaller systems fit into larger ones, and they interact with other systems or units: a person system fits into a family; a family system fits into a community; a community system fits into a state; and so on. As the smaller system fits into the larger, the perspective changes: a person

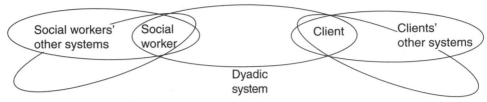

FIGURE 2.2   Dyadic System

system becomes a social unit in the family system; a family system becomes a family unit in the community. Within a system of any size, units react to and interact with other units and their own boundaries.

Social work systems are often two-person, or dyadic, systems, in which worker and client interact about a problem (Figure 2.2). The environmental context may include the dyad, the service-providing agency, relevant community agencies, or the whole community.

The ecological/systems focus fits naturally into the practice of generalist social work. Any social work relationship or partnership is a system that involves at least two people, and often more, interacting. Both (or all) belong to their own set of systems, and the client–worker partnership cannot be isolated from other systems. Both social workers and clients have jobs, home lifes, families, groups, past history, and future expectations, and each of these affect the intervention system and its processes. In addition, social workers are embedded in the agency itself and peer organizations in the community, and both parties in the partnership are further embedded in and interacting with the societal system that has established norms, rules, and the ways of behavior expected of its members.

Exercise 2.5 Your Own Dyadic System

In class, break up into dyads and decide who will be the social worker and who will be the client. Choose a problem setting relevant to your field placement (juvenile court, probation office, school social work, public assistance, mental health office, etc.). Working together and using Figure 2.2 as a model, diagram on a separate paper, first your dyadic system and then the relationships in which both of you partake. On a separate page make a diagram. Discuss and then list at least five complications you can see from the diagram that might limit your work together.

Complications

1.

2.

3.

4.

5.

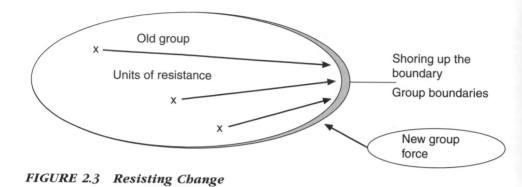

FIGURE 2.3   Resisting Change

In full class, discuss the implications of what you have found.

Whenever a structured system exists—such as a group or an organization with firmly set boundaries—any attempt to permeate the system meets with resistance. Internal units marshal themselves to "shore up" the point of potential penetration. In a person, new ideas are often met with resistance based on old values, attitudes, or past fears. In a group, resistance often takes the form of rejection of new people. In an organization, bureaucratic mechanisms make entry into the organization's processes difficult; for example, in public assistance eligibility workers are "gate keepers" who block access to help for some clients (see Figure 2.3).

The Path through the Agency System

If we look more fully at social work systems, we would see something like that diagrammed in Figure 2.4.[11]

We are given that the community environment, including its demographics, resources, and values, impacts upon the agency in terms of its capabilities, constraints, and its mandate or mission, goals, and objectives within the community. Resources also depend, generally, on the community and the outcomes for clients, consumers, and so on, and will influence the community in a variety of ways. Although no path is set for certain within an agency, generally we can trace the systems framework as follows:

1. The agency mandate sets the mission, goals, and objectives for agency practice, and these become the general operational rules for what the agency intends to accomplish with outputs, or units of work, and outcomes, or projections for change/maintenance for clients.
2. Formal rules and regulations follow from the mandate, and participants within the agency implement these along with more informal practices and procedures. Formal rules and regulations generally set procedures for inputs (3), throughput (4), and intended outputs (5) and outcomes (6).
3. Inputs include everything that comes into the social work setting, including rules and regulations; the people doing the work, including workers and clients; the legitimation

FIGURE 2.4 *The Social Work Organization as System*

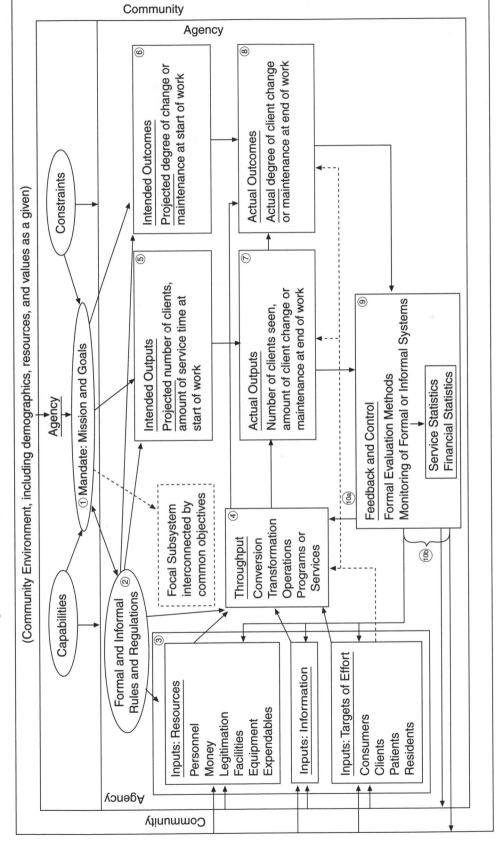

given by community and agency board to proceed with this particular type of work; financing and the constraints placed on agency work by where the money comes from; and the facilities that keep the agency going, including buildings, equipment, and expendables such as computers, paper, and so on. A vital part of the input is information brought in from a multitude of sources, and of course the clients or consumers are essential inputs, including their numbers and the kinds of problems they have.

4. Throughput is what goes on in processing all the inputs. It may transform or change not only the clients but the workers, the programs and services, and the agency itself.

5,6,7,8. While the agency intends certain outputs and outcomes and these intentions direct the processing, the throughput process itself, in combination with its variety of inputs, leads to actual outputs (7) and outcomes (8).

9. The actual outputs and outcomes provide feedback through formal evaluations and monitoring that will moderate all aspects of the agency's system so that its mandate may be served better or more effectively and efficiently.

Exercise 2.6 Walking Through Your Agency's Systems

Using your placement agency as a system, first answer the questions about your community below. Then create a chart following Figure 2.4, filling in the actual information as it applies to your agency.

Community Environment

1. Pertinent demographics

a. _____   b. _____

c. _____   d. _____

2. Community resources available for your agency

a. _____   b. _____

c. _____   d. _____

3. Overarching values in the community

a. _____   b. _____

c. _____   d. _____

Agency

1. Mandate, mission, and goals of your agency.

a. Mandate _____

b. Mission _____

c. Goals and objectives: _____

2. Formal and informal rules and regulations regarding client services *vis-à-vis* target groups, kinds of programs and services, intended outputs and intended outcomes.
   a. Who are your target groups?

   b. What programs are they offered?

   c. How are the services to be given?

   d. What are the expected outcomes?

4. What is the throughput process by which clients/consumers are expected to change, transform, be maintained, or other? That is, what kinds of services will produce the change?

5. How many clients does the agency have? How many could it handle? How long, in terms of contact hours, should the clients be seen?

6. What changes does the agency expect that the intervention will produce?

7. What is the actual output in terms of numbers of clients and hours of intervention? Ask your director for an approximation if the data are not available (i.e., projected success per units of work).

8. How many clients actually reach the goals set for them when the social work intervention is completed? How do you know?

9. What are the formal evaluation methods? Are systems for output and outcome formally or informally monitored? What are the systems for getting the feedback to the agency so that it can be more responsive to clients and outcomes?

Exercise 2.7 Newcomers

Too often we make assumptions about newcomers[12] or "outsiders." Using what you have learned about the systems/ecological perspective, break into groups of about five for the following exercise. Appoint an observer from your group (instructions below). Your objectives are

1. To learn one good thing about each person in your group and explain why a system is in trouble when there is a newcomer or, extrapolating, any change.
2. To understand systems in terms of group cohesion and leadership.
3. To understand the difficulties of newcomers coming into a new situation.
4. To understand resistance to newcomers even if they are welcomed.

A. *Task Instructions*

1. Decide by consensus the most effective way for the group to get to know each person (ten minutes).
2. Put this method into effect in your group (fifteen minutes if needed).
3. Appoint one of your members to carry your method to another group.
4. The appointee's task: Explain the method to the new group.
5. Group decision: Each new group decides by consensus whether to accept the newcomer's method. If rejected, the newcomer goes back to the original group. If accepted, the newcomer brings his/her old group to join the new group. If there is time, the process can be repeated until there is only one group.

B. *Observer Instructions:* Carefully note the following and report to the whole class when the exercise is completed.

1. Who took leadership? How was it assumed?

2. What was the process by which consensus was reached?

3. How did it feel to be an observer?

4. Did you perceive any "networks" in the group you observed?

5. Was group pressure placed on any members in the group? Under what conditions? By what means?

C. *Discussion:* At the end of the exercise, newcomers report on their feelings in their groups, following the guidelines below. Observers report after this, followed by a general discussion on this as a systems exercise.

D. *Appointee's Report*

    1. How did it feel to be chosen by your group?

    2. How did you feel about going to the new group?

    3. How did it feel to be accepted? Rejected?

E. *General Discussion*

    1. What were the reasons for the exercise?

2. What has it to do with social work practice?

3. What have you learned that has increased your awareness of self and others and that you can put to use in your future profession?

Portfolio Building

1. What have you learned about assessment of client problems in this chapter?

2. What have you learned about problem assessment here?

3. In considering social justice, how do client strengths and empowerment relate to this chapter?

4. What is the ecological systems framework, and how is it useful in social work practice?

5. What more do you need to know about client strengths assessment, empowerment, and social justice?

6. What more do you need to know about the ecological/systems framework?

Summary

In this chapter, exercises have provided you with a new perspective on client assessment through the strengths perspective and a new lens—the ecological systems framework—through which to view the contexts of problems. In addition, the problem-solving model became a dynamic process for change, at interpersonal as well as higher systemic levels, while our other theoretical models placed that change within easily pictured frameworks.

Our next chapter looks at values, but we should remember the dynamic processes and contextual frameworks, because all are important to the ways we think about others and about professional social work.

Notes

1. Haley, Jay (1976). *Problem Solving Therapy.* San Francisco: Jossey Bass Publishing, p. 2.
2. Saleeby, Dennis. (1995). *Strengths Approach to Practice*, 2nd ed. NY: Longman Press, p. 50.
3. Paraphrased. Dennis Saleeby, in Schriver, Joe M. (1998). *Human Behavior and the Social Environment,* 2nd ed. Needham Heights, MA: Allyn & Bacon, p. 140.
4. Weick, Ann, and Ronna Chamberlain (1995). "Putting Problems in Their Place: Further Explorations in the Strengths Perspective." In Saleeby, *Strengths Approach to Practice* (1995). op. cit., pp. 39–48.
5. Paraphrased from ibid., p. 51.
6. Ibid., p. 42.
7. Gutierrez et al. (1998). In Schriver, Joe M. *Human Behavior and the Social Environment.* op. cit., pp. 139–141.
8. Fisher, Robert, and Howard Jacob Karger (1997). *Social Work and Community in a Private World.* New York: Longman. p. 43.
9. Ibid., Chapter 3.
10. De Hoyos, G., and C. Jensen (1995). The Systems Approach in American Social Work, *Social Casework*, 66 (8), 490–497; and Greene, Roberta, and Ephross, Paul H., Eds. (1991). *Human Behavior Theory and Social Work Practice.* Hawthorne, NY: Aldine de Gruytere. pp. 278–279.
11. This exercise was created by Professor Ray Koleski, Indiana University School of Social Work, for use in his classes.
12. Revised from Johnson, David, and Frank P. Johnson (1975). *Joining Together: Group Therapy and Group Skills.* Englewood Cliffs, NJ: Prentice Hall.

Chapter THREE

The Internal Process of Problem Solving: Values and Ethics

The Importance of Values

Values must be first and foremost in the minds of social workers without regard to the kind of work they do or the level at which they do it. The practice of social work is a practice of values, and we must become aware of values because, too often in the practice of social work, we only *think* we know what our values are or what values we are furthering with our good works.

A major task for social work education, therefore, is to clarify values about self, the practice of social work, and society in general. With this knowledge, at the very least we will understand that much of what is "known" about self, life, and others is not always fact. As we question the sources of our deeply embedded beliefs, however, we may become uncomfortable or may even feel that our American way of life, our ideas about government's political or economic system, or even that we ourselves are under attack. Remember that to investigate is not to attack: we look at values not to eliminate them but to understand what they are and how they influence our interactions with others. To truly help our clients, we must know who we really serve, and why.

This knowledge is essential to self-awareness. When we find that some of our most cherished beliefs about self and society come from values rather than fact, we may become more effective as social work professionals.

Societal Values and Latent Functions

To understand more thoroughly how we analyze problems, two aspects of our society need attention. First, defining a situation or behavior as a "problem" means that it somehow goes against at least one major societal value. Second, every problem has latent functions for society; that is, it occurs and remains because it serves some purpose, whether that purpose is clearly understood or hidden. For example, racism is certainly a problem in the United States. It violates values of both charity and democratic egalitarianism, and yet it continues because of another value called "social Darwinism." Manifestly, we strive to end racism because of its terrible consequences, but its latent functions, or hidden purposes, keep it alive. Among its latent functions are maintaining a low wage and entry-level work force, giving the majority entitlements or others the tacit permission to look down upon or hate (racism or classism), maintaining a polarized economic/ caste system (classism), keeping a market for used or shoddy goods (sexism, classism), and so forth.

The major societal values in Western culture and in the United States are

1. *Judaeo-Christian Charity Ethics.* We are responsible for one another and have a duty to care for those who are in need.

2. *The Protestant Work Ethic.* Work and wealth are equated with morality, and poverty is not a state of need but a personal fault.

3. *Patriarchy.* Power and authority are vested in an elite group of men, while women and other powerless groups such as children and workers are oppressed and often owned.

4. *Capitalism.* Profit from an enterprise, no matter how it is made or how it exploits, demonstrates virtue. While capitalism is an economic system, it is also a value in our western culture.

5. *Social Darwinism.* Groups that are "different" in race, ethnicity, religion, age, gender, sexual preference, or economic status are stigmatized by the majority population and seen as of lesser or no value compared to the majority population.

6. *Puritan Morality.* Puritan morality is a requirement for honesty and abstinence from vice—which is activity defined as immoral by religion and custom, especially personal or bodily indulgences.

7. *Democratic Egalitarianism and* 8. *Individualism.* We all are equal before the law, and we must attain our goals through individual effort.

9. *Marriage and the Nuclear Family.* Deriving from patriarchy, this belief says that the "proper" American family is a permanent institution consisting of working husband and dependent wife and children.

10. *The American Ideal.* A "looksist" value that dictates conformity to standards set by white, middle-class, middle-income people, this value acts against any who deviate from the "middle of the road" pattern of looks and behavior.

Exercise 3.1 American Values

For each American value above, write at least three examples of how the value affects American life. Discuss your answers in class.

	Value	*Effect 1*	*Effect 2*	*Effect 3*
1.				
2.				
3.				
4.				
5.				
6.				
7.				
8.				
9.				

Exercise 3.2 The Latent Functions of "Isms"

For each "ism" below, list at least five *purposes* or *hidden benefits* (latent functions) to American society or at least a powerful group of Americans. Then discuss your answers in class.

	"Ism"	*Benefits*

1. Racism

    a.

    b.

    c.

    d.

    e.

	"Ism"	*Benefits*

2. Sexism
   a.
   b.
   c.
   d.
   e.
   other

3. Heterosexism or homophobia
   a.
   b.
   c.
   d.
   e.
   other

4. Classism or poverty
   a.
   b.
   c.
   d.
   e.
   other

5. Mental, emotional,
   or physical disability
   (ableism)
   a.
   b.
   c.
   d.
   e.
   other

6. Ageism against people 40–65
   a.
   b.
   c.
   d.
   e.
   other

7. Ageism against people over 65
   a.

	"Ism"	*Benefits*

b.

c.

d.

e.

8. Ageism against children

  a.

  b.

  c.

  d.

  e.

  other

9. Other

Exercise 3.3 Pick a Problem

In this exercise, the whole class should participate, with the instructor leading the discussion. Each person should write his or her answers in the spaces provided and then share them with the class. To begin, choose any social problem. Following the problem-solving process;

1. Identify why this is a problem in clear and concise terms.

2. To whom is this a problem and why? List three entities.

3. Identify the one major societal value that seems most important to the problem.

4. Identify the manifest function of the problem; that is, what do people say is the problem?

5. What is the problem's latent function? Why does it persist in society even though we know it is a problem? What advantages are there to keeping this particular problem in our society?

6. What is the economic basis of the problem? Who benefits or "cui bono"?

Values Awareness

In the following values clarification exercises, two ideas may help you. The first is that our clients are part of our culture. They are, therefore, aware of its values and share them, even though the problem situation may camouflage this. Secondly, any individual, including social workers and clients, can and probably does hold conflicting values very strongly and at the same time. For example, belief that an unborn fetus has a right to life and belief in the value of capital punishment are ultimately polar opposites, yet many people live with both values very comfortably. Problems arise only when choices must be made, and our clients are very often caught between conflicting values. So are we all.

Exercise 3.4 We are Heterosexist Because . . .

Break into groups of from five to seven each. The issue for discussion is homosexuality.

A. One person states a position on the issue. The second states opposition to the first. Go around the group, alternately stating positive and negative positions, at least twice. At your instructor's signal, list and discuss the values that were encountered in the group.

B. In the total class situation, explain where personal values about homosexuality came from. Name the several societal values that are part of those personal values. Discuss.

Exercise 3.5 But My Folks Told Me That . . .

Instructions: In this small-group exercise, each student should answer questions individually and then discuss each issue round-robin style. Class members should discuss *broad values* they all share and then values deriving from students' more immediate family, religious, or ethnic backgrounds.

A. Each of us comes from a specific set of cultural values, and these values may be surprisingly different even among classmates. To find out more about yourselves, think of the immigrants in this country who were your forebears.

   1. When did they come to America, and from what country?

2. What cultural and religious beliefs did they bring? Are these still practiced in your family? Why or why not?

3. Most immigrants were poor. Were your forebears? If so, what ideals about work may they have had? Does your immediate family share these? Do you?

4. What major societal values(s) pertain to your parents' values? To your own?

B. Our most potent source of values are, probably, our parents. Even though schools, religion, and cultural heritage are powerful, our parents transmitted them to us, in all likelihood. What do you know about your parents, especially on the ideas listed below?

1. *Marriage.* Is their marriage intact? How do their feelings on marriage, whether theirs is intact or not, influence your own views?

2. *Religion.* Are they religious in the sense of attending and participating in religious meetings, customs, and so on? What have they taught you about religion, and to what extent do you agree or disagree?

3. *Work.* Who is the breadwinner in your family of origin? Why? What do you think of this? What importance does money have in their household?

4. *Education.* How important is your education to your parents? What education do they have?

5. *Home and Family.* Who makes decisions on major purchases? What kinds of possessions are important? If you had to name one thing to characterize your parents' concept of home and family, what is it? Are your parents outwardly cool or affectionate toward each other? Toward their children?

6. *Sex Roles.* What behaviors and morals do your parents expect of their sons? Their daughters? Are these different? How? How do you reflect these values in your behaviors, morals, and expectations for the future?

7. *Prejudices.* What prejudices, if any, do your parents have (ethnic, racial, social class, etc.)? What do they say? What do they do? How has this affected your own ideas about people who are "different"?

8. *Parenting.* What one word would best describe their parenting practices? Have they been consistent with all the children? How did they train and punish? How do you feel about their parenting? Will you parent in the same manner or differently?

9. What do you most *respect* about your parents? What do you *dislike* most about them?

10. How are you like your parents, and how are you different?

General discussion. How have your parents' values affected yours? List your own values on each issue above. Connect your own values with those of your parents, and then connect those with major societal values. Discuss in class how your own values might affect your social work practice.

Values Conflict in Social Work

All dimensions of reality shift in social work. One of these dimensions consists of practitioners' honest attempts to carry out mandated goals. Inspired to help others in the difficult tasks of social functioning when life has gone awry, we strive past the bureaucratic mechanisms that limit service, go around legislative mandates and recalcitrant policies, and push past negative public opinion and the biased views of mass media. As social workers, we carry on despite frustrations caused by bureaucratic blocks to service and limited resources, seek to modify limited organizational capacities to function in accordance with social work mandates, and deal, more or less graciously, with resistant others with whom we must work.

Our initial value orientation is humanitarian (Judaeo-Christian), but it is transmuted through belief systems, backgrounds, and contending values for every individual. Underlying our agreement that we should help the less fortunate, we may also believe we have the right to choose who is deserving and who is not. In addition, we may agree that some people are "to blame" for their own misfortunes, and so we are obligated to withhold help from them until they demonstrate their willingness to admit their guilt and strive to do better. (How many social workers does it take to change a light bulb? One! But the light bulb has to really want to change!)

We believe that society must assume responsibility for assuring basic sustenance to all, yet we agree that the needy should be given so little that many are undernourished, ill, and poorly clothed and sheltered. We know that institutional inequalities such as racism and sexism limit access to opportunity, yet we also know that "anyone can succeed in America." Finally, we are aware of the limitations of the helping technologies and the tendency toward the self-fulfilling prophecy of those we label deviant. Yet we continue to diagnose, label, and intervene with methods that may or may not work.

Following are several exercises that will help us understand these value dilemmas.

Exercise 3.6 The Other Side of Battering

In small groups of four to seven, discuss the following. You are social workers who have been dealing with battered women for six months, and you now take a highly feminist stand on the issue. You fault our sexist society for the battering, and you do not believe that you can deal with the batterers at all; however, you have just been assigned the task of organizing and leading a group for battering partners or husbands. For each topic below, first write how you feel or think, then discuss the topics with your group.

1. How do you feel about the problem?

2. What direct service skills would you use in this setting?

3. Who are the potential sets of clients?

4. Given your own perspectives and values, what will you do about the assignment?

5. What major societal values are inherent in this problem situation, and how?

6. Discuss the results of your small group meetings with the whole class.

Exercise 3.7 Helping Clients Help Themselves

Recent work with battered women has demonstrated that it is difficult to organize them for group therapy or even support groups. This is a source of frustration to many social workers who feel that the group process would help them become emotionally stronger and able to make better choices for themselves. First write, then discuss the topics below.

1. What are your feelings about battered women's "lack of willingness" to help themselves? What societal values are involved in the way you feel?

2. Discuss the resources you might use to help yourself, not the women, to deal with resistance in those you want to help.

3. What means could you use to maintain objectivity?

4. What values are involved in maintaining the status quo for the women and their batterers? For you?

The Social Control Issue

A more encompassing dimension is that of social control and the values by which we enforce it. As social workers, we believe that the institution of social welfare and the practice of social work are society's mandates for helping the less fortunate. The underlying meanings (or latent functions) of our jobs, however, often put us between client needs and society's dictates, as "middle persons" of social control. As professionals, we are given institutional "power over" clients to regulate aspects of their lives and behaviors on the threat of denying them help, whether or not we do.

Clients are surely aware of that power. Seeking help is their formal declaration of inability to cope, and disempowerment teaches them what loss of power means to them in other, empowered areas, such as their roles as workers, parents, homeowners. Loss of self-esteem, anger, and alienation from the systems in which they live are only some visible results of their erosion of self. Empowerment practice gives clients the right to partnership in plans for their own lives, and unless we subscribe to empowerment practice we belittle their strengths, life experiences, and aspirations.

Exercise 3.8 Losing Power

On each of the ten index cards your instructor will give you, write one thing of great importance to you. With no warning, your instructor will ask for one card at a time, sometime during the class period, and will destroy each. After all your cards have been destroyed, answer the questions in the spaces below.

1. How did you feel about the process when it began?

2. When you handed over your last card, how did you feel?

3. How does this relate to power in the social work profession?

4. Loss of esteem, anger, and alienation from society are only a few visible results of erosion of self. Write down and then discuss with the entire class three other results.

(1)

(2)

(3)

5. When you entered the field of social work, did you expect to be in a position of power over clients? Discuss.

Exercise 3.9 Advocacy Against Values

Break into small groups of from four to seven members each. You (collectively) are a worker in an adoption agency, and a couple has come in seeking to adopt a child. According to the rules under which your agency handles the social and legal aspects of the adoption process, any couple or any single parent who is emotionally stable (according to the discretion of the worker), is financially secure, is able to provide an adequate home, and shows no evidence of wishing to "use" the child (for example, adopting to secure a shaky marriage) may adopt. You, as the worker, have a great deal of discretion under these rules.

Problem Situation. One partner of the couple is a physician with a good income from approximately ten years of practice in the community. The other is a teacher of high school science, has been employed by one school system for the past five years, and has gained tenure and promotion to chairperson of the science department. Their reasons for wishing to adopt is that they feel they have a great deal of love to give a child, enough security to provide well, and would like to "complete" their family with two or three children at intervals. It is obvious to you that they have a great deal of respect and affection for each other, and the home and future they might provide their children seems excellent. They are a lesbian couple.

A. You are aware that this couple as adoptive parents goes against some major attitudes in this country.

1. Write down your own feelings about this, and the several societal values from which those feelings come. Discuss the issue in your group.

2. Because you have the discretion to accept or deny, what will you do? Why? Write your decision in the space below, along with three reasons that led you to that decision.

Decision: _____

Reason 1.

Reason 2.

Reason 3.

3. Name the sources of your value conflict.

B. You choose to accept the adoptive couple, but you find that the administration has many doubts about the placement.

1. According to the National Association of Social Workers (NASW) Code of Ethics, to be discussed later, this should not be a problem. Why is it a problem to your agency administrators?

2. Advocacy is necessary because of a conflict in values. What advocacy skills do you need to help the adoptive parents at the organizational level? Community level? List and discuss.

Skill	Organizational Level	Community Level
(1)		
(2)		
(3)		
Other		

2. What information do you need for good advocacy? Where can you get it?

Information	Where Available?

3. List the steps you will need to take with your administrative superior to advocate for the couple. Then discuss them in class.

    (1)

    (2)

    (3)

    (4)

    (5)

    (6)

    (7)

    (8)

C. In class, discuss what happened in your group. Why? What were the value elements of the process?

Exercise 3.10 If I Woke Up Gay Tomorrow

Divide into groups of four to six people. Each group should appoint an observer, who will report on the group's discussion to the entire class. First, write answers to the questions below in the spaces provided. Then, taking about fifteen minutes, discuss the question "How would life be different if we woke up gay tomorrow?"

A. What it would mean personally

    1. How would it affect relationships with friends, family, colleagues?

    2. To whom would you come out, and how?

    3. How would it affect your social and work lives?

B. General questions

    1. Identify some issues confronting gay people today.

    2. What are your own feelings and stereotypes about homosexuality?

    3. What values have to do with homosexuality, and why?

Exercise 3.11 The Teenage Pregnancy[1]

This is a guided problem solving exercise, done in groups of from four to seven people. Proceed according to the process outlined in Chapter 1.

Problem Situation. Penny Wise, a social worker on her first job after college, is employed at the Community Mental Health Outreach Center (CMHOC), a local county agency. Although she has had previous clients, this is her first experience with an unwed pregnant girl.

Debbie Turpin is a fifteen-year-old girl who is about six weeks pregnant by her boyfriend, an Hispanic American named Juan Santos. Debbie and Juan have been seeing each other without her parents' knowledge for about six months. They know her parents would not approve of Juan as a boyfriend because he is not of her race and is Catholic. Juan is seventeen years old, a junior in high school. He has a part-time job at a gas station and is quite responsible. Debbie is a good student and seems emotionally mature for her age.

Debbie's parents love her, but they belong to a church that believes in punishment for sins committed, and their definitions of sin are very broad. Their ties with the church are very close, and members of the congregation are very aware of what goes on in other members' lives. Debbie's father is a blue-collar worker, and there is not much excess money in the home as Debbie has four younger siblings. He is a rather authoritarian father, and Debbie's mother defers to him in all things, including her role and the roles of the children, discipline for the children, and things religious.

When Debbie first suspected she was pregnant, she called the crisis center for help and was referred to the CMHOC. This is her first appointment. She has told no one of her problem, partly because the full impact of possible pregnancy is only now beginning to hit her. It is, she says, "like a bad dream from which I'll wake up soon." She feels that Juan would support her no matter what she decided to do. She knows that if her parents find out about the pregnancy they will punish her, but she is not as much worried about the physical punishment as the effects on her parents in terms of their sorrow and embarrassment among their friends. She is totally unaware of her options and does not have any preference for action. Her religion has instilled no values about abortion, although she does know she has "sinned." She does not want to go to her parents, but she knows she needs help.

Instruction 3.11.A   Problem Identification

You (collectively) are the social worker, Penny Wise. Naturally, you have your own values and ideas about the "oughtness" of Debbie's behavior and her choices. You are also concerned about her age and the involvement of her family, the problems she and Juan may have because of the pregnancy, and so on. Remember that this pregnancy is not happening to you, and you cannot "put yourself in Debbie's shoes." You must put aside emotions, desire to help, values, and belief systems to offer Debbie your expert help. What you feel and believe are only important in terms of how they can be used to help Debbie. To clarify the situation, *state clearly and concisely what you perceive as the primary problem in this situation.*

STOP! Do not proceed until your instructor has looked over your work.

Feedback 3.11.A

Among the many choices of problems you may have considered are the following:

1. Debbie does not have a good relationship with her family.

2. She will not be able to support a baby or continue with her education.

3. She needs an abortion.

4. She needs help telling someone (Juan, her parents, her minister) about the pregnancy.

5. She needs medical care.

6. She is an immoral young woman or a spoiled brat.

7. Juan needs to go to work so that he can fulfill his responsibilities to Debbie and the baby.

8. Debbie and Juan need to get married.

There are, of course, other considerations, and you probably have listed many more than are above. The problem for Debbie—the reason she has come to you for help—is that *she is pregnant and does not know what alternatives she has.* She needs information and then help in securing the necessary aid. In other words, she needs your help and expertise in learning about her options in this pregnancy.

Instruction 3.11.B   State the Goals of the Work

As with any social work problem, there are preliminary steps. One is to establish relationships so that work can take place; the second is to lay out goals of the social work effort to be undertaken. As a social worker, *what relationship will you seek to establish, and how? What is the goal for this problem?*

STOP! Do not proceed until your instructor has checked the goals.

Feedback 3.11.B

The first contact of a social worker–client relationship is extremely important. Poorly handled, the client might not return even though in great need. Even worse, it may hurt the client. You must begin by developing a sense of trust with Debbie. "Friendship" or sympathy will not do: these are easily seen as transparent or synthetic. Rather, you must make a clear statement of what you can do for Debbie, show willingness to help within the agency setting, and have a nonjudgmental attitude. Such simple amenities as rising to greet her, sitting her beside you rather than across a desk, and having a comfortable office can help to set her at ease in what must be an uncomfortable situation.

In addition, you must see Debbie as worthy of respect and assure her that her strengths will be a major part of your work with her. Further, you accept Debbie's condition and problem without condemnation. Any moralistic feelings or values you have apply only to yourself—you have no right to impose them on Debbie. Judgmental attitudes or remarks are beyond the bounds of social work practice. You avoid labeling, even in your mind, and do not place Debbie in a "client box." For now, you know only that Debbie's situation is unique because she is a unique human being who has come to you seeking the help of an expert.

You know that social workers are powerful in our relationship with clients and that we may unconsciously exploit clients for personal gratification; therefore, you direct your efforts toward a partnership relationship that recognizes what Debbie can offer. She knows her situation and capabilities more than you do, and she is the one who must endure the ordeal of teenage pregnancy. Though you can help her clarify her feelings and lay out alternatives, only she can make decisions about her life.

The social worker's role is to provide information and support so that Debbie can make a well-informed decision, given her stress and lack of experience because of her youth. She is already six weeks pregnant, so time is important. At this first meeting, alternatives and their consequences must be explored for quick decision making. Though you might prefer to deal in depth with the reasons for and consequences of Debbie's condition, that preference cannot interfere with Debbie's need. Debbie is your primary consideration.

You know that the pregnancy's underlying causes may or may not lie in her background—her family, her own emotional needs, her love for Juan, or any number of things. Her problem now, however, is not to explore causes—it is unwed pregnancy, and the partnership goal is to look at alternatives for Debbie's future.

Instruction 3.11.C *Gather Information*

The first session should provide information from Debbie so that the two of you can find alternatives. This (in the "problem situation") is the most important source of information. You have already gleaned other necessary information from your social work education, texts that you have, and library materials.

1. *What are some kinds of information necessary to help Debbie understand her alternatives? Where can they be found?* List both the personal information you need and the resource agencies you can call on.

Personal Information   *Resource Agencies*

2. A second kind of information comes from assessing Debbie's strengths and those of relevant others, such as Juan, his family, and Debbie's own family. *List the strengths of each relevant system, including Debbie.*

STOP! Do not proceed until your instructor agrees that you have enough information.

Feedback 3.11.C

The first kind of information you need is information about Debbie—her feelings, her relationships with Juan and her family, and so forth. She is the most important source of information for this. Have one of your group members play Debbie, another the social worker, and the remainder discussants. Do a role play according to your instructor's advice. Use the information from the role play as part of your data.

Secondly, you need to know the mandates and policies of your own agency (or like agencies) and the legal aspects of Debbie's problem. Your text and class material are good sources here, although you may need to consult other books. Finally, in the community where your social work program is located, find resources available to Debbie. The instructor is available for questions, and some information is presented below.

Further Information

1. To marry, Debbie must have her parents' and the law's permission. Courts can be petitioned to take wardship and allow a marriage if parents will not give permission.

2. Abortion in your locality may require parental notification or consent. Check this out.

3. Courts or certified agencies may deal with adoption, but it requires parental involvement, except if the court takes wardship of Debbie.

4. Your agency, the Community Mental Health Outreach Center, provides a broad range of counseling and referral services, including family counseling, mental health counseling, and psychological testing and diagnoses. It does not provide abortion or adoption services or money for these services, though it can make referrals for such services. The agency's mandate is to provide any assistance within these general guidelines that is legal and reasonable. Among the agencies that might be of referral use in this problem are

   (1) Department of Public Welfare—Provides medical assistance for the indigent and, depending on the state, Temporary Assistance for Needy Families (TANF) assistance to pregnant teenagers and to new mothers.

   (2) Planned Parenthood—Provides abortion counseling and referral, and may provide abortions depending on state laws. No money is available for abortion in the "Debbie" scenario.

   (3) Legal Aid—May provide legal information regarding the rights of the unborn child.

   (4) Schools—School counselors may help if Debbie trusts them. They could also provide counseling for the future education of Debbie or Juan.

   (5) Technical schools—Business/technical schools may help people who qualify to learn trades either during the day or in the evening.

   (6) Department of Public Welfare—Child care services provide adoptive or foster care placement for the child when it is born.

   (7) Salvation Army—Has maternity homes to which Debbie could be referred to live during her pregnancy.

   (8) Family Services Association—Could be of help in consulting on family crisis and in providing information and adoption services.

Instruction 3.11.D   General Constraints

Any problem situation has some general constraints. You know from Debbie's general information of several difficulties she faces now, regardless of her later decision about the pregnancy. These are called "overarching constraints." They lay the background for alternative solutions and their consequences. In this situation, they include the conditions Debbie brings to the social work relationship—her family's economic and religious backgrounds, for example, or the kind of family settings from which she and Juan come. Your task is to *list several overarching constraints,* and *discuss what effects these may have on Debbie's decision.*

Overarching Constraints	*Effects on Debbie's Decision*
1.	
2.	
3.	
4.	

STOP! Do not proceed until your instructor agrees with your constraints.

Feedback 3.11.D

Though you may have found others, among the most obvious overarching constraints for Debbie are

1. Confusion. Debbie is confused about her options.
2. Guilt. She does not wish to hurt any of those who love her.
3. Time.
4. Money. Whatever choice Debbie makes about her pregnancy, it will require an amount of money not easily available to her, her family, or Juan and his family.
5. Health. Debbie's emotional health and her physical condition are at risk.
6. Social realities of unwed pregnancies. Society still has harsh reactions toward a teen mother; there are limited alternatives for Debbie's, Juan's, and their baby's future; societal bias places emotional strains on the families, and so on.
7. Conflicting love and loyalty. Debbie has affection for Juan, and he for her. She also has love for her family.
8. Worry. Debbie's family's possible reaction to her could be very negative.
9. Age. Debbie is only fifteen years old.

Instruction 3.11.E   Generate Possible Solutions

You now have enough information to "brainstorm" alternative solutions, both good and bad, with Debbie. In brainstorming, think of any and all alternatives, not just "acceptable" ones, even though some may go against major societal norms. Several solutions come to mind, which you should list below. Then, under these categories, list how they might be accomplished. In other words, *what are the major alternatives available* to Debbie? *How might each be accomplished?*

Alternative A.

Alternative B.

Alternative C.

Alternative D.

Alternative E.

STOP! Do not proceed until your instructor has evaluated your alternatives.

Feedback 3.11.E

Most of Debbie's alternatives can be classified into three major categories: abortion, have the child but give it up for adoption, and have the child and keep it. Within those categories, you and Debbie developed the following means of accomplishing each.

Abortion

1. Abortion at a clinic, without either family's knowledge.

2. Abortion by family physician, with or without Debbie's family's knowledge.

3. Self-abortion, along with awareness of its dangers.

Adoption

1. Run away and have the child.

2. Stay at home and have the child.

3. Have the child in a maternity home.

4. Move in with Juan's family during the pregnancy.

Keep the Child

1. Early marriage with Juan so that the child will be legitimate.

2. Stay home during pregnancy and plan to keep the baby in Debbie's parents' home.

3. Run away, seek help from an agency elsewhere, have the baby, and bring it to Debbie's or Juan's parents' home.

4. Stay at a maternity home during pregnancy, then bring the baby home.

5. Stay with Juan's family during the pregnancy.

Instruction 3.11.F   Examining Alternatives—Analysis

Debbie by now is feeling overwhelmed, not only by her problem but by the alternatives, none of which seem really desirable. You feel that if the two of you look at the constraints involved with each alternative, she may be able to better understand them to make a more rational decision. At this stage, *list the positive and negative aspects of each alternative. Prioritize the alternatives in terms of feasibility, given the constraints you have discovered.*

STOP! Do not proceed until so instructed.

Feedback 3.11.F

Adoption—Positive

1. The baby will live.

2. A two-parent family, giving love and security for the baby.

3. Generally, adoptive families are carefully screened to be economically secure.

4. Adoptive families are also screened for emotional maturity, giving more of a chance that babies will be loved.

5. This baby will be a wanted baby by the adoptive parents.

6. The baby will have a better home than Debbie could provide, given her age and other limitations.

7. If Debbie goes away to have her baby, friends, relatives, and church acquaintances may not know she is pregnant. This will spare her and her family embarrassment, and she can resume her old life unencumbered by a child in her teenage years.

8. She can return to school and fulfill her educational potential.

Adoption—Negative

1. There will be pain and unhappiness associated with giving up her child, and the continuing worry and anguish about this child she will never know.

2. Whether she remains in her home or leaves during her pregnancy, there are social and emotional consequences to be faced.

3. The physical and emotional effects of the pregnancy and delivery itself are sometimes severe.

4. What are Juan's rights to the baby?

5. Since the child is biracial, it may be difficult to place immediately, creating trauma for the child.

6. What will be the attitudes of those Debbie loves during her pregnancy? They love her and will be sorrowful and hurt.

7. What are the costs of care for Debbie during pregnancy and childbirth?

Keeping the Baby: Early Marriage—Positive

1. Debbie and Juan love each other, and Juan's family is supportive of the relationship.

2. The baby would have a loving two-parent family.

3. If positive financial and emotional support could be obtained from either or both parental families, Debbie and Juan could continue their educations, leaving the baby with loving grandparents.

Keeping the Baby: Early Marriage—Negative

1. Debbie and Juan are probably too young to enter into this permanent relationship and to have such burdensome responsibilities.

2. Chances are that financial problems would prevent both from continuing their education, thus limiting their life chances and the baby's chances.

3. They lose their "teenage growing and exploring" years in a marriage for which neither is as yet prepared.

4. If they live with parents, they would be seen still as children in their parents' home, but the expectations would be different; they would be expected to contribute as adults while being treated like children.

5. Since the baby would be cared for a great deal by grandparents, if they lived in a parental home, this would create role strain and stress for Debbie.

6. The baby would serve as a constant reminder of lost opportunities for both and might be treated as such even if only on a subconscious, emotional level.

7. Religious differences should not be underestimated when the rearing of a child is involved.

8. Cultural and social differences stemming from the different upbringings of the two would be stressful both for the young parents and for the child.

Keeping the Baby: No Marriage—Positive

1. Debbie would have the baby to care for and love, and the baby would have her.

2. Possibly Debbie's parents, if she lived at home, would also come to love the baby.

3. There would be less emotional and financial burden than in an early marriage. This would be especially beneficial for Juan.

4. Debbie's mother could take care of the baby while Debbie continues her education.

Keeping the Baby: No Marriage—Negative

1. There would be embarrassment for the unwed mother and baby and condemnation by church members of the family.

2. The baby would be reared in a home (with Debbie's parents) that considers the baby living evidence of their daughter's sin.

3. The baby would be reared in a one-parent household.

4. There would be additional financial problems for Debbie and her family.

5. The baby would remain a constant reminder and punishment for Debbie.

6. Debbie would lose her "teen years of development and exploration."

7. Debbie would lose the chance for future education that might offer her a better life.

8. Debbie might become isolated from anyone other than the baby; the baby might come to be seen by her as the cause of her isolation and trouble and be treated accordingly.

9. If Debbie moves out and lives alone, she would have even more problems in terms of child care, isolation, lost opportunities, finances, and so on. It is likely she would become a public dependent. Returning to her family after the birth of the baby would be a problem, and you, as social worker, must assure her that you will be there to help her through crises. Perhaps Debbie's family would refuse to take her in, and you would have to find her and the baby a new home.

Abortion—Positive

1. Abortion has the fewest social consequences or stigmatization unless Debbie chooses to tell her family or Juan.

2. Debbie develops normally into adulthood emotionally and socially.

3. This is the "quickest" solution.

4. Debbie would be free to continue her education

5. This solution probably has the fewest unknown factors connected with it.

6. It would prevent inadequate child care.

7. Both sets of families might never know, alleviating problems with them.

8. The child would not serve as a constant reminder of and punishment for Debbie's "sin."

9. Debbie's family would not be embarrassed and ostracized. Juan would be able to continue his education.

10. The financial cost is minimal compared with that of having the baby.

11. Medical problems are fewer than with pregnancy and delivery, especially for Debbie at her age.

Abortion—Negative

1. What are Debbie's beliefs regarding the "humanness" of the fetus?

2. Juan's Catholicism might make him opposed to abortion.

3. Debbie's family's morality includes the belief that sin deserves punishment.

4. Where would payment for the abortion come from?

5. Debbie has to make an immediate decision.

6. Debbie is afraid for her own physical well-being.

7. What are Debbie's feelings for the unborn child?

In any event, Debbie's life chances will be blighted by this pregnancy. Adoption offers the best life chances for the baby but is unlikely, given her parents' feelings and beliefs about sin. For you, as her social worker, Debbie is the primary client, and involvement of relevant others must be on the basis of her knowledge, consent, and desire.

Instruction 3.11.G   Synthesis

Of course you know that Debbie must make her own decision. However, based on what you two have accomplished during this session, one choice appears best. Remember that Debbie, in the final analysis, must live with her decision.

At this point, the instructor will tell you what Debbie has decided. Discuss the societal values involved in the decision and your own value dilemma about implementing her decision.

After the decision is made, you must help Debbie to implement it. You have expertise on community resources, agency referrals, and so on, for both immediate and long-term help of all sorts. You also have expertise on working with Juan, his family, and Debbie's family. Now, together, you must work on implementing her decision. *Given Debbie's choice of alternatives, how will you implement her decision? What resources will you use? What strengths must she call on? How will you help her deal with her emotional needs?*

STOP! Do not proceed until you and the instructor have discussed Debbie's decision.

Feedback 3.11.G

Do a role play in each group, discussing how you will implement Debbie's decision. Report the group's decision to the class as a whole.

Instruction 3.11.H   Evaluation

How will you evaluate the success of the plan? Discuss and report your choice of evaluation to the instructor, either in class or by writing a short paper on the following three areas of concern:

1. The process of decision making that led to Debbie's choice of solution.

2. An analysis of that solution based on Instruction G.

3. The means of implementation of the decisions, based on your work for Instruction G.

Exercise 3.12 Values in "The Teenage Pregnancy"

The teenage pregnancy exercise was obviously a problem in generalist practice at the micro level. It did not deal on a therapeutic basis with Debbie's problem, although it was interpersonal in that the worker–client dyad worked with it. At the point where we left the exercise, no outside social systems were engaged; however, it is clear that wider family systems, community systems, and perhaps even state or federal legal systems might be involved. Values, from the societal to the personal, at client, worker, and family levels moved unplanned pregnancy into becoming a problem rather than a joyous expectation. Discuss in the classroom

1. What societal values led us to define teenage pregnancy as a problem?

2. What values were involved in the discussions at each step of the process?
    a. Problem definition

    b. Information gathering

    c. Setting goals

    d. Considering alternatives

    e. Choosing feasible alternatives

    f. Implementing the plan

3. What values will be involved in evaluating the success of the plan?

Exercise 3.13 Ethical Dilemmas and Issues in General

Throughout our text, our use of the problem-solving model presents a process for reasonable and logical solutions of problems. However, another element exists for social workers—the ethical facets of problem solving. Loewenberg and Dolgoff[2] have provided us a list of the ethical aspects of problem solving, saying that we should check each ethical aspect for each problem-solving step. In the exercise below, we list the problem-solving steps and ask you to consider the following for each:

1. What ethical issues are involved in this step? What principles, rights, and obligations have an impact on these ethical issues?

2. What additional information is needed to properly identify the ethical implications?

3. What are the relevant ethical rules and principles that can be applied? Which ethical criteria are relevant in this situation?

4. If there is a conflict of interests, who should be the principal beneficiary?

5. How would you rank order the ethical issues, rules, and principles that you have identified?

6. What are the possible consequences that result from utilizing different ethical rules and principles?

7. Who should make the ethical decision? When is it justified to shift ethical decision making to another person (not the social worker)? To whom should it be shifted?[3]

Exercise 3.14 Who Makes the Decision?

Go back to the teenage pregnancy exercise. Each student should note some of the ethics of each step according to Loewenberg and Dolgoff. Then the instructor should lead the class in discussing each of the steps.

1. Problem Identification

2. Goal Statement

3. Information Gathering

4. General Constraints: Are there ethical constraints?

5. Possible Solutions

6. Examining Alternatives

7. Synthesis

8. Evaluation

Our next chapter will deal more fully with the interrelated tasks across levels that have been demonstrated in the exercises about Debbie. We should again, however, point out that the "teenage pregnancy" problem is not isolated at the micro level. Not only did the worker's activities affect the client, they would have affected many other systems if continued across levels. The exercise, including values and choices, could be applied to clients with the same kinds of problems (parallel populations at risk). To engage other services for the client through referral, information, or even advocacy would have been the next step in the intervention process. Certainly others involved in Debbie's life would have to be considered. Courts, maternity homes, and legal, medical, and educational systems would have probably become involved to implement Debbie's decision.

NASW's Code of Ethics and Empowerment Practice

Major societal values are, of course, omnipresent in the relationship of social workers with those who seek our help. However, our Code of Ethics constitute a further set of principles, setting social work apart as a profession. The Code of Ethics has as its mission

> . . . to enhance human well-being and help meet basic human needs of all people, with particular attention to the needs and empowerment of people who are vulnerable, oppressed, and living in poverty. . . .[4]

This mission is rooted in a set of core values that embrace social work's unique purpose and perspective:

- Service
- Social justice
- Dignity and worth of the person
- Importance of human relationships
- Integrity
- Competence[5]

Exercise 3.15 Definitions of Core Values

Read the NASW Code of Ethics and then write a definition for each core value listed above.

1.

2.

3.

4.

5.

In the following exercise, you deal with both values and the Code of Ethics, even though they may not be stipulated.

Exercise 3.16 The Dirty Home

Divide into groups of four or five for the following discussion exercise.
Problem Situation. You are a student social worker in field placement at a public health department, and your task is to make a home visit to a family whose three school-age children need vaccinations before they can enter school in the fall. Your goal is to convince the parent to bring the children in for their free vaccinations.

You have made an appointment to visit the home, but on your arrival you find the house in shambles. The front door is off the hinges and several windows are broken. The odor of urine, stale food, and general dirt assails your nostrils. When you knock, someone shouts for you to come in. An old sofa is stained and smelly, with one cushion missing and springs coming out. Two or three rickety wooden chairs, a coffee table covered with papers, dirty dishes, soda and beer cans are placed near a blaring TV set. A dirty, half-naked toddler sits on the filthy floor, clinging to the parent. An older child with stringy hair and runny nose peeks at you from the hallway, and two other school-age children are watching the TV.

The parent seems almost blank in appearance, but seems to rouse herself to ask you to sit down. You don't really want to sit on the sticky and encrusted furniture, but you do need to talk to the parent. Write your notes before class discussion begins.

Discussion A. What is your reaction to the state of house, parent, and children? That is, what do you immediately believe you should do?
Discussion B. What steps will you take when you return to the office? Upon what theoretical material are these steps based?
Discussion C. Upon what values is your reaction based? What stipulations in the Code of Ethics may apply?
Discussion D. The parent is a man. How do you react to him? Based on what values?
Discussion E. The parent is a woman. How do you react to her? Based on what values?
Discussion F. Given your field placement assignment, what will you do? Given your reaction to the situation, what will you do?
Discussion G. What is your reaction to the Code of Ethics in this instance? Does it apply? Is it difficult for you to stick to the Code? In what way? Why?
Discussion H. Dealing with our own values and biases before we impose them on clients is a difficult task. To judge clients by our standards diminishes them in their own eyes, and, given our Code of Ethics, we do not have that right. If our goal really is empowerment, we need to partner with our clients, help them to see alternatives, and then allow them the choices of what will happen in their future. Conclude the above situation by discussing the following:

1. How can we partner with this parent?
2. How would this parent become empowered?
3. What information do we need to help empower him or her?
4. How can we get the information?
5. What must we do? What must we not do?

Exercise 3.17 The Coin of Payment

A "coin of payment" is the price people pay for goods or services, and it is often payment that is not monetary in nature. Social work operates outside the marketplace; that is, payment for services, all or in part, is provided by agents other than the client. Sliding scales, in which clients pay determined on their income or assets, is one "coin of payment"; however, workers who are less than professional in terms of the Code of Ethics often impose another sliding scale, in that the less clients pay or the more they receive, the more nonmonetary payment is expected. Looking again at the dirty house exercise, list the kinds of payment some workers might expect from the parent, and discuss the ways in which these expectations violate the Code of Ethics.

Coin of Payment Expected	*Violations of Code of Ethics*
1.	a.
	b.
	c.
2.	a.
	b.
	c.
3.	a.
	b.
	c.
4.	a.
	b.
	c.

Portfolio Building

1. What do you know now about the importance of values in social work practice?

2. What have you learned about your own values, specifically: values on the "isms" of society—racism, sexism, ageism, classism or poverty, heterosexism—and on your feelings about the results of unwed pregnancy?

3. Have you clarified some of those values, and will you be able to deal with them in social work practice? How?

4. What further information do you need, and what further work must you do, to clarify your values for generalist practice?

5. What do you now know about the Code of Ethics and about ethical problem solving?

Notes

1. Created with the help of Harlan Schweer, Purdue University, 1988.
2. Loewenberg, Frank M. and Ralph Dolgoff (1992). *Ethical Decisions for Social Work Practice*. Itasca, IL: F.E. Peacock Publishers, Inc.
3. Ibid., p. 55.
4. *Code of Ethics* of the National Association of Social Workers, as adopted by the Delegate Assembly of August 1996. Part 1 of 3. In *The Indiana Social Worker*, v. 14, no. 4. Published by the Indiana Chapter, NASW, October 1996, pp. 6–8.
5. Ibid.

ChapterFOUR

Levels of Generalist Practice

Simultaneous Practice across Levels

Generalist practice is based on a generic foundation, which includes a liberal arts base; social work skills, values, and knowledge; an awareness of social work's mission and history; sensitivity to diversity and social justice; and dedication to social action and social change.[1] (See Figure 4.1.)

Effective and competent social work practice addresses social dysfunctions at all levels of a manifested problem. We serve clients and populations-at-risk across a variety of fields and levels, yet often forget the commonalities of practice tasks from the interpersonal to social policy. Rather than seeing only clients' immediate problems, we must be continually conscious of underlying problems and the possibilities of change across levels from the individual to the societal.

Awareness of the simultaneous nature of practice across levels makes us better social workers. Though we often separate our practice into micro, mezzo, or macro levels for clarity while dealing with clients' immediate problems, we look at implications of other levels—what can be done at the group or family level, how the community could be activated to help parallel populations, or how organizational policies or state or national legislation could be changed to provide social justice for similar clients' problems. *Simultaneity* presumes that individual, family, and community are always tied to the widest environment. It suggests that social workers must connect the individual to the larger environment *and* to their own personal social circumstances.[2]

By *levels of practice* we mean the following, recognizing that there is overlap among the levels:

1. Micro-level or direct practice
   a. Therapeutic counseling: individual psychological or emotional counseling, rarely done by generalist social workers
   b. Direct practice in problem-solving partnerships, on which specific tasks are agreed and worked with client systems (individuals,

FIGURE 4.1. A Conceptual Model of Generalist and Advanced Generalist Social Work, March 1988

GENERIC FOUNDATION

Liberal arts base: social work knowledge base, biological, socio-cultural, psychological, human development, systems & ecological perspective; social work & social welfare history; social work mission & purpose; focus on person in environment; professional use of self; social work values; basic communication and interpersonal helping skills; cultural competency; commitment to social action and social change; strengths perspective within problem-solving approach; and understanding of human relationships.

GENERALIST

PERSPECTIVE: informed by socio-behavioral/ecosystems knowledge; ideologies that include humanism and empowerment; methodology open; client-centered and problem focused; direct and indirect intervention; research based.

COMPETENCIES: 1) engage in interpersonal helping; 2) manage change process; 3) utilize multilevel intervention modes; 4) perform multiple practice roles; and 5) examine/assess own practice.

CONCENTRATION

Advanced social work practice skills & knowledge in an area of concentration

Practice emphasis based on:
• Frameworks & perspectives (conceptual framework built upon relevant theories)
• Populations-at-risk
• Practice contexts/perspectives
• Intervention methods/roles
• Traditional values

ADVANCED GENERALIST

Population groups & common base transferable among settings problem areas.

In addition to generalist perspective and competencies, practitioner will:
1) apply critical thinking skills; 2) demonstrate professional use of self;
3) understand strategies of change that advance solid justice; 4) apply knowledge of bio-psycho-social variables; 5) analyze impact of social policy; 6) communicate effectively; and 7) seek organizational change.

Shelly, S., 1998, with excerpts from 1994 CSWE Curriculum Policy Statement and Mona Struhsaker Schatz, Lowell E. Jenkins, and Bradford W. Sheafor. Colorado State University.

groups, families), and referral, education, modeling, and information sources are given

c. "Case advocacy," which "runs interference" for clients to argue their cases to powerful others.

2. Mezzo-level practice

a. Indirect practice, in which practitioners influence wider systems to serve both individual clients and parallel client populations

b. "Cause advocacy," or advocacy to insure clients' rights when they interact with more powerful systems and institutions. Indirect practice generally takes place in organizations and in communities and aims to change structures and policies to benefit client systems.

c. Community action or community practice, which is the mobilization of client groups to make social change for problems they have identified.

3. Macro-level practice is indirect practice at the broadest level, where there may be no client contact at all. Its facets include

a. Administration of human service organizations

b. Program development and evaluation

c. Research, writing, and educating future social workers

d. Lobbying, testifying, and taking political action to change policies and legislation

e. Policy formulation, implementation, and evaluation

Although social workers tend to individualize problems and solutions, this makes *good* social work impossible, while turning away from individual work completely and adopting *only* macro practice is impractical and problematic. The individual is (usually) the base of practice, but the emphasis is on how wider levels of the environment serve as resources for individual problems.[3] A simultaneous model of practice can help you, the social worker, to view all levels as you work on any one. The central challenge to social work is to connect the individual and the collective, the personal and the social.[4] Figure 4.2 shows the simultaneity model. Using a simultaneous perspective presumes an ideological tie among individual, family, community, and even societal problems. Though the levels are artificially separated for ease in understanding, try to see the simultaneous nature of the work that could be done.

Just to make it easier to see the simultaneous nature of crises, let's look at a problem (or set of problems) that has little to do with social work itself.

Exercise 4.1 Now What Do I Do?[6]

You are driving to your social work night class and realize how hard it is raining. Out of nowhere, your right front wheel hits a large pothole that causes you to veer into the curb, and

FIGURE 4.2   *Simultaneity Model Revisited*[5]

A. Micro/Intrapersonal Practice
Work: client–worker dyad on personal/intrapsychic
  problem
Method is clinical or therapeutic counseling, education,
  and referral
Purpose: to gain information about client and the client's
  problem
	B. Micro/Direct Interpersonal Practice
	Work: client within social systems, awareness of other
	  clients in similar situations
	Method: case advocacy, may include clinical and
	  therapeutic work
	Purpose: partner with client to solve problem

C. Indirect Practice (Mezzo Level)
Work: insure delivery of services for parallel
  populations-at-risk
Method: cause advocacy, coalition building, grassroots orga-
  nization, lobbying etc.
Purpose: social action to develop programs and policies
  for populations-at-risk
	D. Indirect Practice (Macro Level)
	Work: no direct client contact
	Method: administration, policy, education
	Purpose: influence government to change policies and
	  programs for populations-at-risk

your car abruptly stops. You are okay, but the right wheel is a mess; it will not turn. You know without doubt that you need to arrange to have work done on your car. What are the steps it will take to get your car fixed? Does your auto insurance policy cover this type of damage? Is the city liable for the damage? If so, how do you collect? But first things first; let's start out.

Discussion Questions

1. First you need to get the car towed to a garage. How do you determine which garage?
2. What are the steps it will take to get your car fixed?
3. What barriers might you encounter? Which ones are within your control? Which barriers are beyond your control?
4. Which barriers beyond your control might delay your ability to get the car fixed?
5. Where do you find out about liability? Will your own auto insurance pay for repair?
6. Because you need your car every day to commute to classes and to your part-time job, how will you get and pay for a rental car?
7. Could you have avoided this accident? Whom do you blame?
8. What feelings do you have after discerning the cause of the accident?

Now let's look at an exercise in social work practice across all levels.

Exercise 4.2 Working Across Levels

Divide the class into groups of four or five persons. Groups then pick a person in need of social work intervention: some possible candidates might be a learning disabled child, a person with AIDS, an elderly person, a poor person, and so on. Discuss and assume strengths for the person, which you will then include as resources at every level of practice.

A. Elements of the situation
    1. Describe the problem situation.

    2. Describe the practice level requiring the most immediate attention.

    3. Decide what information you will need and where you can find it.

    4. Describe the resources you and the client have available to your work.

B. Using the chart in Figure 4.2, develop your own chart of practice across levels for this person.

A. Micro/Intrapersonal Practice	B. Micro/Direct Interpersonal Practice
C. Indirect Practice (Mezzo Level)	D. Indirect Practice (Macro Level)

C. Report on your work in class, and lead the discussion on the client you have chosen.

Exercise 4.3 The Abused Spouse

General Instructions. This is a guided problem-solving exercise. Break into groups of from five to seven students. Take one step at a time, reach consensus, and write your conclusions in the space provided. Do not proceed to the next step until the instructor has reviewed your work.

Problem Situation. You are a worker at a crisis hot line for domestic abuse, located in a small Midwestern town. Annie, who identifies herself as a young wife with two small children, has called your center several times, at first anonymously and later giving only her first name. Her husband is a well-known, highly regarded basketball coach, and she is afraid to tell anyone about his abusive behavior because she fears people will think she is lying or blame her. She talks of his explosive temper, jealous rages, and physical violence. He has tried to choke her and has threatened to kill her. The battering has destroyed her self-esteem. Even her family and members of her church, including the minister, believe she has a model family, and her husband is perceived as a model husband, church member, and community servant. Finally, afraid he will succeed in killing her, Annie asks you for help.

Instruction 4.3.A   *Problem Identification*

In behaviorally specific terms, *what is Annie's presenting problem?* What other problems do you believe she has, from your conversations? *Prioritize and list them.*

Presenting Problem:

Other Problems

1.
2.
3.
4.
5.
6.

Prioritize Problems

1.
2.
3.
4.
5.
6.

STOP! Do not proceed until the instructor has discussed your answer.

Feedback 4.3.A

The presenting problem is that Annie is afraid her abusive spouse will kill her. The emotional problem is a drastic loss of self-esteem and feelings related to survival. She is also likely experiencing depression, anxiety, and suicidal or homicidal ideation.

Instruction 4.3.B   State the Goal of Your Work

Having quickly assessed Annie's situation, her fear, and her past reluctance to leave her spouse, you ask her to come for an interview. When she comes in, the two of you discuss her priorities, using the tentative list you developed in problem identification. Now, *state the goals of your work* in levels of priority; that is, state the immediate goal for Annie, then future goals at wider levels that you will try to attain.

1. Immediate goal

2. Other micro-system goals

3. Mezzo-level goals

4. Macro-level goals

STOP! Do not proceed until the instructor has checked your goals.

Feedback 4.3.B

Even though you know that building, enhancing, and improving her self-esteem is a major goal, the severity of her situation means that future goals must take a back seat. Safety is an important issue, and low self-esteem is secondary in nature. The immediate goal is to find ways to protect Annie by developing a plan for her safety.

Instruction 4.3.C   Gather Information

You find that Annie has no real skills for supporting herself but that she is an intelligent woman who has risen from poverty before marriage to achieve a bachelor's degree in humanities. She married right after graduation and so has no work experience except for clerking in Wal Mart and various jobs in fast food restaurants. Her parents respect her husband and she believes that if she leaves him they will disown her. Her loss of self-esteem has destroyed much of her motivation, but you encourage her in believing she can retrieve it. Even with her fear, she has had enough strength to come to you for help. Assess Annie's needs, strengths, and priorities. Develop a list of each.

Needs	*Strengths*	*Priorities*

What are her resources at the levels of practice?

Micro-Resources	*Mezzo Resources*	*Macro Resources*

STOP! Do not proceed until instructed to do so.

Feedback 4.3.C

Annie and you first determine what she wants and assess her strengths, needs, priorities, and corresponding resources, including background information on her life circumstances, capacity and motivation for change, and the real danger she is facing at the present time. Possible categories of resources include family, church, financial, transportation, educational resources; real and present danger laws; opportunity to access assistance, and so forth. What do you notice about how sometimes resources can also be part of the problem?

You might define the resource categories as micro, mezzo, and macro, or you could look at them as immediate, primary, and secondary, or in other ways, such as local agencies, personal and social, or laws, procedures, and regulations. The categories themselves are not as important as to be able to designate clearly the kinds of information you need. If you decide to partialize by levels, the information you need at the smallest level would come from Annie herself, details as to what her husband might do, what kinds of emotional or financial support she would need, whether her family would really disown her or help, and if she could rely on her church.

At the second level, you would look at agencies available to help Annie and the level of each one's effectiveness. For example, if the court ordered a restraining order, to what extent would the local police be able to enforce it? Would the court order financial support? What agencies might be able to help in terms of carrying out her safety plan? There may even be information you need at the widest level, including, for example, networks of people nationwide who help abused wives, legislation in process, agency directories, and so on.

You will need to connect with your local Information and Referral service or access the Internet or library to get the information you need. On other micro levels, you assess what her family, outside groups, church, and so on might provide for her. On the mezzo level, you look at the community to find local police and court procedures governing spouse abuse, community shelters, financial and counseling assistance she might access. At the macro level, you find the state laws and protection given in cases of spouse abuse, stalking, attempted murder, etc.

Instruction 4.3.D   Brainstorming Solutions

Given the information you have, *Annie and you brainstorm solutions* to her present danger. Neither limit your imagination at this point nor choose an obvious solution without considering others (called the Iron Law of Specificity). By looking at many possibilities, you might find the one best solution for Annie. At the same time, you must *brainstorm solutions at mezzo and macro levels* so that Annie and wives like her, called "populations-at-risk" will be able to work with the information and solutions you and Annie have developed. Using the chart on the following page, *list the possible solutions for Annie at present,* at micro, mezzo, and macro levels.

Level	Problem/Goal	Resource Information	List of Alternatives
Micro Problem 1.			
Micro Problem 2.			
Mezzo Problem 3.			
Macro Problem 4.			

STOP! Do not proceed until the instructor has checked your information.

Feedback 4.3.D Brainstorming Solutions

Level	Problem	Goal	Information	List of Possible Alternatives
Micro 1	Safety	Develop safety plan	Resources, strengths, life circumstances, capacity for change, and real danger.	Coming to shelter Staying home, taking chances Moving in with family or neighbors Asking minister to talk to husband Getting a gun for protection Going underground Kicking husband out Moving out on own Filing restraining order or battery charges
Micro 2	Low self-esteem	Improve self-esteem	Same as above	Meeting with individual counselor Joining community support group Doing it on own Enhancing her education Joining self-help projects and programs
Mezzo	Limited protection for battered women	Rouse community for protective laws	Populations-at-risk Present legislation How to create change Community resources and strengths Action systems	Forming a coalition Contacting the state for possible expansion dollars Working with local churches to provide safe houses Setting up lobby for change Eliciting help from legislators, relevant others Educating police about domestic violence Demanding protection on restraining orders

Macro	Current policies do not insure protection for women being battered	Change policy to insure protection	Political climate
			  Strengths and resources at group, family, coalitions, and community levels
			Organizing network
			  Political interests of policy makers
			Opposition to change in families, churches, police, community
				Lobbying
				Testifying
				Demonstrating
				Involving concerned groups, such as NASW, NOW, other agencies
				Becoming involved politically

Instruction 4.3.E   Choosing the Most Feasible Alternative

You have developed a list of solutions at the different levels of practice. Because your first priority is to protect Annie, you now need to look at solutions for her safety. The first step in this solution is to *prioritize the solutions in order of feasibility.* Next, *assess each in terms of Annie's strengths and the resources of the community.* Finally, look at *barriers to Annie's success.*

Solution	Strengths	Community Resources	Barriers
1.	1)	1)	1)
	2)	2)	2)
	3)	3)	3)
	4)	4)	4)
2.	1)	1)	1)
	2)	2)	2)
	3)	3)	3)
	4)	4)	4)
3.	1)	1)	1)
	2)	2)	2)
	3)	3)	3)
	4)	4)	4)

Solution	Strengths	Community Resources	Barriers
4.	1)	1)	1)
	2)	2)	2)
	3)	3)	3)
	4)	4)	4)

STOP! Do not proceed until the instructor has evaluated your work.

Feedback 4.3.E

Assess the strengths, resources, and barriers according to your own community. Annie decides to come to shelter.

Micro-1-Level Solutions	Strengths	Resources	Barriers
Coming to shelter Staying home, taking chances Moving in with family/ neighbors Asking minister to talk to husband Getting a gun for protection Going underground Kicking husband out Moving out on own Filing restraining order or battery charges			
Micro-2-Level Solutions Meeting with individual counselor Joining community support group Doing it on own Enhancing education Joining self-help projects and programs			
Mezzo-Level Solutions Forming a coalition Contacting the state for possible expansion dollars Working with local churches to provide safe houses Setting up lobby for change Eliciting help from legislators, relevant others Educating police about domestic violence Demanding protection on restraining orders			
Macro-Level Solutions Lobbying Testifying Demonstrating Involving concerned groups, such as NASW, NOW, other agencies Becoming involved politically			

Instruction 4.3.F   Implementing and Evaluating the Solution

Annie takes the car one night when her husband is sleeping and drives to the shelter. In measuring your success in helping her take this action, answer the following questions:

1. How well do you think this plan will work? Why?

2. What is the next step for Annie?

3. What are your next steps at different levels?

Discussion on "The Abused Spouse" Exercise

Once Annie is safe in the shelter, you and she can set other goals. The first would probably be to increase her own strengths, particularly in the area of self-esteem. To do this, she might see an individual counselor or join a community support group. She can also set her own goals—what she really wants for her life—and this could take the form of divorcing her spouse, enhancing her education, moving away from the town, and so forth.

At the same time Annie and you are partnering on the goals of safety and self-esteem, another part of your professional task is to consider action on mezzo and macro levels for parallel populations at risk. Your goals may be to organize community action to demand better police and court protection, provide more shelters in the area, set up a training program to educate police on spouse abuse, establish a coalition in the community, and so on. At the macro level, you know the problem is that the law is lax and unspecific about interfering in domestic quarrels, so your goal may be to change policies by setting forth exact definitions of what constitutes abuse. At this level, you would formulate plans for lobbying the legislature and testifying, involving all your relevant constituencies in your proposed social action.

Problem Solving and Practice Levels

Our brief example points out the uses of the problem-solving method in a multitude of ways, looks at the strengths perspective, and notes the simultaneous concerns and actions of generalist practitioners across levels—thoughts, concerns, and actions perceived simultaneously to help clients, populations-at-risk, and the community, and to better society as a whole. Obviously, relationships across levels have many of the same characteristics.

1. The personal becomes political at mezzo and macro levels because of resource allocation, mobilization, changing public sentiment, and leverage with political entities.
2. Defining the problem and setting goals are essential steps to action.
3. The identified problem—in Annie's case, immediate danger—must be handled first, even though we may also be concerned about the client's other problems (for Annie, her emotional and mental health).
4. As we gather information from many sources, the most important are obviously client strengths and community resources.
5. A number of alternatives might solve any one problem, and it is our professional responsibility to consider alternatives and their consequences in partnership with clients.
6. While some solutions might seem easier or better to us, the partnership requires that clients make their own decisions. Our job is to lay out alternatives, along with the pros and cons of each, that the clients may not see. Selecting a feasible solution considers the problem's severity, client strengths, and client needs and self-determination. Though we may prefer a particular alterative, the partnership model requires us to respect clients as the experts on their own lives.
7. Mezzo and macro levels of action work for the whole population-at-risk, and helping one client with social action and social change makes that help available for the many in need.

Exercise 4.4 Relevant Constituencies

Social action requires coalitions and groups to support the plans and programs of professional social work. Relevant constituencies are those people and groups who support you and those who might act against your planned social action. Your first task is to identify these groups. Then you must inform and inspire those who will help and plan to convince the others to at least not fight against you. You will have to gather enough support and persuasive information to neutralize their arguments.

In the abused spouse exercise, you identified a parallel population-at-risk—those women who, like Annie, are in danger of abuse from their spouses. Using that example, first identify positive and negative constituencies. Then identify the strengths of each constituency and at least one persuasive tactic to either gain their support or neutralize their opposition.

Constituency	*Positive?*	*Their Resources*	*Your Tactic*
1.			
2.			

3.

4.

5.

6.

Exercise 4.5 Hoop Dreams[7]

General Instructions

You have just watched the documentary movie *Hoop Dreams*. Now complete the following exercise, supporting your statements with specific information such as quotations and clear descriptions of what you observed in the movie. Your goal is to demonstrate that you understand and can apply social work concepts to Arthur's family.

Problem Situation

The documentary movie *Hoop Dreams* shows two families over a period of several years, looking at the impact of inadequate schools, the effects of living in poverty, and the influence of readily available drugs in the neighborhood. The story also addresses violence in the neighborhood and inadequate housing, and racial issues are especially highlighted.

1. At the time that Arthur's father leaves, the family faces many challenges. What are they? Identify these challenges at each level: micro 1, micro 2, mezzo, and macro in the chart below.

Level	Problem/ Goal	Resource	Strength	Roles	Possible Alternatives
Micro 1	P: G:				
Micro 2	P: G:				

Level	Problem/ Goal	Resource	Strength	Roles	Possible Alternatives
Mezzo	P: G:				
Macro	P: G:				

Use the previous chart in completing the following exercises:

2. What strengths are apparent at each level? In Arthur's mother? In Arthur's father? In the family? In the community? In the culture?

	Micro	*Mezzo*	*Macro*
Arthur's Mother			
Arthur's Father			
Family			
Community			
Culture			

3. What resources are available at each level?

	Micro	*Mezzo*	*Macro*
Arthur's Mother			
Arthur's Father			
Family			
Community			
Culture			

4. At each level, what would be your goal in working with the family? The community? The culture?

	Micro	*Mezzo*	*Macro*
Family Goal			
Community			
Culture			

5. Assume that you are a social worker employed at a multiservice agency assigned to work with Arthur and his family. What social work roles and action would be appropriate if you were helping resolve micro-level problems that affect this family?

6. Assume that you are a social worker employed at a multiservice agency assigned to work with Arthur and his family. What social work roles and action would be appropriate if you were helping resolve mezzo-level problems that affect this family?

7. Assume that you are a social worker employed at a multiservice agency assigned to work with Arthur and his family. What social work roles and action would be appropriate if you were helping resolve macro-level problems that affect this family?

8. Assume that you are a social worker employed at a multiservice agency assigned to work with Arthur and his family. What possible alternatives and solutions would you assist the family identify at each level?

9. What additional information would you need to know about the family to fully understand its situation?

10. What feelings do you think are being experienced by individuals in the family at this time of crisis?

11. Think about what the family seems to value or think is important. In what ways are these values strengths to the family?

12. Enter into a class discussion about the environmental stressors the family is facing. What are they? How do you think cultural, ethnic, racial, background, gender, and class affect this family? How would these differences between you and members of the family influence forming a professional social work relationship with the family as a whole or with members of the family?

13. Perceptions of social work
   a. How do you think the family would perceive a social worker?

   b. How would that perception facilitate or limit the work together?

   c. How will *your* biases, stereotypes, or view of them affect *your* work with the family?

   d. How would you prepare for the first meeting with the family?

Looking at the Levels

By now, you should have a good perspective on the levels of social work practice using the generalist model and the problem-solving perspective. In our next sections, we will put these ideas to work even more, looking at the individual client, groups, organizations, and finally policy as practice.

Portfolio Building

1. What are the levels of practice? How do you work with them?

2. Explain the simultaneity model. Why is it important for social workers to understand the simultaneous levels of practice?

3. How do levels of practice and the simultaneity model fit into the systems framework? How do they fit into the ecological model?

4. Problem solving is the overarching method for social work practice in this book. How do the concepts of levels of practice and simultaneity model fit into that model?

Notes

1. Schatz, Mona Struhsaker, Lowell E. Jenkins, and Bradford W. Sheafor (March 1998). *A Conceptual Model of Generalist and Advanced Generalist Social Work*. Colorado State University: Unpublished manuscript.
2. Fisher, Robert, and Howard Jacob Karger (1997). *Social Work and Community in a Private World*. New York: Longman Press.
3. Op. cit.
4. Fisher and Karger, pp. 39–42.
5. The original Simultaneity Model appeared in the first edition of this book. The present model was developed from the original by Professor Shelly.
6. This exercise was developed by Harry J. Macy, Ph.D., Director of the Department of Social Work, Ball State University.
7. Exercise developed and contributed by Valerie Nash Chang, Ph.D., Indiana University School of Social Work.

Section TWO

Micro Practice with Individuals, Groups, and Families

ChapterFIVE

Working with the Individual Client

In Section II, we will be looking at the interrelated tasks of social workers and the ways in which they must be aware of and work across levels. If we intend to work for empowerment and social justice, micro-practice, as illustrated in most of the exercises in the values chapter, is tunnel vision. While working with individual clients, families, or groups is certainly an essential and rewarding, kind of practice, systems work, ecological practice, and problem solving through the mezzo and macro levels makes our practice professional social work.

An important task of direct practice is psychosocial assessment, but before even beginning, certain tasks involving trust must be accomplished by the worker. These are basic "client approach" techniques and processes such as trust, disclosure, listening, and so on. The following exercises explore consequences of disclosing problems and describe characteristics of those to whom we feel comfortable with our problems.

Exercise 5.1 Who Can We Trust?

Individually, take a few minutes to think about a problem or worry you had but could not discuss with anyone. There may have been no one available, or you might have been afraid to talk about it, or the nature of the problem might have been too difficult to discuss. In the space below, write your feelings about the problem. Do not state what the problem was.

1. What *feelings* did you have about the problem?

2. What were your *fears* about discussing it? What were the *obstacles* to discussion?

3. What were the consequences, either in your life or in your feelings, of not disclosing this problem?

Join together in groups of three or four people, and, in about three minutes each, read your lists one at a time to the group. Don't disclose the problem itself. Discuss only the feelings and consequences you each experienced because you felt you could not tell anyone about your problem.

1. What kinds of feelings did this discussion bring out?
2. Did disclosure of your fears and feelings, even at this late date and without talking about the problem itself, make you feel different about yourselves or your problems? How?

Exercise 5.2 Who Can We Tell?

Form small groups of three or four people. Without discussion, take about five minutes to answer the items below.

Think of a problem or concern that you *did* disclose to someone, but make sure it is a problem that you are comfortable in sharing with others. Then write down, in the spaces below, the following:

1. If you were upset by the behavior of the person to whom you went for help and regretted telling your problem, list at least three *behaviors* he or she exhibited that made you sorry you told. Then say how those behaviors made you feel.

Behavior	*Feeling*

1.

2.

3.

If you found the person helpful and were glad you disclosed the problem, list at least three *behaviors* he or she exhibited that made you feel good about disclosing the problem.

        Behavior   *Feeling*

1.

2.

3.

Go around your group and read your responses, then discuss the following:

1. What must it be like for people with no one to turn to for help?
2. What obstacles did you face in telling others of your fears, problems, concerns, and worries? How would those who come to us for help feel?
3. What must we, as social workers, be careful to show in our behaviors when others talk about their problems to us? Why? List the relevant behaviors below and then discuss why you chose them.

Relational Skills

As social workers, we have learned a set of relational skills called the Carkhuff model.[1] They include:

1. Empathy—the ability to "walk in another's shoes," to understand a person's situation and respond to it with appropriate concern.

2. Respect—the ability to accord another person belief in his or her uniqueness and to trust that person's potential to cope with life problems.

3. Warmth—an attentive, non judgmental response to another person's humanness.

4. Concreteness—the accurate labeling of feelings, experiences, and behaviors.

5. Genuineness—honesty and authenticity in dealing with others—a perception that, because of their status as valued human beings, they merit such sincerity.

6. Self-disclosure—appropriate use of the worker's self that allows the client to perceive the worker's ideas, attitudes, and relevant experiences.

7. Confrontation—the ability to point out discrepancies between thought and actions without engendering emotions destructive to the relationship (e.g., fear or shame in the client that might result in anger toward the worker or an increase in the client's anxiety).

8. Immediacy—the ability to respond to the state of interaction as it exists in the "here and now" between client and workers.

In the following exercises, there are two ways to proceed. Your instructor will direct you. Each role play should last about five minutes, with another ten minutes spent on discussion.

Method 1. All members of the class choose a partner and conduct interviews, with one person the respondent listener and the other the one with the problem. You may switch roles for the separate exercises or switch partners.

Method 2. Two people are chosen from the class to do each role play. One is the grievant; the second is an interviewer who is attempting to use relational skills to help the first. The remaining class members observe the interaction and note examples of each relational skill they see in the role-play process.

Exercise 5.3 Kicked Out by the Computer

You are a university freshman and you have just been kicked out of school by a computer error that says your financial aid has not come through. The financial aid secretary says she thinks it has. You are very upset and go to the bursar, to your academic counselor, and to the financial aid counselor. They say only that there must be a mix-up somewhere. You go to a friend for advice and consolation.

Begin simply by saying that you are upset. Let the friend draw out the facts and your feelings. List below those behaviors that demonstrate the friend's relational skills. Afterwards, discuss in class.

Relational Skills	Behavior	Behavior	Behavior
Empathy			
Respect			
Warmth			
Concreteness			
Genuineness			
Self-Disclosure			
Confrontation			

Relational Skills	Behavior	Behavior	Behavior
Immediacy			

Exercise 5.4 The Roommate Problem

You are a college junior and have been assigned a new roommate, a freshman from your home town. The roommate has no friends and depends on you for everything. Although you like the person, you don't want to be a babysitter, but you don't want any hurt feelings between you. You are feeling constrained, strangled, and manipulated. You go to the dorm counselor for advice.

Begin by saying that you're fed up. Let the counselor draw you out. Say anything you like. After the role play, fill out the exercise sheet below.

Relational Skills	Behavior	Behavior	Behavior
Empathy			
Respect			
Warmth			
Concreteness			
Genuineness			
Self-Disclosure			
Confrontation			
Immediacy			

Discuss in class the skills used in the exercise.

Exercise 5.5 The Vanishing Lover

You are a college sophomore and your lover has just ended your relationship. You are understandably upset and need a listening ear. Make up your own details. Begin by saying that you're shocked, and let the interviewer draw out everything else. After the role play, fill out the exercise sheet and then discuss the problem in class.

Cognitive Skills

Cognitive skills are those mental functions used to analyze not only the factual information given but the less overt information obtained from the interaction. That is, we observe such things as eye contact, body language, emotional and behavioral actions, and our feelings and those of the client about what is happening in the context of the interview. Thus, as we are

Relational Skills	Behavior	Behavior	Behavior
Empathy			
Respect			
Warmth			
Concreteness			
Genuineness			
Self-Disclosure			
Confrontation			
Immediacy			

ourselves "experiencing" the session, an analytic part of our minds notes the "what is happening" as another important source of information.

The cognitive skills of generalist practice are defined in the problem-solving model. Because of the complexity of most "people in situation" problems, however, we seldom have the luxury of laying out such a careful analysis while the work itself (the intervention session) is in progress. Rather, we usually note problems, situations, factors, and emotions as we proceed, and our minds sort through these both during the process and after to make sense of the input. Though we use the problem-solving model as an abstract, we must break it down to put it into practice.

The following are cognitive skills:

1. *Analyzing a "person/problem/situation" (the social situation) in terms of commonalities across society.* Regardless of where you are in the process, particular human reactions occur—anger, depression, fear—and the ability to identify them to point out commonalities.

2. *Interpretation of verbal and nonverbal content of the relationship.* Being able to see and interpret them for information is the difference between being a friend and being a professional social worker. We must realize that the analysis includes reactions of both client and worker, and that the ongoing internal dialog in the worker's mind should include not only "he or she feels . . ." but "my reaction to that statement/emotion/behavior is . . ."

3. *Identifying personal and social constraints that prevent well being.* In formulating any action plan, outside constraints such as time, money, legality, and so on may prevent action. Internal constraints—inability to become motivated or to take action if motivated—obscure goal directions and prevent action. Ambiguity of feelings is one example, as in a love–hate relationship or guilt about pursuing a personal goal of happiness. Fear is another emotion that obstructs action, and you can probably find many others.

4. *Breaking down the problem.* Partializing a whole set of concerns helps clients to clarify what may have seemed one whole hopeless mess. Separating out different areas of concern to work on them one at a time often relieves free-floating anxiety that accompanies an unclear definition of problems, and it gives clients direction on which tasks can be accomplished first.

5. *Verbalizing in clear statements the essences of clients' concerns.* Too often an overwhelming problem results in a diffuse mixture of fears, anxieties, and "I don't know whys." Picking out common threads, verbalizing them, and reinterpreting what you perceive so that clients can agree with or deny your assessment, is an important cognitive skill.

Although there are many such skills, these are among the most useful in generalist practice. The following exercises, based on the scenarios presented in the three preceding exercises, emphasizes their use in ordinary and professional situations.

Exercise 5.6 Cognitive Exercises

Refer to any or all of the three role plays above. In one sentence

1. Identify the problematic social situation.

2. Identify the primary emotional problem.

3. What has *this* person/problem/situation in common with other such scenarios?

4. Name the obvious emotions of the person with the problem.

5. Name the emotions of the listener/interviewer.

6. How are these emotional affects important to the context of the exercise?

7. What social constraints on action did you perceive?

8. What personal constraints did you notice?

9. Break down the problem to see its relational issues: what emotional problems must be dealt with before the problem can be solved?

10. Break down the whole problem into a series of smaller tasks. What particular concerns can be worked on to solve the larger problem?

(1)

(2)

(3)

(4)

(5)

(6)

(7)

(8)

Social Diagnosis: The Art of Social Assessment

People come to social workers because they need to achieve a goal. The initial interview, once called the "social diagnosis," sets the tone of the entire helping relationship. Our job in the initial interview is to assess, or make a preliminary appraisal of, the "person in environment" and his or her "presenting" problem, along with strengths and resources. Figure 5.1 is a format for social diagnosis.[2]

FIGURE 5.1   Elements of Social Diagnosis

Diagnosis
  Identifying information
  Social and ecological systems (individual, family, community)
  Presenting problems
  Strengths and resources, hopes and desires
  Referral and collateral information
  Social history
Assessment
  Structure of all systems
  Mood and emotion
  Development
  Competence and resources
  Resilience and risk
Goals
Summary

Shelly, S., 1998, with excerpts from Barry Corner (1991) *The Social Work Skills Workbook*. Belmont, CA: Wadsworth, Inc. Unpublished exercise.

Clearly, we can only begin to "fill in the blanks" for a social diagnosis in the initial interview. We can obtain some basic "description" information in the interview itself, including parts of the social history. However, "assessment" information usually comes as we write up the interview or discuss it with our supervisors.

The complexity of any problem situation makes it difficult to carefully analyze everything going on—the interaction complete with physical, emotional, relational, and social factors. More often, we note problems, situations, and relating factors as we proceed and sort through them both during and after the process. That is, we interpersonally guide an interaction while we think of what we ask, providing an atmosphere in which social work intervention can take place.

A social worker's problem-defining skills are at the forefront of assessment. The following exercises look at the essential elements of social assessment: content (what the client says is going on), process (what goes on in the interview in addition to the presenting problem), and how to do the assessment itself.

Exercise 5.7 The Intake Interview Scenario: Introducing Don Duguid[3,4]

General Instructions

Break into groups of four or five students. The following exercise is based on the guided problem-solving model, so do not proceed to next steps until you have sought advice from your instructor.

Problem Situation

Don Duguid, a social work student, was placed in his family services field placement two weeks ago. It was pretty exciting, he thought, to launch into an illustrious career in mental health. He was anxious yet eager. Hadn't many of his friends in high school and college sought him out to tell him their problems? Hadn't they told him they felt much better after hearing his advice? No doubt about it, he had all the raw materials for becoming the greatest interpersonal social worker ever.

The actual job of counseling didn't seem all that difficult. He had seen Dr. Burroughs, the psychologist, simply sitting and listening, occasionally uttering a comment or asking a question. He had also sat in on a session with Ms. Hilfman, the director of the agency, and had seen her effortlessly wend her way through a client's difficulty. Ah, yes! He knew he had many of the same qualities as Ms. Hilfman and Dr. Burroughs. Yet, how did they know the right thing to say?

Feeling full of himself, he walked to Hilda Hilfman's office, expecting as usual to be assigned to go to a meeting or to observe a counseling session. After a few minutes, however, Hilda's countenance became serious. "Don," she said, "you've heard at staff meetings that we've been operating with a skeleton staff because of budget cuts. Ellen, the intake worker, is sick, and I must work on the budget for the board meeting tonight. It will take me all afternoon. I know you have been here just a short time, but do you think you could do an initial interview?"

Don felt a surge of elation. "Hmmm," he said. "I think I can handle that."

"Good!" replied Hilda. Because initial interviews are aimed at getting enough information about the client's difficulty to decide whether the agency can be of service, she felt that Don could collect the information and then consult with a more experienced worker.

Instruction 5.7.A   *Problem Identification*

Remember that the problem identification step asks the question "What?" Do not confuse this step with that of setting goals. At this point in the exercise, *What is the problem Don faces?*

STOP! Do not proceed until so instructed.

Feedback 5.7.A

The problem is that Don, an inexperienced field placement student, must conduct an information gathering initial interview. As we have learned, there are both relational and cognitive tasks in any social work setting. For the present, because Don is having difficulties with relational skills, we will deal only with that facet of the problem. That is, this exercise will work with relational skills. The next exercise (5.8) addresses the cognitive skills involved in information gathering in the initial interview.

Instruction 5.7.B   State the Goals of Don's Work

Don picked up the green sheet from the receptionist and saw the name "Judy Loescher" neatly printed at the top. He called out in his most professionally assured voice "Judy Lesher?"

A rather heavyset woman in her mid-thirties looked up from a book, nervously crushed out her cigarette, and corrected his pronunciation. "You mean Judy Losher?"

"Oh yes," he said, wishing he had been just a bit more tentative.

As they walked to the interviewing room, he could feel his "natural" abilities as a conversationalist begin to fade. But once in the room, he felt more confident. He began with the first question on the sheet—age—and then worked his way down through marital status to presenting problem. Suddenly he remembered he must put the client's problem first, before the paperwork. He inquired, "Well, Judy, how may we be of service to you?"

"Well, uh, gee, I don't know," she replied, squirming uncomfortably in her chair.

Anxiety seized Don, but after a few seconds of silence, he recovered. "Well, I mean, like . . . like are you having trouble with your teenage son?" He was banking on the high probability that teenage sons generally give mothers trouble.

"No."

"A problem with finances?"

"No."

"Are you fighting with your husband?"

And so the interview went for the next fifteen minutes. To say that the interview did not flow smoothly would be an understatement. Don found out that Judy's husband "was becoming a drunk" and that he had been fired from his job as a warehouse worker. Having run out of questions, he resorted to giving advice. He suggested that her husband join Alcoholics Anonymous. She said she had already told him he should. He asked if she had thought of getting therapy for him, but she returned, "Do you think he's crazy?"

"Don't you think it would be good to start communicating?" he asked.

"About what?" she countered.

By now Don was completely demoralized and felt as if he had a bigger emotional problem than did his client. Although he knew that part of his task was to get a worker client relationship started, he simply did not know how to do that, let alone to survive the rest of the interview.

After a few more moments of silence, Judy finally said, "I hate to ask, Mr. Duguid. I mean I think you are like my doctor, and I couldn't ask him, but . . ."

"Yes, go on, what is it that I can help you with?" he replied excitedly. Thank heavens she was finally going to ask him for something he could get his professional teeth into!

"I'm parked in a fifteen-minute zone. Can I please go and move my car so I won't get a ticket?"

Don was taken aback for a moment. But, he thought, here's my chance to run across the hall and talk to Hilda. "Yes—yes, of course, go move the car. We wouldn't want to be responsible for giving you another problem to worry about," he said in a nervous attempt at humor.

As she left, he rushed to Hilda's office. Attempting not to betray his anxiety, he explained that he was having trouble "getting the interview off the ground."

"I'm sensing some 'first interview panic,'" she said, feeling guilty about having misperceived Don's readiness. She knew she must allay his anxiety, for she had forgotten how hard it is to translate practice courses into real practice.

"Well, I did get nervous. Judy, my client, is really resistant. No matter what I try, she doesn't respond." Don was caught in a bind. He needed help but did not want to appear incompetent.

"So," Hilda said, "when the interview got sticky, you got angry at Judy and frightened about getting across to her. It must have been rough."

"She understands," Don thought in a burst of relief. He began to tell her what happened and soon found himself saying that he was not sure what the goals of the work (assessment goals) were.

Help Don out. In a few sentences, *what are the relational goals of the initial information gathering interview? What behaviors demonstrate those skills?*

Hilda asks Don to prepare a "relational skills chart," and you should fill this one out also.

Relational Skills	Behavior	Behavior	Behavior
Empathy			
Respect			
Warmth			
Concreteness			
Genuineness			
Self-Disclosure			
Confrontation			
Immediacy			

STOP! Do not proceed to the next feedback until you consult with your instructor.

Feedback 5.7.B

Don filled out the chart, rating himself pretty poorly on all skills except, perhaps, confrontation. He had really tried on "immediacy" but was on the wrong track with his advice-giving. After having looked at his results, he protested, "Well, it seems obvious that I'd want her to tell me her problems so I could give advice. That's what professionals do. When I go to my doctor, I tell her what's wrong and expect her to make a diagnosis and tell me what to do—give me advice. I'm in training to be a professional, am I not?"

"Well, yes," Hilda replied, "and many clients do expect you to tell them what to do. And you're right that the general goal of the initial interview is to gather information so that a social diagnosis can be made. However, the social work perspective is that of a partnership—both client and worker are involved in the problem's exploration."

Don looked down. "Yes, I guess I did jump the gun by launching into advice based on very little information."

"Your advice may have been good," said Hilda. "The point is, it came from *your* frame of reference. Unfortunately, telling the client what *you* think about the problem may cut off further collaboration. However, just having identified those skills and realizing the difficulties of immediate assessment and advice-giving means you have come a long way toward your goals in the initial interview."

Instruction 5.7.C Gathering Information about the Client

Hilda continued. "Don, in addition to just having relational skills, professional social workers integrate knowledge of relationships cognitively; that is, they assess relationships as they occur and use the knowledge to evaluate clients' emotional tone, reactions, and motivations. This information, which has to do with how the client feels about telling his or her story, facilitates disclosure. However, disclosure is painful, and social workers must be aware of that. Because disclosure is the first step to gathering information, how could you help Judy to tell you about her problem situation? *What are some of the conditions for free client disclosure, and what can the social worker do to create an atmosphere where clients can discuss their problems?* Don thought about what he had learned about disclosure and the use of relational skills, and then about his own feelings when he had to tell Hilda he couldn't handle the interview. Help him out again. *List some of the elements of disclosure.*

1.

2.

3.

4.

5.

6.

7.

8.

9.

10.

STOP! Before you proceed, consult with the instructor.

Feedback 5.7.C

You probably listed such things as the client's perception of worker's impatience, lack of trust or caring, and so on. To make the client comfortable in the interview situation, such core skills as respect and approval, a willingness to listen, empathy, and listening without giving your own ideas or values are important.

Don's response to the question was "People just naturally feel better in getting things off their chests. I guess it could just be cathartic."

"There is also a reason in terms of just gathering complete and accurate information," Hilda said. "People have a hard time feeling intensely and thinking logically at the same time. You said that no matter what you advised, Judy either had tried it, said it wouldn't work, or was resistant. Why do you think she responded like that?"

"Gee, I don't know," he replied. "The advice I gave seemed pretty reasonable. I mean, I would have followed it if I found myself in that difficulty. It seemed like common sense to me."

"Exactly!" she said. "And that suggests a plausible explanation for what you imagined was Judy's resistance. By the time Judy hit your door, she had probably done considerable thinking and solution-finding on her own. If she hadn't thought of some of these solutions being "common sense," as you put it, something must have gotten in the way."

"Well, what, then? It wasn't stupidity! Judy seems pretty bright."

"It's been my experience with people—me, clients, or anybody—that it is generally *affective* factors that preclude effective coping. Just remember, it's very hard to think logically and feel strongly at the same time. Fear, despair, or hopelessness more often get in the way of figuring out problems in living than anything else. So to facilitate problem solving, we must try to reduce the client's destructive affect.

"So to get her to really open up, I simply need to ask her how she feels!" Don felt that he had discovered some kind of professional key.

"Well, it's not quite that simple, Don," Hilda cautioned. "We have to realize that clients not only have feelings and perceptions of their problems but also feelings about talking about those problems to a relative stranger. In gathering information, those feelings may be a barrier, because if we are highly anxious, we may deny or exaggerate problems, especially if we are talking with someone who might judge us."

Instruction 5.7.D   *Gathering Information from the Client's Perspective*

Hilda said, "Don, "social work is not easy, and understanding a problem from the client's perspective is often the hardest part. What we need to do now is be more specific about Judy's problem. Did she say anything that indicated her problem situation?"

"She made a very strong statement about Jack, her husband. She said 'Somebody has got to do something about Jack's drinking! He comes home sometimes late at night and lots of times misses dinner. He never plays with the kids any more. Even though I still love him, he's changed. I just don't know what to do!' "

"That *is* a pretty strong statement," said Hilda, "and it's full of emotional overtones, which will have a bearing on the assessment you make of her problem situation. What I would like you to do now is take that statement and do four things with it."

Help Don again with the following steps.

1. Write three statements that demonstrate Judy's emotional state from what she said. Use the format "It sounds like you feel (a little, pretty much, really) . . .

(1)

(2)

(3)

2. Write three statements about the perceptions and thoughts Judy might be implying. Use the format "You think that (. . . some conclusion . . .) because of (. . . her evidence . . .).

(1)

(2)

(3)

3. Write three statements that would help Judy clarify why she feels as she does. "You feel (. . . emotional state . . .) because of (. . . what she feels is happening in her life . . .).

(1)

(2)

(3)

4. Write three responses you would make to let Judy know you are hearing what she is really saying to let her know you understand her distress. Such statements usually take the form "That must be (. . . description of how you perceive she feels . . .)," or "I hear you saying that you feel (. . . description of what you think she is feeling . . .)."

(1)

(2)

(3)

STOP! Do not proceed until instructed.

Feedback 5.7.D

You may have come up with many statements in addition to the ones below. These are examples of responses that Judy's statement might imply.

1. Emotional state
   (1) It sounds like you feel a little confused about the whole situation.
   (2) It sounds like you feel really angry.
   (3) It sounds like you feel awfully sad and upset.

2. Perceptions and thoughts
   (1) You think that Jack doesn't love you because he doesn't spend much time at home.
   (2) You think that your marriage is falling apart because Jack doesn't spend much time with the kids.
   (3) You think that Jack is an alcoholic because he drinks so much.

3. Clarification of feelings
   (1) You feel depressed because you can't seem to get through to Jack.
   (2) You feel angry because he never plays with the kids.
   (3) You feel afraid because Jack has changed and you don't know him any more.

4. Empathetic responses.
   (1) That must be very painful for you.
   (2) I hear you saying that you are confused and hurt.
   (3) I understand how that could make you feel afraid.

Instruction 5.7.E   Generating Alternative Responses to Content

"Now," Hilda said, "try a few responses to the *content* of what Judy seems to be saying. She is probably telling you lots of things about her thoughts, perceptions, and feelings. The trick here is to read between the lines without engaging in idle speculation or heavy interpretations. What you're trying to do is get her thoughts and opinions about her situation, along with her reasons for those opinions. These responses generally take the form 'You think that (. . . her conclusion . . .) because (. . . her reason for that conclusion . . .)'." *List your thoughts about Judy's perceptions and how her feelings may impact her behavior.*

STOP! Wait for the instructor to evaluate your work before proceeding.

Feedback 5.7.E

Don began hesitantly, gathering steam as he continued. "You think that

1. Jack is drinking too much because of his behavior.
2. Jack is being inconsiderate because he misses dinners that he knows you have spent much time preparing.
3. You've tried just about everything.
4. A good father should spend time with his children, and Jack's not doing that.
5. Jack's losing his job doesn't give him the right to act like this.
6. If Jack really cared, he wouldn't act like this.
7. The kids might lose their father's companionship.
8. Jack should know that you worry about him.

Instruction 5.7.F   *Generating Alternatives in Response to Content and Feelings*

"Often," said Hilda, "it is enough to respond only to content, as you have just done. Many times, though, we want to respond to both feelings and content. Again, these responses generally take the form 'You feel (. . . something . . .) because of (some aspect of the situation)'." *For each response to content you listed above, make a statement that includes perceptions both of the content and Judy's feelings.*

1.

2.

3.

4.

5.

6.

7.

8.

STOP! Do not proceed to next feedback until so instructed.

Feedback 5.7.F

"This isn't as hard as I thought," Don said as he began.

1. When Jack comes home late, you feel angry because it means he doesn't care.
2. You feel impatient, because if Jack would only quit drinking, the problem would be solved.
3. You feel disappointed in Jack because he's not being a good father.
4. You feel at a loss because you've tried just about everything.
5. Because nothing seems to have worked, you're afraid that the problem might be insoluble.
6. It hurts you to see Jack not eat meals you have prepared.
7. You're confused about Jack's abrupt change in attitude and behavior.
8. You're suspicious about what Jack is doing late at night.

Instruction 5.7.G   *Generating Sharing Affect Response Alternatives*

Don knew that the next response type was "sharing affect," or showing that he empathized with Judy. This is what people do to show they really *understand*. Social workers demonstrate this understanding by sharing something of themselves while keeping the interview focused on the client.

Hilda said "Okay, Don, now give me three statements that would indicate to Judy that you empathize with what she feels about her situation."

Don thought a minute and said, "I know exactly how you feel! Boy, one time I had a girlfriend who said she loved me one day and then the next day told me to kiss off! Let me tell you how I felt! God, was I afraid and confused!"

"Whoa," Hilda interrupted. "First, you really don't know what Judy feels. Second, Judy is not here to find out about your life. That's what we mean when we say social work is *client centered*. What you want to do is communicate understanding of how she might feel. Now, in your mind, it might be that one of your own experiences would help you to understand, but the client doesn't need to know that experience. You only use a little of yourself in showing empathy with Judy. Try again." *Write three sentences that would let Judy know that you know what it feels like to be hurt.*

1.

2.

3.

STOP! Do not proceed until instructed to do so.

Feedback 5.7.G

The ideas Don had are below. You may have others.

1. It must be really confusing for you to see Jack change.
2. I'd be scared too, if I though my wife didn't love me any more.
3. You must feel powerless with Jack's drinking seemingly out of control.
4. I can imagine how angry you must feel, sitting at the table with Jack not there.
5. It's hard to be so angry at someone you really love.

Instruction 5.7.H   Limitations of Relational Tasks

Don's confidence had returned. He felt that wonderful confidence in knowing what to do. It seemed simple enough: Follow what Judy was feeling and perceiving and demonstrate his understanding by using these techniques. By simply responding to Judy's feelings and perceptions, and by throwing in an occasional "sharing affect," he could quickly establish that they were there to talk about feelings, perceptions, and more feelings. *That's* what social work was all about: getting people to talk about *feelings*.

He returned to the interviewing room and saw Judy sitting in her chair reading her book. He breathed a sigh of relief when she told him that she had just got back, as parking spaces were very hard to come by at this hour downtown. Don replied that they would have to leave at one o'clock (fifteen minutes away) because the room was scheduled for another interview.

"It sounded to me from what you said before that you think that you've tried about everything imaginable and are about at your rope's end, like nothing will make this nightmare go away, is that it?"

Mixed feelings of elation and sympathy rushed in as he saw tears welling up in Judy's eyes. He handed her a tissue. "I can imagine how difficult it is not knowing what else could be tried," he continued as she fought for composure. She began sobbing and told him her fears about Jack's drinking and its effect on the kids. She and Jack still seldom fought, but the kids were getting very hostile toward him. She had considered divorce and had even had thoughts of moving out, kids and all, without so much as telling him where she was going (for which she felt intense guilt). The passing but nevertheless ugly thought of suicide had crossed her mind.

After the fifteen minutes, Judy said that she felt better but wasn't really sure of what they had accomplished. In spite of the glow Don was feeling, he wasn't all that sure either. He asked her if she could come back tomorrow and continue, not unaware that he would have a chance once again to talk to Hilda.

The next morning he told Hilda what had transpired and said that he really still didn't know what they had accomplished, nor what more they could accomplish going on in the same vein. Hilda, remembering her days in training as a client-centered therapist, had some inkling of what Don and his new client were feeling. Those many years ago, she had been taught to help people by simply facilitating their own awareness of their subjective realities. She knew, however, as a social worker, that client-centered counseling had certain limitations.

She threw the question right back into Don's lap, as she seemed to want to do most of the time, by asking, "What are the general constraints you can think of for relying exclusively upon relational techniques for gathering information in the initial interview?" *Help Don by listing general constraints of relational techniques.*

STOP! Do not proceed until so instructed.

Feedback 5.7.H

Don said he felt there was a circular quality to the interview, and he knew Judy felt this too. In fact, he said, there were a couple of times she said that she seemed to be repeating herself. Hilda responded, "What you and Judy were feeling was that the interview had become *unfocused*. Though Judy was probably feeling *person-centered satisfaction*—feeling free to talk and feeling understood, she wasn't feeling much *problem-centered satisfaction*—that is, the feeling of progress toward problem solution. While you were gaining information about her perceptions and feelings, she was helped to express them, but we also help clients by giving them the subjective sense that some light has been shed on the problem. What else did you see?"

"Well, though I felt progressively sure of how she sees things, I don't really feel I have a workable handle on what is her social situation. I only know what it feels like to her on the outside."

"That is a further limitation: counseling methods lean heavily on the premise that problems stem largely from what goes on inside people's heads, so the logical solution is to straighten out inner thoughts, feelings, and perceptions. Then the problem will 'solve itself.' However, social workers believe that social situations, which are an external constraint on their clients, are at least as important as factors in social functioning as are personality factors."

"But one thing I did was get entirely into Judy's frame of reference. I can see things from her point of view."

"Well, not entirely, which brings me to the last constraint. I'll admit you have a better idea of her perceptions and feelings, but this false sense of security can be damaging—it can blind you to other possibilities. When you pick one possibility as opposed to another, or respond to certain statements as opposed to others, you implicitly guided the conversation, thus influencing your client. You need to be aware of that.

"Remember, no matter what technique is used, if workers hold rigid notions of right or wrong or harbor unresolved personal troubles, no amount of techniques will make them good facilitative social workers. Basically, helpful versus unhelpful 'instant responses' will depend on who you are as a person. Improving in this area can come only from an honest and constant examination of your own values and beliefs."

Don's problem now is that, though he's had a small taste of competence as a social worker, it is simply not enough.

Instruction 5.7.I   Synthesis

To understand Don's problem, each class member chooses a partner and does a five-to-ten minute role play. One person is Don, the other Judy. Remember, Judy is highly upset about her situation at home and doesn't really know what to do. Have Judy start off with her statement: "I don't know, but somebody has got to do something about Jack's drinking! He comes home sometimes late at night and lots of times misses dinner. He never plays with the kids any more. Even though I still love him, he's changed. I just don't know what to do."

During the role play, use whatever responses you normally use, and at least one each of the following:

1. Response to feeling only
2. Response to perception.
3. Response to feeling and perceptions.
4. Sharing affect response.

After the role play, write those responses you used and discuss them with your partner. In class, discuss what you have learned about relational information gathering.

In the following exercise we emphasize cognitive tasks within the interpersonal context.[5] Among the tools we use are the "dimensions of assessment"—the What, Where, When, Who, and Why of the situation:

1. **WHAT.** The *focal* dimension refers to the stressful event that caused the problem.

2. **WHERE.** The *spatial* dimension or behavioral setting refers to the physical attributes of the situation.

3. **WHEN.** The *temporal* dimension refers to the time boundaries of the situation as a whole, including episodes or events within that general time frame.

4. **WHO.** The *structural* dimension includes the cast of characters and the reciprocal roles they play and under what rules. Rules can be psychological "games" or be dictated by norms, values, and traditions.

5. **WHY.** To whom is the situation a problem and why. Each relevant actor needs a *behavioral specification*.

In the past, cognitive and relational tasks have generally been separated and handled as two distinct activities. However, it is more realistic to do both at the same time; that is, we interpersonally guide an interaction while we think of what to ask. *That* is what you should look for in this exercise. How does Hilda tell Don to guide but not control the interview while getting information from Judy?

Exercise 5.8 Cognitive Tasks and Goals

General Instructions

Break into groups of four or five to proceed with this guided problem-solving exercise.

Problem Situation

Don has just finished his first interview with Judy. He had difficulty helping her tell her story, but he learned a few principles used by social workers to encourage clients to open up. During the discussion of limitations of using purely relationship-centered techniques, however, Hilda and Don concluded that although the client may have experienced freedom to tell her story, something was lacking. Also, though he had obtained lots of information, he was not sure it was all useful in helping Judy eventually solve the problem.

Instruction 5.8.A   Identify Cognitive Goals

Although interpersonal relational skills were perhaps *necessary* for facilitating as accurate and undistorted an account as possible, they were by no means *sufficient*. In addition to relational tasks, there are cognitive tasks and skills that must be performed if information is to be *gathered*. *What cognitive expertise does Judy have a right to expect from a social worker? What are the cognitive goals and tasks for the initial interview?* Discuss and write your answers below.

STOP! Do not proceed until so instructed.

Feedback 5.8.A

When Don was asked what rights Judy had in the relationship, he replied, "I guess Judy has the right to expect a sensitive social worker but also a social worker with at least some expertise in knowing what avenues of inquiry are better than others and how to actualize inquiry in the most client-centered way possible. In addition, the client has a right to a partnership relationship with the worker, in which she is considered the expert on her own life."

Hilda went on to explain that the *cognitive tasks* of the initial interview are to *organize its content by the management of information*. By using our cognitive skills, we help ourselves and our clients make sense of what is happening in their social situations. The *cognitive goals* of the initial interview are *to obtain specific information* to help clients understand their difficulties. While we *facilitate* the client's disclosure with relational tasks, we also *guide* that disclosure by performing cognitive interviewing tasks.

Instruction 5.8.B   Gathering Information: Guiding the Interview

Hilda told Don that gathering some kinds of information was more valuable than gathering others, and, therefore, guiding the direction of the interview was essential. Moreover, she said, "You reflect upon and analyze in retrospect from the sometimes amorphous information you receive." To get started, however, you need information about the dimensions of assessment. You already learned about them (see p.xxx). Therefore, for Judy's situation, you should *analyze the dimensions of the situation* to clarify whose problem it is and why. Then *write one or two questions to elicit information on the dimensions*.

1. What is the focus?

2. Where does it take place?

3. When do events take place?

4. Who is involved and what are their relationships?

5. Why does the situation come to be defined as a problem?

Questions to elicit information on:

1. Focal dimension.

(1)

(2)

2. Spatial dimension

(1)

(2)

3. Temporal dimension

(1)

(2)

4. Structural dimension

(1)

(2)

5. The "why" of the problem.

(1)

(2)

STOP! Do not proceed until the instructor evaluates your assessment dimensions.

Feedback 5.8.B

1. The focal dimension is, very likely, Judy's husband's drinking.
   (1) What brings you here today?
   (2) What's been going on?

2. The spatial dimension: The home situation.
   (1) Does your apartment seem empty at night without Jack there?
   (2) Where does Jack do his drinking?

3. The temporal dimension: How long this has been perceived as a problem, when did episodes occur, and for how long will Judy put up with it?
   (1) How long has this been going on? (General time frame.)
   (2) What happened the last time Jack came home drunk? (Episode.)

4. The structural dimension: A systems network would be very helpful to you at this point.
   (1) How do the children react when he comes home drunk?

   (2) Who manages the money in your family?

5. Behavioral specification: The definition of the situation as a problem is a perceptual consideration, and, though you have many of Judy's situational definitions by having used your responding skills, there are other actors in the situation. It would be helpful to learn *their* definitions of the situation. In this case, three sets of role actors are focused on Jack's drinking and behavior; that is, three different sets of problems in one situation. To Judy, Jack's drinking is a problem because the change has her confused. To the kids, it may be that he no longer spends time with them. To Jack, the problem may be figuring out why everybody else is having a problem. The "why" of the problem includes
   a. Judy's personal obstacles in solving her problem (fear, despair, discouragement, inability to cope with anxiety, etc.).
   b. An objective description of her situation.
   c. How the situation is being defined as a problem by its role actors—she, her husband, and their kids.
   (1) What does Jack say about his drinking? Your concerns? His job loss?
   (2) Can you tell me what you mean by "never plays with the kids"? By "late at night"?

Instruction 5.8.C   Gathering Information: Assessment Content

In addition to the above content, Don also needs some facts about the family and the general situation. He also needs to clarify the presenting problem: even though Judy is talking about Jack's drinking, she has not clearly specified the focus of her problem. Also, Don has to assess the many different levels of meanings of what Judy is telling him and the overall situation that was defined as "problem." *Below, write the kinds of assessment content information Don needs.*

Presenting problem

General family information

Levels of meaning Judy may have about Jack's drinking

Why the situation is defined as problem

STOP! Do not proceed until so instructed.

Feedback 5.8.C

Generally, the initial interview should produce four kinds of information. The first is simply data—things like the client's marital status, number of children, general level of income, address, phone number, place of employment. It is important, however, not to start off an interview just reading the list and getting responses, and it is not necessary to get all the information in the first interview.

Second, Don must clarify the presenting problem—what brought the client to the agency. The stated problem may or may not be the primary one. To have a clear statement of why the client believes help is needed is the first step in examining the whole "problem/person/ situation" interaction.

Third, Don must not only look at the emotional elements of the interview but cognitively assess Judy's feelings and behaviors as functions of her situation. Many levels of meanings can come from a simple statement. For example, Judy's primary complaint seems to be Jack's drinking. To stop at this level—to deal only with her reactions to his drinking—would completely fail to get at the less obvious but more painful distress she feels at the idea that her marriage is falling apart.

Finally, Don needs to figure out why this overall situation is defined as "problem." Remember, a situation itself is a neutral entity. It becomes a problem only when infused with feelings and behaviors that cause difficulty for someone. The ecological systems perspective gives us a kind of "diagram" for a focused sense of what's going on apart from the client's immediate distress.

Instruction 5.8.D   *Frames of Reference*

Don was beginning to overload on terms as he reflected on his first interview with Judy Loescher. He had difficulty helping her tell her story, but he learned a few principles that social workers use to encourage clients to open up. He knew that listing *types* of information helped, but he really wanted to know how to draw forth the kinds he needed. He said, "Hilda, it seems like I got so much information I don't know what to do with it. It's really hard to take everything in and then to try to fit it into categories. Isn't there some way I can direct the interview to get just the information I want?"

"Well," said Hilda, "the problem with that is that in an interview your information comes in at many levels. For example, during the first part of your interview with Judy, you gathered all sorts of information about her *as a person*. You noticed that she is taciturn when confronted with the interviewing situation; that she is overweight; that she is so anxious that her emotions may hinder problem-solving; that she attempts to control emotional outbursts; that she feels discouraged and beaten; and a host of other things.

"You gathered that information from what you saw and heard while talking. That is the kind of information that becomes grist for your cognitive mill *after* the interview, when you write down some of what you have perceived. However, you need to process it cognitively while in the interview too, and generally speaking, social workers will have a framework by which to process information."

"Framework?" asked Don.

"Yes, a theory or combination of theories—a psychodynamic model, for example, would look at Judy's contribution to the problem because of her unconscious conflicts and motives. Behavior theory looks at problems from the perspective of conditions that reinforce maladaptive behaviors. It's not so important which theory you use, as long as you have some evidence of its effectiveness and enough knowledge about it to use it effectively."

Don was a little taken aback. He had read about different perspectives on social work practice, of course, but still had not developed one of his own. He asked, "What perspective do you use, Hilda?"

"I use a social psychological framework in viewing personality as interpersonal and behavior as a function of the situation. In this, behavioral traits can best be conceived of as habitual reaction patterns to, and ways of controlling, others. I also interject the strengths perspective, which asserts that the client's 'problem meaning' counts for more in the helping process than do scientific labels. Individuals are seen in the light of their capacities, talents, competencies, possibilities, visions, values, and hopes. In Judy's case, we believe in her ability to know what is best."

"Wait a minute," Don interrupted, "I'm confused! You tell me to impose my own frame of reference in helping Judy figure out her problem, but you've also told me to get the story from *her* frame of reference."

"That's right, Don," Hilda explained. "The frame of reference you impose is not your personal frame of reference but the problem-solving techniques of social work practice. You cannot force the client's process into a particular mold, but the problem-solving method will help you to gain the information you need in a caring and yet objective manner."

Hilda also went on to explain to Don that he also needed to understand social situation and Don asked what that was. Hilda replied, "Social situations influence us—people and objects in a time–space circumstance, or a group of role-related people in some setting for some period of time, focusing on something. However, to identify a problem, you must look at Judy's social situation and its dysfunction. You must define Judy's problem in terms of 'social situation' and 'dysfunction'."

Help Don again. *Identify Judy's social situation and describe how it is dysfunctional.*

STOP! Do not proceed until so directed.

Feedback 5.8.D

Don asked for more advice. "What is her social situation, and how is it dysfunctional?"

"You don't know that yet, and you can learn that only from Judy. Judy is experiencing a problem, but that does not make the situation a problem. It depends on point of view. What you can learn here is *what kinds of things make situations dysfunctional for most reasonable human beings,*" Hilda replied, handing him a photocopied sheet from her desk drawer. "A situation becomes dysfunctional or problematic when a person's instrumental or expressive needs are not met. Here are some characteristics of dysfunctional social situations."

Don scanned the list.

A social situation is dysfunctional if:

1. It is structurally and culturally inadequate or disorganized;

2. It is aimless, unfocused, ambiguous, contradictory, threatening, or harmful;

3. It lacks needed resources and opportunities;

4. It presents insurmountable barriers;

5. It stimulates unaccepted stress or impulses;

6. It generates severe interpersonal, role, or value conflicts;

7. It requires performance, knowledge, and skills that are beyond an individual's capacity;

8. It does not validate identity.

"Whew," Don exclaimed, "I can't remember all of that. That's information overload."

"It might seem so," Hilda answered, "but with practice you will learn to listen for and gather only the valuable information."

Instruction 5.8.E   Generate Alternatives for Open-Ended Questions

Don now had a framework to guide him, but he needed a few more specifics. Knowing that Hilda would expect him to generate questions, he began to think of open-ended questions to get at the three areas of person, situation, and problem. Think of two questions each to get information about

1. Judy's personal obstacles in solving her problem
   (1)

   (2)

2. What makes the situation problematic?

(1)

(2)

3. What questions deal with the problem itself?

(1)

(2)

Exercise 5.9 Writing the Social Assessment

General Instructions

Break into groups of four or five people to deal with Don's problem. Try not to have many of the same persons in the group as there were in the previous exercise. Follow the guidelines for guided problem solving, and do not proceed through the steps without consulting with your instructor for feedback.

Instruction 5.9.A   Identifying the Problem

Don now has to write out a social assessment as part of his learning experience for Hilda Hilfman, his field instructor. *What problem do you perceive for Don?*

STOP! Do not proceed until you have conferenced with the instructor.

Feedback 5.9.A

The problem is that Don, an inexperienced field placement student, must write a social diagnosis and he does not know how.

Instruction 5.9.B   Setting the Goals

Before Don begins writing, Hilda talks with him about looking at the setting of the interview, his approach to it, and the kinds of things of which he must be aware; for example, his own personal values, beliefs, and general biases along with physical, social, and emotional behavior that might lead him to a more inclusive assessment. She advises him that, in his written social assessment, she will be looking for those elements. *What is Don's educational goal from the initial interview? What factors does he need to assess to reach this educational goal?*

STOP! Do not proceed until so advised.

Feedback 5.9.B

Don's educational goal is to learn to write a social diagnosis that has within it the setting of the interview, his approach to it, and the kinds of things of which he must be aware; for example, his own personal values, beliefs, and general biases along with physical, social, and emotional behavior that might lead him to a more inclusive assessment. He should also be aware of Judy's perspectives, values, and beliefs and have a social work perspective based on knowledge, skills, and values.

Instruction 5.9.C   Gathering Information

Don doesn't know how to do an assessment. He asks Hilda what kinds of information he needs, and she suggests that he analyze the dimensions of assessment and that he look at the following questions to "flesh out" his assessment. *What information does he need? Where can he find it?* When you have looked at information needs and resources, help Don again by answering the questions below.

Information Needed   **Resources**

Questions to ask.

1. What is the primary situational problem?

2. What is the primary emotional problem?

3. What has this person/problem/situation in common with other such scenarios?

4. What are the obvious emotions of the grievant?

5. What are the emotions of the listener/interviewer?

6. How are these important to the context of the assessment?

7. What social constraints were there on action in the problem situation?

8. What personal constraints might have been involved in actions on the problem?

9. What are the relational issues of the problem? What emotional problem(s) must be dealt with before the problem can be solved?

10. Break down the whole problem into a series of smaller tasks. What are particular areas of concern that can be worked on to solve the larger problem?

Feedback 5.9.C

Don needs to know a frame of reference to use, the dimensions of the problem, and the problem-solving model. All these are available in your social work classes and the many fine texts you have in your library, but probably Hilda is his primary source of information.

For feedback on the essential questions of the assessment, first answer them in the group and then call on your instructor for consultation.

Instruction 5.9.D   Creating the Framework and Implementing the Plan

Don wonders how he can remember frame of reference, dimension, framework, and the problem-solving model all at the same time. As he understands all the components necessary to a good assessment, he knows that he has to gather yet more information on assessment for a successful completion of his assignment. He decides to lay out the assessment in the format of the problem-solving model. *What are the steps of the problem-solving model for this exercise? Using that framework and the knowledge you have gleaned from these exercises, write a brief assessment on separate page.* Ask your field instructor to help you. On a separate page, write your client assessment.

STOP! Do not proceed until so instructed.

Feedback 5.9.D

Feedback will come from the evaluation given by your instructor.

Instruction 5.9.E   Assessing the Assessor

Self-evaluation is a process necessary in all social work practice. *What should Don remember and what can he use to evaluate his behavior and the information gathered and compiled in his first social assessment? How does he know whether or not he was successful?*

1. How will Don evaluate his behavior?

2. How will he evaluate the information he gathered?

3. How does he judge his success?

Call on the instructor to discuss your answers for this step in the problem-solving process.

Portfolio Building

As we see, the practice of social work, particularly in the assessment phase, is not easy. Paramount constraints are the feelings of uncertainty and anxiety of social workers themselves on first contact. However, if we are aware of all aspects of the interaction, we are less likely to be as unprepared as Don. Review the following:

1. What skills are necessary in the assessment phase of problem-solving?

2. What aspects must be considered in problem solving?

3. Putting these together, discuss the importance of content, process, and style in an information-gathering or assessment interview.

4. What more do you need to know about assessment?

Looking Ahead

Having looked at some of the facets of social work with the individual and the initial interview, we move forward to working with wider systems. Remember, of course, that there is much more work with individual clients beyond the initial interview and assessment. The practice of social work in groups is different only in that the social worker is not so focused on the individual. Still, interpersonal skills are imperative for the successful group process. Group interactions become the focus of the group process, and group members themselves become part of the helping process. Social workers, in addition to facilitating group process, insure that process goals and tasks are clear and that groups do not become destructive to their members.

Notes

1. Taken from Joseph Anderson (1981). *Social Work Methods and Processes.* Belmont, CA: Wadsworth, Inc., pp. 71–81.
2. Barry Cournoyer (1991). *The Social Work Skills Workbook.* Belmont, CA: Wadsworth, Inc.
3. The Don Duguid exercises are based on an earlier version created by Gene Jackson, Purdue University, 1984.
4. This exercise uses a social situational framework adapted from Max Siporin (1972). Situational Assessment and Interaction, *Social Casework* 53, pp. 91–109.

Chapter SIX

Social Work with Small Groups

What Is Small Group Practice?

Social work practice with groups is an important social work competence area because there are many settings in which groups are the medium for service delivery.[1] A group approach can be used to accomplish goals common to all social work practice.

1. To prevent individuals from developing dysfunctional ways of coping with their situations

2. To rehabilitate those who have developed handicaps in social and personal functioning.

3. To accomplish tasks.

Essentially, there are two broad categories of groups for which social work group practice is effective: the treatment group (socioeducational), which enhances the group members' social functioning to improve interpersonal and social relationships; and the task group, which may focus on social change and action or supervision and training. The first works for personal change of group members, the second for change in the environmental context.

Brown[2] identified four types of groups, forming a continuum from enrichment and socialization to task accomplishment (Figure 6.1). This chapter provides practice exercises for both treatment and task groups.

Group practice skills help individuals learn new information and behaviors, practice new ways of relating to others, and work together to accomplish stated group goals. They are based on concepts from small group research, role theory, individual psychology, social psychology, sociology, sociobehavioral and psychoanalytic theory,[3] and a growing body of theory within social work itself.[4]

This chapter is a collaboration between Phyllis J. Day and Lisa McGuire.

FIGURE 6.1   *Continuum of Groups*

Personal Growth and Change <————————> Environmental Change
    Enrichment and Socialization   Task Accomplishment

<——>
Treatment   Socio-Education   Social Action   Administrative

Dynamics of the Treatment Group

Shulman's practice model (1992) for mutual aid, which is consistent with the strengths/empowerment perspective, helps us to conceptualize the group work process[5] in which workers help people to help each other. Within it, each group member can be a potential "helper" *and* a "client" or "recipient." Every group, even informal ones, has a potential for mutual aid. For example, people riding an elevator together might ask others where an office is, push a button for another rider, or commiserate on the weather, all of which are "helpful" activities. The mutual aid process may not always emerge naturally, but social work skills can facilitate the process to achieve group goals.

Social group work practice assumptions include the concepts that

1. The group is a mutual aid system facilitated by members helping one another to achieve both individual and collective goals;

2. Group practice takes place within social agencies, and this context affects both group purpose and group actions;

3. Groups follow predictable states of development, each with distinct processes;

4. Group practice is goal-oriented, with goals expressed in concrete and measurable terms;

5. Group practice utilizes the social work knowledge/values/skills configuration;

6. Group workers carefully consider and actively facilitate each sequential phase of group development to achieve both individual and group goals.

Shulman's model requires social workers to have a basic understanding of the dynamics of mutual aid, the role and function of the group leader, and the phases of the group work process.[6] Its basic concepts are

1. Sharing information—group members and leaders share information about strategies and resources related to group purpose.

2. Discussion/debate process—an exchange of ideas, with identification of agreements and disagreements.

3. Discussing taboo topics—problems in group process may arise unless discussion of taboos, such as addiction, prejudices, sexuality, takes place.

4. "All-in-the-same-boat"—discussing difficult areas, members draw strength from finding they are "not the only one who feels that way."

5. Developing a universal perspective—identification for oppressed group members that their problems may lie in the environment, not in themselves.

6. Mutual support—group members may empathize and offer encouragement to others experiencing the same challenges.

7. Mutual demand—they may also confront other members about facing up to situations they might have avoided.

8. Individual problem solving—working on a problem presented by one group member may give insights into other members' situations.

9. Rehearsal—practicing new ideas or skills with support and feedback from others.

10. "Strength-in-numbers"—group members may band together to address a problem that affects many of them.

Phases of the Group

Every group process has four distinct phases:

1. *Pre-planning:* The worker sets up the group on a particular issue, such as mutual support, education or training, social action, and so forth. Considerations include group size and composition, referrals to group, voluntary or involuntary status of group members, and a general practice goal to be filled in by the group process later.

2. *Beginning stage:* Group formation, with issues of relationship of group to agency, group membership and composition, group structure, and the development of group goals (outcome-focused and measurable). Setting tasks and defining roles, clarifying individual goals, and encouraging interaction among the members are group work goals.

3. *Work phase:* Taking into account the previous session's work, discussion proceeds along the lines of Shulman's concepts.

4. *Ending or transition phase:* Evaluation of the group by its members, dealing with feelings about ending the group and mutual support in the future, and identifying transitional steps for each member.

The following exercise provides an outline for planning for a therapeutic group.

Exercise 6.1 Writing a Pre-Planning Design

Take your field placement population, and, using the outline below, develop a group that will fill a particular need of that population. Your goal is to write a planning process to be handed in to your field director or instructor for his or her evaluation.

A. Client Population

1. Identify the specific population of the group.

2. What are their common needs?

3. How did you become aware of these commonalities?

B. Relationship to agency

1. How does your practice group relate to the overall mission and purpose of the agency?

2. What kind of staff and administrative support exists to develop this group?

3. Would your new group become an ongoing service of the agency?

C. Goals and objectives: What goals will you set for the group?
D. What theoretical knowledge/concepts will you need to work with the group?
E. What are the expected themes and issues the group will pursue?

F. What activities and programs do you propose to help the group reach its goals?

G. Membership

  1. What are the criteria for membership in your proposed group?

  2. How will group members be selected or recruited?

  3. How will they be informed of or screened for the group?

H. Role of worker

  1. What will be your initial and ongoing role in this group?

  2. How could you work with a coleader to maximize effectiveness?

I. Diversity issues

  1. Are there racial, ethnic, or sexual diversity issues related to the client population, worker(s), or agency orientation? What are the issues?

  2. How will these issues relate to group functioning?

J. Size of Group

1. What size should your group be?

2. What is your rationale for the group size you have chosen?

Exercise 6.2 Pre-Planning: Families with a Future

You have been assigned to plan the first session of a new parenting group offered by "Families with a Future" (FF), an agency that provides individual, group, and family counseling to clients referred from child welfare or juvenile court for neglect or abuse of their children. Attendance is required as a condition of returning children returned to parents. The purpose is to enhance parenting skills by identifying barriers and stressors that negatively impact parenting; increasing knowledge of child development and age-appropriate expectations for children, along with learning new skills that are age appropriate for children; and increasing knowledge of positive support resources. As you work, consider values and social work ethics for these involuntary clients.

1. Write a two or three sentence introduction to clarify the purposes and objectives for the group's new members.

2. Write a paragraph to explain the role of the group worker, including some information about society's view of child abuse and neglect and how the worker might be helpful to group members.

3. Develop an activity to introduce group members to one another.

4. List three ways the group worker can encourage interaction among members at the first session.

a.

b.

c.

Exercise 6.3 Planning a Growth Group

General Instructions

Divide into groups of four or five. Sloan House is a residential treatment and shelter home for girls in trouble. Originally it was a home for unwed mothers; however, it has become a kind of "institution of last resort" for girls ages 10 to 18 who can no longer live at home, those who were made wards of the court for "status offenses," and those wards of the state who cannot be returned to their homes or placed in foster care. You are child care workers at Sloan House and you must plan an orientation for four girls recently admitted. They are Janice, age 12, who ran away from home and was court-committed as incorrigible; Denise, age 15, whose father has sexually abused her; Ellie, age 13, slightly retarded and pregnant; and Lisa, age 13, who has been "hanging around" with a group of older teens who shoplift and steal cars for kicks.

Your task is to list what you want to accomplish in each of the four phases of your group's six meetings. Discuss the phases until you understand them, what you want to accomplish in each, and tasks that must be accomplished.

Phase	*Goals for Each Phase*	*Tasks*
1. Pre-planning	**1.**	**1. a.**
		b.
		c.
	2.	**2. a.**
		b.
		c.

Phase	Goals for Each Phase	Tasks
	3.	3. a.
		b.
		c.
2. Beginning	1.	1. a.
		b.
		c.
	2.	2. a.
		b.
		c.
	3.	3. a.
		b.
		c.
3. Working	1.	1. a.
		b.
		c.
	2.	2. a.
		b.
		c.

Phase	*Goals for Each Phase*	*Tasks*
	3.	**3. a.**
		b.
		c.
4. Termination	**1.**	**1. a.**
		b.
		c.
	2.	**2. a.**
		b.
		c.
	3.	**3. a.**
		b.
		c.

Exercise 6.4 Planning an Independent Living Program

Again, you are a social worker from Sloan House. Increasingly, older adolescents who cannot return to their parents' homes are being admitted to Sloan House for short periods of time, then released at age eighteen to independent living situations. Your director is concerned about two points. The first is that they do not know how to go about living on their own, and the second is the stress they feel on leaving the emotional comfort of the home and striking out on their own. Your task is to develop a social group work program that is designed to meet both needs. Write your conclusions in the spaces below the questions.

1. What information will the girls need on living independently in your community? List it below.

2. What emotional stresses can you expect the girls to feel, both about leaving Sloan House and about living independently?

    Termination Stress   *Living Independently*

3. What group processes will give them support in the termination process?

4. What will be the role of the social worker in the group?

5. Briefly discuss the overall elements of your new program, including group size, number of meetings, informational format, and expected group processes.

Exercise 6.5 Why Me? Mothers with HIV/AIDS: Group Formation

General Instructions

Form into groups of about seven people. One member is the social work professional and one is the observer, who will record the dynamics laid forth in Shulman's model (see p. 147). At the end of the group session (about twenty minutes), the observer will report on those dynamics to the group. The social worker will report the group process, including the observer's report, to the class as a whole.

Problem Situation

Each person has been referred to the hospital Pregnant HIV/AIDS Group by her gynecologist for mutual support in having and caring for her expected child. Each member is in her second trimester of pregnancy. Members, aside from the social worker and the observer, include

1. Emily, age 17, unmarried, infected and impregnated by her high school boyfriend, HIV positive.
2. Judy, age 30, married with three children, a hemophiliac, developed full-blown AIDS in her first trimester of pregnancy.
3. Jane, age 23, a college-educated, drug abusing, middle-class wife, HIV positive.
4. Abbie, age 35, married, infected with HIV during her promiscuous teenage years, in remission.
5. Lily, a divorced woman with one child age 4, infected by her former husband, near AIDS stage of HIV infection.

They have agreed to come to the group voluntarily. The task of the social worker, who intends to use the Shulman model, is to acquaint them with one another and to enable them to set group goals. The original goal is to establish an ongoing group for mutual support after their children are born.

1. Begin the discussion with round-robin introductions that include short descriptions of each member.
2. Each member should explain what she expects from the group. Write your expectations (as the group member) below.

3. Work on goal setting. At the end of the session, agree on and write down a goal in measurable terms.

4. Discuss the process in the groups and then in class.

Leadership Processes

Bales (1950)[7] identified two distinct leadership processes: task or instrumental and socioemotional or affective leadership. Task leadership focuses groups upon stated goals and objectives, while socioemotional leadership focuses on feelings and interpersonal relationships between and among group members. Group workers must be aware of and facilitate both processes in leading groups. While the social worker is identified as formal group leader, typically informal leaders emerge from the group members. They also take on task and socioemotional leadership roles. In the mutual aid group model, the worker's role is to mediate interactions between each group member and the group itself.

Schwartz conceptualized group workers as having two clients: individual members of the group and the group itself. This helps to avoid what

Shulman calls "casework with an audience," in which group members relate to the group worker but essentially ignore the potential assistance they might receive from other group members. The challenge to group workers is to assist the group in moving through its developmental stages effectively. Many groups have two assigned coleaders to aid in the group process.

Exercise 6.6 The Work Phase in Group Work: A Role Play—Not with My Daughter . . .

General Instructions

This exercise is designed for the entire class and will take at least one hour to complete. The role play itself takes about twenty minutes. You may find it helpful to videotape it for later processing. Having "stock" characters enables moving into strong emotions very quickly, and we suggest deciding on roles immediately before beginning the exercise, rather than preparing them earlier. Place seven chairs in a circle for the session. Students not actively involved in the role play should write down specific skills they observe, along with elements of the Shulman mutual aid model (p. 147). In addition, they should list and identify task and socioemotional leadership roles, both those of the social workers and those arising from the group. There are two "worker" roles and five "client" roles.

Problem Situation

Two students, a boy and a girl, inform their high school social workers that the girl is pregnant, that both their families are very upset about the situation, and that the emotional stress is hurting them so much they cannot cope with their lives, let alone their schoolwork. They and their families have agreed to meet with the social workers to discuss the situation.

Worker Roles

The workers take about five minutes outside the room to discuss how to begin the session and how they will work together as coleaders.

Client Roles

1. *Julie, the pregnant girl.* You are sixteen years old, a high school junior, and a good student, who has been dating Kevin for eight months and cares for him deeply. Your pregnancy is four months along, and you have many mixed feelings about what to do.

2. *Kevin, the teenage father.* You are very confused about the situation, and your feelings change from one minute to the next. Sometimes you feel like a real man, making a baby; other times you feel that Julie trapped you with her pregnancy. You like her a lot but never expected it to get this serious. A senior, you want to go to business college, but now you may have to marry her and take care of the baby.

3. *Carole, Julie's mother.* You have a good relationship with Julie and thought she would come to you to talk about sex before engaging in it, even though you believed she was too young

for it. You would have made sure she had contraceptives. You are so disappointed in her—you married young, and you hoped she would go to school and have some fun before having a family. You feel you are too young to be a grandmother, but you love babies and want to help Julie.

4. *Ron, Julie's father.* You have just found out your baby is pregnant, and you think her boyfriend has taken advantage of her innocence. You are terribly angry with him. Though you have always been proud of Julie, now you wonder what kind of a girl she really is. You thought you had been a good father; now you are angry and want all of this to be over.

5. *Pearl, Kevin's mother.* Kevin is your only son. His father died when Kevin was a baby, but you remember how proud he was of Kevin, and how he talked about him going to college to make something of himself. You thought Julie was nice before she got pregnant, but now believe she may have trapped Kevin. You are angry they had sex, but also angry at Kevin that he didn't use condoms.

Student clients should read their assigned roles and introduce themselves. Discussion begins with the social workers and plays out as it will for about twenty minutes with no interruptions from instructor or viewers. After it comes to a close or is ended by the instructor, each student should answer the following questions for class discussion:

1. What did you feel during the session?
2. What skills did the workers use? Both workers and onlookers should report on skills.
3. How did coleadership work (or not) during the session?
4. What would have been the "next step" for the group?
5. What might the workers have done differently if they had to do the session over again?

Exercise 6.7 Out of the Nest: Terminating a Treatment Group

Break into groups of six, in which one member is the social worker, one an observer, and four are clients you have met before, at Sloan House in Exercise 6.3 (p. 152)—Janice, Denise, Ellie, and Lisa. They will soon be released from Sloan House and are both fearful and happy, exhibiting the ambivalence and emotional upheaval of termination of a part of their lives. Janice and Ellie (who has given up her baby for adoption) will return to their parents' homes, while Denise and Lisa will enter foster homes. The social worker's job is to use the group process and his or her informational skills to help the girls through the termination process. The observer's task is to write down group interaction, leadership patterns, cohesiveness, and mutual support efforts, to discuss them both with the group and in the class as a whole. The role play takes about fifteen minutes; then observers and social workers in each group report to the class.

Exercise 6.8 Role Play: A Celebration of Life

General Instructions

The whole class will participate as members of a bereavement group for people who have lost a loved one recently, with the instructor as worker and leader. It is intended as an example of positive termination rather than a skill-building exercise. Students are encouraged to share their personal experiences as participants in the role play if they are comfortable doing so. The instructor should supply a large plant or small tree in a large bucket, a bag of potting soil, and a small shovel.

Situation

The setting is a bereavement group sponsored by a hospital. Its goal is to provide emotional support and development of coping skills for people whose loved ones have recently died. This is the final session of a ten-session group, and group workers have planned a celebration of life to commemorate the lives of their loved ones. Participants imagine that they have been members of that group, and will meet outside to plant the tree. Group members stand in a circle around the tree, and participants take turns saying the name of their loved one, identifying one quality they will remember, and putting a shovel of soil around the tree. The instructor then provides a short statement that the purpose of the group has been met and how its members are now transitioning into a new phase of life.

Processing the Experience

Write your answers to the discussion questions in the spaces provided below, and then discuss them and the celebration experience with the class.

1. What were your feelings about the celebration role play? List several below.

2. What positive and negative experiences have you had in saying goodbye to a group?

3. Why are ceremonies and celebrations important to people?

4. What are some methods of encouraging positive terminations throughout the group process?

Exercise 6.9 Facilitating Sloan House's Independent Living Program

General Instructions

Form groups of from four to seven people for this guided problem-solving exercise. It will take about two class periods to complete, although the instructor can shorten it by setting time limits on each step.

Problem Situation

Sloan House has developed an Independent Living Program (ILP) for girls who will soon leave the house. The ILPs have two functions: to ease termination stresses and to give information on community resources. The informational part is fairly simple, because in the past members of community agencies have come in as a panel to answer questions and to offer agency help to the girls when they are on their own. You, collectively, are a child care worker who is fairly new to Sloan House. You have cofacilitated several ILPs and are now assigned to do one alone for six girls who will leave Sloan House within three months. Remembering all you have learned, you decide to first identify your problem.

Instruction 6.9.A   Problem Identification

A problem identification specifies exactly what you must do. Be careful not to set your goals first. Generally, you can break the step for this instruction into two kinds of problem identifications. First, *what is the task* assigned you, and second, *what is the best way to go about it?*

STOP! Do not proceed until the instructor has discussed your work with you.

Feedback 6.9.A

What you must do is to design the ILP program for six girls. From past groups you have cofacilitated, you know that a good design includes

1. Preliminary planning for the content of group sessions.

2. A pregroup phase in which you design beginning objectives and think about the tasks that might meet them.

3. A convening phase—the first meeting, where goals and tasks are decided.

4. A working phase, in which the work of the group is actually carried out.

5. A termination phase that prepares the group members to leave the group.

You decide to stick with this plan because you feel a little shaky about designing one all on your own.

Instruction 6.9.B   Gather Information

Although you have worked with groups before, you want to do a really good job but are not quite sure how to proceed. You know that you need both theoretical and practical information and decide to *list the kinds of information you need and the purposes for which you need it.*

STOP! Do not proceed until you have checked your information with the instructor.

Feedback 6.9.B

You need several sets of information. While the first and most obvious is information about the girls who will be in your group, this exercise is not set up to deal with their interrelationships. Rather, it is to plan the overall process by which the program will be carried out. Although you will keep in the back of your mind that this program is for the girls, their characteristics and interactions will not be crucial at this step.

The second set of information is about community resources. You can obtain the files from past ILPs and with them find out the people who can provide information to you.

Third, you need to know theoretical information on both the group process and its meaning to the girls involved.

Instruction 6.9.C   Setting the Goals

Now that you have clarified the problem and have a sense of the kinds of information you need, you must set both goals and subgoals. From previous experience you know how ILP sessions have been conducted and the phases through which such a group must proceed. *State, in behavioral terms, the overarching goal, and list the phases of the group process,* which actually constitute your subgoals for this exercise.

Overarching Goal _____

Phases of Group Process

1.

2.

3.

4.

STOP! Do not proceed until so instructed.

Feedback 6.9.C

The overarching goal is to produce a fully synthesized "plan of action." The subgoals involve the phases of the group work; that is, the first subgoal is to specify planning for the preliminary phase, the second for the beginning stage, and so on.

Instruction 6.9.D   Group Objectives for the Convening Phase

Probably the most important purpose of the ILP is to meet the needs of the residents. These needs include

1. Specific information to help them meet daily living problems;
2. Assistance with psychological ambivalence related to wanting to leave Sloan House but not wanting to give up its security;
3. An opportunity to explore their expectations and to practice independent behaviors in a socially protected setting.

An information/support group is an efficient means to disseminate information and gives much opportunity to focus on self-concept and social learning. The group also gives an opportunity for members to assume responsibilities while maintaining access to sources of emotional support—they don't have to go out on their own for a while yet.

You have gathered preliminary information that both assesses the situation the girls face and provides initial direction for your meetings. You are now ready for the convening step, where the group will become the medium by which the girls receive both information and emotional support. With this in mind, *identify the objectives for the convening phase of group development.*

STOP! Do not proceed until the instructor has discussed your objectives.

Feedback 6.9.D

The objectives for the convening phase of group process include

1. Identification of group purpose, based in part on the common concerns of the group members;
2. Clarification of the benefits of the group meetings as resources for individual members;
3. Preliminary identification of some of the concerns related to leaving Sloan House and being "on your own";
4. Clarification of the role of social worker as a resource person rather than a group leader;
5. Promotion of beginning relationships among the girls by identifying mutual concerns and promoting openness.

Instruction 6.9.E   Objectives of the Organizing Phase

You have now completed two group sessions. Surprisingly, things went very smoothly. The girls were able to identify their fears about leaving Sloan House and about being on their own, and you identified some informational needs. Most agree that getting together for these sessions is helpful, and the group is beginning to become cohesive. Now you must plan for facilitating the group during the organizing phase. *Identify the skills you need to move the group smoothly through the organizing phase.*

STOP! Do not proceed until so instructed.

Feedback 6.9.E

The concern of many group members during the beginning of the organizing phase is to find a mutual group experience, be democratically oriented particularly toward the social worker, and shape the patterns of the group in ways positive to the individual members. The skills needed by the worker in this stage include

1. The ability to hold the group steady, to turn the issues being expressed back to the group, and to help the group to continually clarify its purpose;

2. The ability to "refocus" on the original goal, hold the group to its purpose, and ensure that tasks are carried out;

3. The ability to facilitate the internal processes of group cohesiveness and consensus building. This is done by using a combination of affective and leadership skills including guiding as opposed to controlling and the continual expressing of an acceptance and belief in the group's capacity to manage its own processes;

4. The ability to assess the progress of individuals and to give support for their work.

Instruction 6.9.F   Working Phase of the Group

The ILP group has now completed six sessions. Members have called in speakers from community agencies to speak on employment, job training and educational opportunities, and apartment hunting. They are obviously beginning to have a sense of being a group and are evolving into the middle maintenance phase—working—of being a group. To effectively manage the group during this phase, you must identify some expected or typical patterns that might emerge. *What might be the emotional patterns that might emerge? The task/maintenance patterns? What are the practice skills you need?*

STOP! Do not proceed until the instructor has looked at your work.

Feedback 6.9.F

During earlier stages the girls worked through some conflicts and settled into the program on which they had agreed. The group is carrying on its activities with feelings of closeness, commitment to goals, and an emphasis on its common problems rather than differences. The dynamics here relate to leadership and group tasks. Internal processes include bonding and cohesion among members, who desire now to be together, and an emphasis on task-oriented roles that move the group toward its goals. Girls have assumed both socioemotional (group maintenance) and task roles. Decision making is by consensus and open cooperation is in evidence.

The practice skills at this stage include guidance in terms of information and counsel, the supporting of members' strengths and differences in their movement toward independent living, and assessment of how well the girls are carrying out their tasks to help the group remain focused. Maintenance skills include encouraging members to participate, active listening, and identifying obstacles as well as giving information to overcome them.

Instruction 6.9.G   Work in the Termination Phase

The ILP has completed nine of its eleven scheduled sessions. Group members have received information on employment, housing, home and money management skills, and community social services. They have decided that the final two sessions would be discussion about termination and a fun trip to the YWCA. Your supervisor reminds you that termination is an essential part of the helping process and that it is your professional responsibility to assist the group through it. To facilitate the group during this phase, your supervisor suggests that you *list the group dynamics that are likely to occur in this phase* and *identify the helping skills you will need.*

A. Group dynamics
   1.
   2.
   3.
   4.
   5.

B. Helping skills
   1.
   2.
   3.
   4.
   5.
   6.

STOP! Do not proceed until you are instructed to do so.

Feedback 6.9.G

Termination for the ILP was a planned and anticipated event. This awareness shaped the program, the depth of relationships, and the goals. It also possibly served as motivation for the girls because the information received was a useful step in preparing for independent living. Even though the time of termination may be known, there are problems associated with this phase. These include

1. Separation—with the ending of the group system, emotional reactions occur that are associated with loss or grief. They may vary in intensity and sequence and include denial, anger, bargaining to continue the group, and depression. Group members may experience strong ambivalence, hoping the group will continue but also pleased to see it end.

2. Maintenance failure—in the face of termination, the group begins to lose its goal structure and a return to relational processes appears. Decision-making deteriorates, cohesiveness lessens, and roles shift to more self-oriented ones.

Helping skills include the processes of identifying and assessing what has occurred over the life of the group, with opportunities to share positive elements from the experience. They must be helped to generalize accomplishments, transfer gains to their new lives outside the house, and regain a sense of stability in being alone. Workers consciously point out the ending of the group, review the process of information acquisition, and identify how new social skills can be used in outside situations. Feelings of sharing, loss, separation, and abandonment are very strong here and need to be expressed. Social workers thus enable the group members to use these, to feel a sense of accomplishment, and to know they will be able to establish future relationships.

Instruction 6.9.H   Evaluation

With the termination of the group, you must focus on the effectiveness of the intervention. *List the ways the program can be evaluated.*

1.

2.

3.

4.

5.

STOP! Do not proceed until you are instructed to do so.

Feedback 6.9.H

Formal evaluation of the project focuses on both emotional and educational gains. Methods used might include

1. A summary by each group member of gains made from the group experience;

2. Assignment of each member to a particular task that would use the gains of the group experience, along with a self-report of outcome;

3. A behavioral checklist of self-rating completed by members or significant others;

4. A full-blown program evaluation conducted at a specified time after concluding the ILP to assess whether it had been effective in helping the girls enter independent living.

You probably have others. Discuss them in the class to find how well they would work as evaluative mechanisms.

Dynamics of the Task Group

Group workers also facilitate the efforts of people who join together to develop improved services for groups of clients or for taking on neighborhood or community tasks. Such *task groups* include, for example, fundraising groups, groups that testify before policy-making bodies, and groups that develop or change programs to make them more relevant to client services. For our purposes, a task group is *a collection of individuals joining together in a communicative work effort toward a common goal.* Participants bring diverse interests, commitments, and perspectives to a given situation, while the social worker provides technical and informational resources to the group. Task group leadership is somewhat different than that in mutual aid groups, with more attention given to furthering the task, although socioemotional leadership is still present.

Exercise 6.10 My Own Task Groups

Using the space below, identify task groups of which you have been a part. Then describe the manner in which decisions are made. Finally, describe your primary role in each group, that is socioemotional leader, task leader, follower, observer, and so on.

Task Group	Decision-Making	Primary Role
1.	1.	1.
2.	2.	2.
3.	3.	3.
4.	4.	4.
5.	5.	5.

Social group workers in task groups must attend to the following:

1. The dynamic movement of the group as it moves through the phases of planning (convening), organizing (beginning), working, and termination;

2. The nature of work relationships among group members;

3. The leadership processes as the group moves toward its goals; and

4. The nature of decision-making processes within the group.

Task groups, like mutual aid groups, go through stages of group development, and skilled leadership through those processes maximizes task accomplishment.

As in treatment groups, *pre-planning* by the social worker before the task group is actually assembled is essential. Setting the agenda on such issues as problem definition, goal identification, assessment of current situation including present and future resources, elements of consultation and information gathering are part of the pre-planning work. The *convening or beginning stage* presents special challenges as people are introduced, goals and purposes are clarified, and allowances are made for the diverse perspectives that will enrich rather than inhibit group process. At this time, plans are set and tasks assigned to move toward the goals. During the *working phase,* problem solving and change implementation occurs, and this often requires a sophisticated level of conflict resolution. The *termination phase* considers issues of evaluation of progress, celebration of success, and identification of issues for further attention.

In summary, task group participants share common concerns and represent a diversity of talent, interests, abilities, and levels of commitment. The degree to which they optimize this diversity may be a function of the social worker's capabilities. The social worker's goal is to maximize the group's potential to facilitate high quality outcomes.

Exercise 6.11 Planning a Task Group

Divide into groups of four or five members. You are workers at the Yorkwood Community Center, whose mission is to "empower community members to enhance the quality of life for all residents of the Yorkwood neighborhood." The center has emergency services for food and clothing, a family counseling program, and an after-school recreational program for children ages six to twelve. At a recent staff meeting, people expressed concern about local families' alcohol dependence. The administration then assigned you to develop a work group to study the problem. In turn, they learned that there is a great deal of alcoholism in the neighborhood. Your work group's task is to develop an alcohol awareness group for the after-school program youth in fifth and sixth grades.

Discuss the following to provide a basic outline for the group. Write the gist of your discussion in the spaces provided:

1. What do you need to know about the agency's function? What should you consider about its mission? How might such a group influence its members?

2. What social problem led to a need for this group? What do you need to know about the social and institutional barriers that may impact upon the development of a group?

3. What issues are associated with the group's composition? What constituencies do you believe need to be represented?

4. What do you know about the human life cycle and its relationship to the potential members' needs?

5. What type of group will best serve its members' needs?

6. What cultural factors influence potential members' lives? Will these factors impede on their ability to engage in the group and relate to others?

7. What is the proposed outcome? Who will be changed and how? Develop a plan that will evaluate the effectiveness of the group for its participants, its leaders, the agency, and the community.[8]

Leadership in the Task Group

While the social worker may plan for the group, usually as part of his/her assignments in an agency, the charge is generally to facilitate rather than lead the task group. In fact, when the group begins its work, leadership emerges from among its members: task-focused leadership, which is goal-directed toward the completion of the problem-solving process; and socio-emotional leadership, which tends to the group's needs for cohesion and continuity and the members' needs for emotional support. With this in mind, let's look at leadership capacities of lay persons—those who are not employed by agencies but generally make up their boards.

Exercise 6.12 Lay Persons Developing Client Programs

There are advantages and disadvantages in working with lay persons to develop programs that will ultimately serve vulnerable and dependent clients. List below the advantages and disadvantages you can think of, and then discuss them in the full class.

Program Type	*Advantages*	*Disadvantages*
1. Substance abuse	**1.**	**1.**
2. Teenage pregnancy	**2.**	**2.**
3. Community mental health	**3.**	**3.**
4. Runaway youth	**4.**	**4.**
5. TANF (Temporary Assistance to Needy Families) work programs	**5.**	**5.**
6. Homeless shelters	**6.**	**6.**
7. You name it!	**7.**	**7.**

Where there are leaders, there are also followers—people who contribute in the problem-solving process with their ideas, their input, and their votes but do not assume leadership roles. Many times, conflict occurs among them or between them and task leaders, and this calls for conflict resolution skills and the ability to lead groups toward positive outcomes. Commonly, there are five ways to solve problems in the group:

1. Elimination—getting rid of all options but one;
2. Subjugation—majority rule suppresses all but one option;
3. Compromise—creating new options from pieces of those initially presented;

4. Alliances—creating a majority by joining subgroups in the whole group;

5. Integration—creating consensus among all options presented.[9]

Exercise 6.13 Leadership in Conflict

In a local Community Mental Health Organization (CMHO), an organizational task group has been formed to create a new program, funded by the state, in substance abuse for cocaine-addicted women. A problem arises concerning this population: some members want to serve only cocaine-addicted, pregnant women, some want to serve women who abuse alcohol, others feel that not enough attention has been given to senior women who abuse prescription drugs, and some believe that substance abuse prevention and programming is the correct choice. You are the chair of this task group and you know that there are five ways to solve conflicts in the group. For the next meeting, you consider the five methods to resolve conflict. What kinds of leadership style would you use for each method? Write your ideas below and then move to class discussion.

1.

2.

3.

4.

5.

Exercise 6.14 Evaluating the Sloan House ILP

General Instructions

This is a guided problem-solving exercise, to be carried out in groups of from five to seven students. You are already familiar with the Sloan House program for girls with problems and with the Independent Living Program (ILP) developed for those moving out on their own.

Problem Situation

During the past year, twenty-four residents of Sloan House participated in ILPs before being released on their eighteenth birthdays. A recent survey of these girls identified that 40 percent of those who had tried independent living were unsuccessful despite participating in ILPs. Some had returned to Sloan House, some went to live with their parents against the recommendations of professional staff, and some had entered or been placed in other treatment facilities. Most had continuing serious emotional adjustment problems; four were in trouble with the law. Therefore, the agency director requested a thorough evaluation of the ILP.

Sloan House has a standing Program Evaluation Committee (PEC) made up of board members, and the director asked that they evaluate ILP. The PEC is composed of five board members and a member of the professional staff appointed by the director. You have been appointed to that position. Your task is to assist the committee in its examination of the ILP and to help it develop recommendations based on its findings. The other members are

> Jay Martin, attorney,
>
> Jim Scott, director of another social agency,
>
> Mary Edwards, wife of a prominent businessman,
>
> Sylvia Spencer of Spencer Manufacturing Company and PEC Chair, and
>
> Margerie Blake, high school teacher.

Instruction 6.14.A   *Problem Identification*

As the social worker assigned to assist Ms. Spencer, the chair of PEC, you review the membership list and begin to think about planning. Although you know the problem for the PEC is to evaluate the ILP, you need to clearly state *your* problem as technical assistant. Remember, the evaluation is a committee responsibility, not yours. *What is your problem? What are its facets?*

STOP! Do not proceed until so instructed.

Feedback 6.14.A

Your problem is to provide technical assistance and information to the PEC. That is, you are the professional consultant to the group. In addition, you have the chores of arranging times and places for meetings, helping the chairperson to plan the agenda, and trying to ensure that the potentials of the committee members are utilized. You will not be able to know much more about them than their business roles in this exercise, but you will need to clarify your roles with them.

Instruction 6.14.B   Goals of Your Work

Having identified the problem as a professional planning assignment, *what is your long-range goal* in terms of the task group? *What are your immediate goals?*

STOP! Do not proceed until the instructor checks your goals.

Feedback 6.14.B

The long-range goal is to ensure that the group remains task-oriented and goal-directed until it develops a plan for evaluation of the ILP. Short-range goals are to plan the process of the task force, dealing with both cognitive and relational aspects to the extent possible.

Instruction 6.14.C   Assessing the Situation: the Planning Phase

Though the work of the task group must remain flexible, a general plan for overall progress is essential to keep the group task-oriented and goal-directed. Two planning areas must be considered. The first is cognitive in nature, that is, a general outline of the entire work, from goal setting to end—identifying goals for the committee and the tasks that must be assigned and the possible means by which the tasks can be accomplished. The second is socioemotional awareness—an assessment of the individual members' potentials, resources, and the probability of them working well together. Finally, you must work with the chair to clarify your own role in relationship to hers and to the committee as a whole.

1. What is your general outline of the whole process?

2. What kind of socioemotional assessment can you make at this stage?

3. What is your role in relationship to the chair? To the committee as a whole?

STOP! Do not proceed without feedback from the instructor.

Feedback 6.14.C

Cognitive tasks include

1. Orientation, that is, problem identification and goal setting;

2. Discussion and assessment of the situation; provision of statistical information;

3. Discussion of constraints faced by the ILP that limited its success;

4. Developing new ideas that would lead to success;

5. Choosing the best plan and the ways to implement it.

These cognitive tasks are in fact the problem-solving model you have used throughout these exercises. Relational tasks include

1. Gaining some information on the people;

2. Assessing, in a preliminary manner, how they would work together;

3. Ensuring that group members know one another and that they each have a beginning sense of how they can work together;

4. Understanding your own role and making that clear to them.

In a "real" setting, you would probably know about each of these people, but here you need not worry about their characteristics. Assume that they will work well together because they are concerned about the program and dedicated to the success of Sloan House.

Role clarification. Social workers, regardless of practice settings, methods, or client populations, always "talk with someone" about a "problem situation." Consequently, practice requires the development and management of a variety of relationships, and it also requires an assessment of the social worker's particular role in each new setting. In this case, your role is that of consultant to the chairperson and resource consultant to the committee as a whole. You must realize that this places you in a *secondary* relationship; that is, you are *not* the group leader. That role belongs to the chairperson, and you must be sure that you do not usurp it.

Instruction 6.14.D   The Elements of Consultation

Having established your role as that of program consultant, look at the areas of consultation. These are, generally, program consulting and process consulting. *What are the elements of program consultation? Process consultation?*

STOP! Do not proceed without feedback from the instructor.

Feedback 6.14.D

Program consultation consists of helping the committee to focus on the charge the director has set for it, committee goals and tasks, and methods by which to proceed. The consultant also does relevant research and presents research conclusions and theories, along with statistical data on the problem at hand, to the committee. Process consultation is a set of activities that helps the committee members perceive, understand and act on communication patterns, roles, policies, procedures, and decision-making processes within the work. The dynamics of action fall under process consultation.

Instruction 6.14.E   *Planning in the Pregroup Phase*

Very aware of your responsibilities to Ms. Spencer, the committee, and the needs of the girls in your organization, you decide to do some initial planning to ensure that the group is successfully launched. You have already done some reading on evaluative methods and successful programs of the sort Sloan House wants to have, and you discuss these with Ms. Spencer. She asks you to prepare an initial agenda for the first meeting. *What should be included in the agenda?*

STOP! Do not proceed until the instructor has discussed agendas with you.

Feedback 6.14.E

The agenda you have prepared should include the following, although you may have more items.

1. Introduction of group members, including comments about areas of expertise relevant to the needs of Sloan House

2. Explanation of the charge of the PEC, including an idea of the background of the problem and the time frame in which the work should be accomplished

3. Discussion by committee members of the problem, its goals, possible alternatives, and tasks

4. Discussion of resources available to assist the committee, including data about Sloan House residents

5. Task assignments and scheduling of future meetings.

Instruction 6.14.F   The Convening Phase

The initial meeting is critical in the work life of a task group: A frustrating experience by members can delay or reduce its effectiveness; therefore, it must be a productive and satisfying experience. Ms. Spencer is a bit uncertain about what the group can realistically accomplish, even with your agenda, and she asks you to clarify for her what to expect. Because of your experience in group work, you understand that there will be two levels of process going on at the same time—cognitive tasks and socioemotional juggling. *Specify for Ms. Spencer how you intend to handle each level;* that is, the program work (agenda tasks) to be undertaken and the dynamics of group interaction and leadership tasks that will produce a working group.

Program Work: Agenda Tasks

Group Interaction and Leadership Tasks

STOP! Do not proceed until the instructor provides feedback.

Feedback 6.14.F

On the program level, realistic expectations are that the group will define and discuss the charge to the committee, set some time limits for work accomplishment, get some idea of the background of the present ILP and some information on programs that have been successful, and look at how they can begin to organize around tasks. Group dynamics in this phase include an approach/avoidance dynamic, for even though the members have volunteered to serve on the committee they now begin to assess the responsibilities that membership requires in relation to other obligations. There will also be a kind of emotional "milling process" as members seek to develop interpersonal alliances with one another, and a kind of inventory-taking process as members assess the resources they have in relationship to the goals and tasks.

Instruction 6.14.G   Work in the Organizing Phase

After the first meeting, in which time was spent getting an understanding of the ILP and generally discussing how to proceed, there was consensus that the orientation process had been completed and that at the next meeting the committee would lay out plans and assign tasks. Ms. Spencer has requested that you gather and distribute the information the group needs, and she wants to know what the dynamic processes are likely to be. *What kinds of information will the group need? What dynamic processes are likely to occur?*

Information needed

Group processes

STOP! Do not proceed without the instructor's permission.

Feedback 6.14.G

The critical need of the committee is information that they do not have. This would include a report of the ILP in past years, verbal reports and discussion by the director of past successes and failures, research and evaluations of similar programs, feedback by clients on what services they found valuable and what were not, and information on both the behavioral and emotional issues faced by the girls leaving Sloan House for independent living.

Group processes at this stage are marked by the emergence of group norms and the differentiation of members into specific roles that help the group maintain itself internally and move toward its goals. Functions of the group at this stage include patterns of decision making, leadership, role performance, and communication.

Instruction 6.14.H   Working in the Middle Phase

The PEC has collected a variety of information and consensus at the last meeting. They plan to devote the next meeting to reviewing alternate ways to prepare residents for independent living. The members also want to define recommendations that might eliminate some of the problems of residents in future ILPs. Ms. Spencer would like you to explain *what are the expected task (program) needs of this phase and what are the expected group dynamics?*

Expected tasks of work phase

Expected group dynamics

STOP! Call on instructor for feedback.

Feedback 6.14.H

1. *Group Dynamics.* This work phase is marked by the strongest period of cohesiveness and coalescence among the group members. The group goals and members' objectives are blended. Group norms have provided the relational and decision-making processes of the members to the point that interactions are predictable, for example, seating arrangements, communication patterns, and levels of support and confrontation. Decision making moves to a consensus type. Maintenance and task roles are integrated so that both socioemotional and the task/leadership roles are evident.
2. *Program Needs.* Program needs center on those that support or facilitate consensuslike decision making, strengthen members' feelings of participation, and support the roles of the members. Informational needs continue to be a central need.

Instruction 6.13.I   Termination Phase

The PEC has spent nine two-hour meetings formulating recommendations about the ILP. Extensive discussion of program alternatives, options, and impact has been completed. There was agreement at the end of the last meeting that you would put into writing their final recommendations, and at the next meeting these would be approved and then sent to the director.

Ms. Spencer has asked to meet with you to go over her plans for the final group meeting. She sees that the group has evolved into a very close, hard-working committee and has accomplished a great deal within a short period of time. With the goal of the group in sight, she is determined that their final meeting be a meaningful experience that will encourage them to continue their work with Sloan House and perhaps work closely with her again. She believes that the experience has reinforced her belief that volunteers working together with professional staff can make an important contribution to the overall operation of Sloan House. As you reflect on Ms. Spencer's comments and think about the group dynamics and group needs during the termination phase, what will you tell Ms. Spencer? *What are the dynamics of this phase, and what are the program needs?*

Program needs at termination

Group dynamics at termination

STOP! Wait for instructor's feedback before you proceed.

Feedback 6.13.I

1. *Group Dynamics.* The characteristics of termination have two levels: member reactions to ending and the reaction of the group as a whole to ending. It is from these levels that the characteristics must be understood.

Member reactions—dissolution of relationship means separation and is marked by emotional reactions to the event. Expression of feelings covers a range of emotional expressions filled with considerable ambivalence, for example, mixed feelings about leaving an experience and yet relief that the work is done. Members may feel denial or anger or simply want to avoid dealing with feelings.

Group as a whole—reactions to termination produce a number of changes within the structure and process of the group; for example, a lessening of role performance of task and maintenance functions. The decision-making process may deteriorate, and there is a reduction of cohesion.

2. *Program/Group Needs.* Program needs complement the group processes during termination. There must be plans to explain recommendations to the executive director. Informal group processes center on evaluation and recapitulation. This can provide useful evaluative information as well as a means for individuals to discuss ending relationships as group members.

Portfolio Building

1. What are the processes of group practice?

2. What are the differences between treatment and task groups?

3. What phases must groups go through, and how do social workers affect those phases?

4. What leadership processes are necessary to group practice, and what is the place of the group worker in them?

5. With what areas of group practice do you need more experience?

Looking Ahead

With our work on consultation we have moved out of the area of direct interpersonal services. In working at wider systems levels there will be less intensity in terms of relationships but more cognitive efforts toward social change and social action. In the following chapters, we will deal with social work at organizational, community, and, finally, policy levels that might effect change at state and national levels.

Notes

1. Garland, James, Hubert E. Jones, and Ralph Kolodney (1965). "A Model for Stages of Development in Social Work Groups," pp. 1–28. In Saul Bernstein, Ed. *Explorations in Group Work*. Boston: Boston University School of Social Work.
2. Brown, L. (1991). *Groups for Growth and Change*. White Plains, NY: Longman Publishing Group.
3. For a review of roles carried by individual members in groups, see Johnson, David W., and Frank P. Johnson (1975). *Joining Together: Group Therapy and Group Skills*. Englewood Cliffs, NJ: Prentice Hall.
4. See Margaret E. Hatford (1972). *Groups in Social Work: Applications of Small Group Therapy and Research to Social Work Practice*. New York: Columbia University Press, pp. 218–227.
5. See Bales, R.F. (1959). "Small Group Theory and Research," in R.K. Merton, Leonard Broom, and Leonard Cottrell, Jr., Eds., *Sociology Today*. New York: Basic Books.
6. See Shulman, L. (1992). *The Skills of Helping: Individuals, Groups, and Families*. Itasca, IL: F.E. Peacock Publishers, Inc.
7. Schwartz, William (1977). "Social Group Work: The Interactional Approach." In J.B. Turner, Ed., *Encyclopedia of Social Work*, Vol. II, New York: NASW Press.
8. Standards for Social Work Group Practice (1999). AASWG, Inc. Association for the Advancement of Social Work with Groups, Inc., University of Akron, Akron, OH. Adopted 10/17/98.
9. A review of the kinds of functions performed by members of a task group was originally listed by Benne, E.D., and P. Sheets (1948), "Function Roles of Group Members," *Journal of Social Issues, 1948*, 4:2, pp. 41–49. A modified listing is presented in Johnson and Johnson, Op cit., pp. 26–30. Johnson, David, and Frank P. Johnson (1975). *Joining Together: Group Therapy and Group Skills*. Englewood Cliffs, NJ: Prentice Hall.

Section THREE

Mezzo and Macro Practice Levels

ChapterSEVEN

Working in Organizations

The Social Work Organization

Most social work takes place in organizations because organizations are fundamental to every day life. We are born in organizations, worship in organizations, are educated in organizations, work in organizations, and die in organizations. As social workers, we face not only client problems but problems in agencies or communities that affect our ability to serve clients. Poorly functioning organizations do not serve clients well. Understanding this means that at this level we should learn about both policies of the organization and the underlying bases of administration. Netting et al. say that

> Social workers with little or no idea of how organizations operate, how they interact, or how they can be influenced and changed from both outside and inside are likely to be severely limited in their effectiveness.[1]

An awareness of mission, goals, means, structure, resources, and process is primary to understanding organizations. We understand organizations through their histories, underlying ideals, and the prevailing problems that make up the organizational culture. Our earlier chapters acquainted you with awareness of organizational structure. Now, we will concentrate on missions, goals, and problems in organizational settings.

Generally speaking, any organization is created as a means to reach specific goals. For example, a business organization may make shoes to obtain profit; a human service organization works with people in need to empower them to meet those needs; a prison holds criminals to punish them or take them out of society. As Schermerhorn[2] says, *missions,* or the basic purpose of organizations, give them societal reasons for existence: They are written statements that identify the organization's official objectives, populations it intends to serve and services it will provide, and the underlying philosophy by which it will operate or ways it intends to fulfill a unique role in society.[3]

Goals set forth expected outcomes to carry out the mission. The mission of a school, for example, is to educate students, and goals might be that every student would graduate with a basic and evaluable set of information. The *means* to insure that students would get such information might include setting up an appropriate curriculum, finding teachers who can educate, getting enough students, and providing for the physical needs of the educational process, such as desks or chairs or the school cafeteria. Goals of a human service organization in which the mission is to provide health care for the homeless might include accurate assessments of health needs among the local population and appropriate health care resulting in well-being for at least a majority of clients, with staff, medication, and individual health care as the means to those goals.[4]

Organizations have both stated and unstated, or latent, goals. For example, in the new Temporary Assistance to Needy Families (TANF) program, a stated goal is to provide clients with work training and job placement so that welfare dependency can be eliminated. However, because training can be provided for only a short time, and jobs available to that population are limited and unlikely to pay enough to end a family's poverty, the stated goal (eliminating welfare dependency) is not the true goal. Therefore, we must assume some latent goals, such as government control of work behavior, for whatever purposes that might entail. Another manifest goal of TANF is "reducing illegitimacy," but we know that the birth rate for mothers on public assistance is lower than that in the general population, and that women in all walks of life, not just those who are public dependents, have children out of wedlock. The latent function, then, is not to reduce illegitimacy but to control the sexual behavior of public dependents.

Exercise 7.1 Commitment to Children

Most social agencies are concerned with children, and most of us believe that the United States is highly child-oriented. Yet if this were true our goal in TANF (or some kind of support for needy children) would provide adequate income at least for their food, shelter, clothing, and medical and educational needs. TANF's goal, however, is to put adult recipients to work. It barely mentions the needs of their children. TANF's manifest plans for day care will not occur because adequate and sufficient day care seems beyond the scope of most states. In fact, TANF supplies even less subsistence for children than did the AFDC (Aid to Families of Dependent Children) program, and the two-year limit on receiving it makes no allowance for children. Are we really child-oriented?

General Instructions

The exercise will take at least one class period, with the instructor listing on the board the decisions class members make about the problem.

Problem Situation

A mother with three dependent children has just been deserted by her husband. He has taken the car and all the money, but she has the household goods and her house payment (or rent) is paid for the next month. Her children are a boy, age fourteen, a girl of ten, and a four-year-old girl. The family has no other resources and no family in town. Though she may be able to find work later, the mother's skills will not give her a well-paying job. Right now she is in crisis deciding what to do to make ends meet for the next several months.

This is your family, collectively, so you may decide what the family members need, and how much, with a low-budget income, they will have for each need. Use the county in which your social work program is located as a basis for costs and revenue.

1. Discuss in the class and list on the board all the needs such a family will have on a monthly basis. You may decide on a rented or purchased home, subsidized or not, and on such details as a car or public transportation, washer and dryer or laundromat, and so on. Do not forget such details as birthdays and Christmas, which should be listed as "entertainment." Prorate heat as it might cost in March, and figure annual clothing expenses and divide by twelve for your monthly rate. After figuring all expenses on a monthly basis, multiply by twelve for an annual income.

2. What could local agencies supply? Remember that most will not help for more than a month, and any emergency donations must be divided by twelve to derive an annual income. For housing, look into the requirements and costs of public housing and check the waiting list for HUD Section 8 housing.

3. What are local TANF regulations, for what could the family apply, and what would be the requirements? How much is the local allotment while the mother is looking for TANF employment?

4. On a separate page, make columns for "List of Needs," "Expected Cost," "Wage Revisions." and "TANF Revisions." Then, taking local TANF allowances for a family of four, apply them to this case. After that, at low-wage work the mother might find, and apply. Discuss and revise the costs listed above until the expenses fall within the low wages she might receive and within the TANF allowances.

5. Discuss what effect this poverty and resulting poor health will have on the children. What may be the costs to society in the long run?

6. What are the likely effects of this deprivation on the mother? Discuss.

7. Are we a child-oriented society? What are the latent goals of TANF in terms of families?

Another kind of goal is agency survival. Once an organization becomes established, a major goal is simply to keep it going. For example, the National Foundation for Infantile Paralysis's initial mission was to cure and prevent poliomyelitis. Once that was achieved, with the Salk and Sabin vaccines, its organizers changed its purpose to that of elimination of birth defects. Obviously, its originators and workers valued the organization itself beyond its goals, and chose to maintain the working relationship among the organization's ecology, its professionals, and its March of Dimes volunteers. This "organizational maintenance," or survival, activity may even come to take precedence over service goals, so we cannot discount its importance in organizational behavior.

When we become part of a service-providing organization, one of our most important tasks is to discover the mission, both manifest and latent goals, and the means by which it meets its goals. Part of the "organizational culture" are values the organization holds regarding its structure and processes. The concept of organizational culture helps us understand an organization's internal strengths and weaknesses, along with its opportunities for growth and threats to meeting its mission.

Exercise 7.2 Know Your Organization

Look at your field placement organization or another organization where you work or play.

1. Where can you find the mission statement? Read it and write it below. Why was the organization first established? Is the mission statement visible and available to all? Is it still relevant to the agency's work today?

2. Mission statements should be very concise, often only a sentence or so. Below, condense your agency's mission statement by eliminating all verbiage not required to fulfill the elements mentioned by Schermerhorn: underlying philosophy, official objectives, population to be served, and ways it will serve. Why was the organization originally established? What purpose did it serve, and for what community? (A community may be a town or a neighborhood, but it might also be a group with like interests or concerns.)

3. What values are apparent in the mission statement? Why are those values important to the mission?

4. Below, write the organization's stated goals. Are the goals still in line with the mission? Does the organization effectively meet its goals?

5. Do you see other, less visible goals that seem more important? What are they? Write the maintenance goals you have found. Are there also latent goals?

Maintenance Goals	Latent Goals
Maintenance Goals	*Latent Goals*
1.	1.
2.	2.
3.	3.
4.	4.

6. You can usually tell what the most important goals are by the amount of resources given them. Very often just a look at the budget—money for service goals versus money for administration—will indicate the most important goals. If you can, look at your agency's budget and see what share of it goes for agency maintenance and what share for client service.

7. Look at the internal strengths and weaknesses of your organization in terms of how it fulfills its mission, and list them below.

Strengths	Weaknesses
Strengths	*Weaknesses*
1.	1.
2.	2.
3.	3.
4.	4.
5.	5.

8. Look externally at the organization's environment and note its opportunities for growth and the threats to meeting its mission.

Opportunities for Growth	Threats to Mission
Opportunities for Growth	*Threats to Mission*
1.	1.
2.	2.
3.	3.
4.	4.
5.	5.

Discuss all these ideas in class.

Organizational Structure, Processes, and Culture

One of our most useful tools as workers is, simply, the organization chart. This is a map that shows who reports to whom, how many people report to one supervisor, and how many levels the organizational structure has. There are formal charts, which indicate how the hierarchy works, and informal charts. Formal charts show the positions each worker holds in the structure and the level of power or authority in each position. You can usually obtain a formal chart from the agency, but you may have to make up your own.

However, formal charts do not always show how the structure really works, because of informal structures and processes such as information flow. Most agency workers may be aware of informal power—who you go to when you need something. A good way to find out who has power is to chart who reports formally and informally to whom, who are gatekeepers (such as secretaries and receptionists), and who control access to others. We find out the informal structure by questions and by observation.

Exercise 7.3 Your Organization's Structure

For this exercise, look at your field agency.

1. Look at your agency's formal organization chart and on a separate page, diagram it, showing where you are on the chart, what positions you supervise (over whom you have authority), and what positions supervise you (who has power over your position?). Does the organization have a flat or hierarchical structure?
2. Again on a separate page, draw a chart showing informal connections and power. Informal connections could be drawn in blue, lines of information in red, and lines of power in green.
3. Write a short paragraph analyzing the differences you have found between formal and informal charts. How do the factors of information flow, formal power, and informal power affect how you respond to your tasks in the organization?

Significant events in an organization's history include (1) the establishment of new policies and programs, (2) new sources of funding, (3) economic and political activities that impact on the organization from the environment, and (4) significant changes in process or structure.

Exercise 7.4 The Organization's Timeline

In the space below, develop an organizational timeline for your field placement agency. Begin with the crucial crisis on which it was based and show at least one significant event from each of the three categories above: 1) establishment of new policies and procedures, 2) new sources of funding, and 3) economic and political activities impacting the organization.

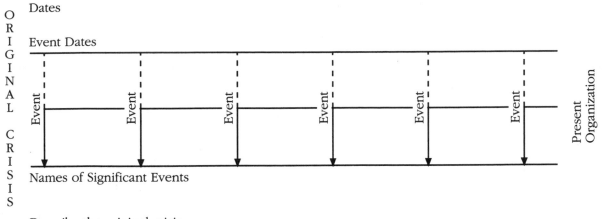

Describe the original crisis

Exercise 7.5 Your Agency's Culture

Many separate forces have an impact on an agency, and in the natural order of things, a culture forms within the organization based on those forces. In society, norms, mores, ways of knowing and being, roles, and expectations appear with societal evolution. In the same way, an organizational culture will emerge over time. Continuing to analyze your field agency, complete the following chart depicting its organizational culture.

Another important element in analyzing a human service organization is knowing its funding resources. Generally speaking, funding resources determine power and authority in organizations. Private, not-for-profit agencies developed within a community for a specific purpose, and funded by local fund drives are usually responsible to their boards, who have authority over budget and practices in the agency. Public organizations are paid for

Values	*Structure*	*History*	*Rules*

by taxes and so are responsible to the legislatures that established them. Private, for-profit agencies are usually responsible only to their owners, who set the goals not on service bases (although they may be concerned with services) but on profit lines. Where there are mixed funding lines, different authorities slice up the funding and reporting responsibilities.

Exercise 7.6 Money Is Power

Identify your field agency (or some other agency in which you are involved) as public, not-for-profit, or for-profit. On a separate page, diagram the hierarchical money and power system from your local organization to as high as the funding goes. Where there are several sources of funding, indicate that in different colors.

Exercise 7.7 The Hierarchical Element

Taking the same agency, on a separate page, draw a diagram of the relevant funding, power, and information systems on which your agency relies for its money, clients, and maintenance as a social agency.

Just as direct practice workers use theory bases for assessing and working with individual clients, knowledge of organizational theory can help us work with the structure and processes of organizations. Your instructor can teach organizational theory in more depth, but here Figure 7.1 presents a few of the major theorists and their concepts.

Exercise 7.8 Organizational Theory Game Show

Decide in advance on a prize for the winning team, such as a trip to the local ice cream store, pizza, a free lunch, a book, and so on (if there is a cost, class members contribute before the game begins). Choose one person to moderate a game of Questions and Answers. Divide into three teams, and run the exercise as if it were a game show. The instructor is the judge. Keep track of which team knows the most answers so that they can win the prize. The questions are

1. What are the themes of scientific management?
2. What are the traits of bureaucracy?
3. What are two components of human relations theory?
4. What is the theory most applicable to social work practice?
5. What are issues of consensus decision making for direct service workers?
6. How does scientific management manage diversity?
7. How does the decision-making model manage diversity?

FIGURE 7.1   Major Organizational Theories[4]

Theorist	Theory	Major Concepts
1. Weber[5]	Bureaucracy	a. Hierarchy with structured chains of command b. Efficiency in tasks c. Structured and elaborate rules and procedures d. Goal rather than service oriented
2. Taylor & Fayol[6]	Scientific management	a. Workers become "cogs in a wheel" b. Decreased initiative and worker satisfaction c. Procedures and protocols specify work parameters d. Little acknowledgment of individuals
3. Mayo[7]	Human relations	a. Attends to needs and interests of workers b. Emphasizes importance of teamwork, cooperation, leadership c. Treats people well for increased productivity
4. Drucker[8]	Management by objectives	a. Clearly states expected outcomes b. Breaks goals into tasks c. Monitors progress by time d. Proactive program planning
5. Michels & Selznick[9]	Organizational goals model	a. Begins with organizational goals b. Recognizes system maintenance goals c. Organizational survival goals take precedence over client service goals
6. Simon & March[10]	Decision making	a. Step-by-step problem solving b. Information management c. Ignores informal structures
7. Burns & Stalker[11]; Morse & Lorsch[12]	Contingency theory	a. If this happens, then do that b. Organization's response to environment c. Organizational survival a key
8. Thompson[13]	Managing diversity	a. Identifies center of power b. Effective use of power by various individuals and groups in leadership c. Organization's ability to understand and change its culture.

8. How does contingency theory manage diversity?
9. Under what theory does your university fall?
10. What are the disadvantages of human relations theory for social work practice?
11. Any other questions the instructor might want should be listed before the game begins.

The Worker in the Organization

As we have seen in some of our past exercises, we cannot isolate the client-worker partnership from everything else. Clients' other systems—work, home, family, groups, past history, and future expectations—affect the intervention system and its processes. In addition, social workers themselves are embedded in similar systems and in the agency, other organizations, peer groups in the community, and so on. Both workers and clients interact with the societal system, with its norms, rules, and the ways of behavior expected of its members.

A major problem social workers face is the organization that has become so bureaucratized it dehumanizes client services. For our profession, quality of service must be the criterion, but in today's people-processing organizations, quality service may be neglected in the pressure of setting unit costs on services. When a formal bureaucratic structure is based on such components as efficiency, hierarchy, division of services, and formalized rules and regulations, it becomes difficult to interject humanistic elements into them, but

> . . . if a human service organization is functioning in a manner that is disrespectful or detrimental to clients, the professional social worker has an obligation to try to change those practices and not simply walk away in favor of a more attractive work environment.[14]

This is a daunting task. Even more problematic are organizations in which social workers have little real authority, such as in host organizations like schools and hospitals. In them, social work is at most ancillary, and workers have almost no status in terms of care *vis-à-vis* teachers or doctors. While social workers can make some changes, in host agencies they walk a fine line trying to do so, and their interactional skills may be as important as are their problem-solving skills.

In the following exercise, set in a hospital, be aware of difficulties in dealing with entrenched policies and people who have formal power.

Exercise 7.9 The Dying Patient

Do the following guided problem-solving exercise in groups of four to seven people. It will take two or three class periods.

Problem Situation

You are a social worker in a hospital where two policies concerning dying patients are paramount. First is that the doctor has the right to decide whether to inform patients that they are dying; and second is that hospital personnel are not given any kind of instruction, support, or help in dealing with the emotions surrounding dying—their own fears and frustrations or those of their patients. The policy is generally simply not to mention dying and to deal with patients as if they were not dying, so as to save them undue emotional stress and pain.

Mrs. Andrews, age forty-two, was recently admitted to the hospital with cancer. Although her family (husband and two teenage children) have been told that she has about a month to live, her doctor refuses to inform her, saying that it will only hurt her to know.

Because her family doesn't know how to deal with its own grief in a manner that would keep the bad news from Mrs. Andrews, they stay away from her. When they do visit, their conversation is light and nonmeaningful, and they seem to exclude her from their plans. This hurts and angers her, seeming to indicate an uncaringness that she cannot understand. She takes out her anger by being demanding and unhappy with the hospital personnel who work with her. They understand what is happening but are unable to respond to her because of the hospital's policies and so protect themselves by being distant and somewhat sharp with her.

At this point, you are appointed to her case. Though you have been at this hospital for some time, you have not worked with a dying patient unaware of impending death. You have been assigned to help her become a "better patient" so that she will not upset hospital routine or irritate those who work with her. You are also instructed to help her and her family as much as possible.

Instruction 7.9.A   *Identification of Client Systems*

In any problem situation, there may be several sets of potential clients of which social workers must be aware. That is the situation here: you are assigned to work with Mrs. Andrews, but she is not the person expressing the need, nor is she a voluntary client. On the other hand, she is the central focus of the problem. Your first task, then, is to specify all potential clients and on that basis choose a primary client. *Who are your potential clients? Who is your primary client, and on what basis have you made that judgment?* List below the possible clients and the reasons they are potential clients.

Client   **Why?**

1.

2.

3.

4.

5.

6.

STOP! Wait for instructor feedback before proceeding.

Feedback 7.9.A

Certainly Mrs. Andrews is the most obvious client, despite the fact that she has not asked for help and is thus an involuntary client. The list of potential client systems, aside from Mrs. Andrews, includes

1. The members of her family, either separately or together, who cannot deal with their grief;
2. The hospital staff who do not know how to deal with Mrs. Andrews and with other dying patients;
3. The doctor, who may not have the information he needs concerning death and dying;
4. Other patients who are dying;
5. The families of such other patients;
6. Groups of doctors who may need the information you will accumulate;
7. The hospital itself, which requested that you deal with Mrs. Andrews;
8. The community and society in general.

Because you see that Mrs. Andrews is the immediate focus of the problem for all other people and because the hospital administration has asked you to intervene, she is your primary client.

Instruction 7.9.B Problem Identification

Because of the many areas of emotional stress, and because you are relatively powerless in the hospital setting, identifying this many faceted problem is complicated. As with other social work contexts, much depends on your perceptions and values. You are a generalist practitioner, and so you know that the focus of intervention lies in relationships of relevant systems. You also know that your primary responsibility lies with Mrs. Andrews but that she does not have the information she needs to work with you in making decisions. Your first step, then, is to specify—without her help, since you are forbidden to inform her of her coming death—what the problem is of which she is the central focus. *What do you perceive as the central problem in this situation?* State the problem and why it is central.

STOP! Wait for instructor feedback before you proceed.

Feedback 7.9.B

It is very easy to see that the policies of the hospital and the power of the doctor are keeping Mrs. Andrews from the knowledge you think she should have; however, neither the hospital nor the doctor has asked for your help. They are not your clients, and, therefore, in this exercise at least, it is not your job to help them to find solutions. Although they are targets and perhaps potential clients, your first duty at this point is to Mrs. Andrews.

As you perceive it, the heart of the matter is that there is very little honest communication among the systems involved. This creates difficulty in all systems, but for your primary client you believe that the problem is that Mrs. Andrews does not know she is dying. There is little or nothing that you can do to assuage the grief of the family, which is in turn causing her to feel isolated, without her assistance. Hospital personnel cannot deal with her in a caring and comforting manner unless they can deal with her impending death. Moreover, since you believe that people have a right to make their own decisions, and your job is to help them through their problem situations, withholding such vital information, then, is a violation of Mrs. Andrews's right as a client.

Instruction 7.9.C   Goal Setting

Having determined the problem, you are now faced with several difficulties. First, it would be unprofessional simply to inform Mrs. Andrews she is dying. Although you see the problem clearly as a lack of honesty, you cannot advise a doctor on what is best for his patient. The doctor may be right that knowing, for Mrs. Andrews, might be too painful. Moreover, her family has rights, and you can do nothing to harm them. Because they are depending on the doctor's advice, you could damage relationships significantly if you are not careful. Finally, because you are an employee of the hospital, you have certain responsibilities toward it and its policies. Whatever you do, it should not be in violation of these many issues.

Nevertheless, you have a professional and ethical obligation to *set a goal that will, in the most direct way, solve the sets of problems surrounding the lack of honesty about Mrs. Andrews's prognosis to the extent possible.* Discuss possible goals and list them below. Then choose the most appropriate one, given the total situation.

STOP! Wait for instructor feedback before you proceed.

Feedback 7.9.C

Because lack of honesty is causing problems for all persons involved, your goal is to see that, in the most appropriate way possible, Mrs. Andrews is informed of her impending death. In this way she can understand her family's apparent lack of caring and share with them the grief surrounding her dying. She will know that they love her and can help them rather than allow her depression and anger to hurt them. A secondary benefit to the hospital system is that personnel will also be able to freely give comfort and support to Mrs. Andrews in the difficult time ahead. Though they may still have difficulty dealing with their own feelings, they can be open with Mrs. Andrews.

Instruction 7.9.D   Problem Assessment: The Interactional Systems

Before beginning any strategy that will fulfill your goal, you must clarify the problem's ramifications. At least three processes are involved: looking at the interactional systems that you will focus on; determining the constraints you already face; and insuring that you have enough relevant information to proceed.

The work for this step is to carefully lay out the interactional systems, which need your attention. Remember, the focus of social work intervention is not the people themselves but *their relationships*. Social work practice is aimed at enhancement of these relationships so that they become more positive or beneficial to the people involved. Given Mrs. Andrews's situation and the problem context, *what are the interaction systems with which you must be concerned? What are the problems most crucial for each interactional system, and which system should receive first attention?*

Interaction System   *Crucial Problem*   *Priority*

STOP! Do not proceed until instructed to do so.

Feedback 7.9.D

The four relevant interactional systems are, at this point:

1. Mrs. Andrews's interaction with her family;
2. The doctor–patient relationship and the relationship of the doctor with all the family members;
3. The relationships between Mrs. Andrews and the hospital personnel;
4. The client-worker relationship that you must establish with Mrs. Andrews. Although you will be interacting with the others in the context of your work, your primary client—involuntary at this point—is Mrs. Andrews.

The most important relationship at this stage is the one you must establish with Mrs. Andrews, to help her recognize you are there to help, that you care, and that you will support her. From your standpoint, you must be able to go along with the hospital policy of withholding knowledge from her while you determine what she perceives as her problems. At the same time, of course, you will be working with her family and other relevant systems.

Next, of course, is the interfamily relationship. Mrs. Andrews feels rejected, and that is difficult for even a well person to deal with. Although her family knows how she feels, they cannot reassure her for fear they will allow her to see the depth of their grieving. There is some evidence, according to Kubler-Ross and others, that people who are dying realize this at some level of consciousness and need to have the problem in the open so that, in love and dignity, they can prepare themselves and their loved ones for the dying.[6] Whether or not Mrs. Andrews knows she is dying, the family knows it. Certainly, they can make their own decisions about honesty with Mrs. Andrews.

The doctor–patient relationship is one of societally legitimate power. This is not to say that the doctor is unaware of or unsympathetic to the needs of his patients; however, it does mean that for all practical purposes he is the final authority for the patient and the patient's family. It would be most difficult to breach this kind of authority. His concern, although you may believe it is misplaced, is to save Mrs. Andrews from more suffering than she already has. The grief this causes her family and the problems for hospital personnel are, he believes, a small price to pay to give her comfort.

The least important of the relationships is that of hospital personnel to patient. That is not to say, of course, that they are unimportant. Bound by the need to act only in accordance with doctor–patient relationships, the hospital system and its personnel are unable to deal fully with Mrs. Andrews. Her outbursts of temper and anguish are upsetting to the personnel and to hospital routine. Their reactions, though they are aware of her pain, are as much to protect themselves as to work through the situation with her. Thus she is becoming alienated not only from her family and her doctor but from those who will be her final companions at the end of her life.

Instruction 7.9.E   Problem Assessment: Constraints

There are certain "givens" attached to any problem, though they may be more complicated with social work problems. At this point you need to look at each constraint—things that may limit your action and intervention over which you have no immediate or powerful control. *List the constraints that impinge upon your actions but over which you have no control or little possibility of control.*

STOP! Do not proceed until your discussion with the instructor.

Feedback 7.9.E

The problem has many constraints and you may find more than are listed here. Please feel free to do so. The easily observable ones include

1. The power the doctor has over informing Mrs. Andrews, both in terms of what he will tell her and what he will "allow" the family to tell her.

2. The legitimation of that power given by the policies of the hospital. That includes limitation of the work of social services; therefore, you are as constrained by the doctor's orders with regard to Mrs. Andrews as are other hospital personnel.

3. Time. Mrs. Andrews has about a month to live. If she is to become reconciled with her family it is necessary that reconciliation take place within the next two weeks. After that, because of her physical pain, she will not be conscious enough most of the time to give attention to the problem.

4. Mrs. Andrews is an involuntary client. That may mean that she will reject your help. Moreover, although the family is likely to look for comfort and help to lay out alternatives, they may reject you, your ideas, your plan.

Instruction 7.9.F   *Problem Assessment: Gathering Information*

Before you can proceed, you need several areas of information. You already know hospital policy, doctor's orders, and your own function in the hospital in terms of what you can and cannot do. You are a trained social worker, and so you also know your mission, and you have certain skills, knowledge, and values with which to work. However, this is your first intervention with a dying client. Now you must consider *what information you need and where you can get it*. List below the information you need and where you can find it.

Needed Information   *Location of Information*

STOP! Wait for instructor's discussion before proceeding.

Feedback 7.9.F

Perhaps the first information you need is information on death and dying, the emotional reactions of patients and their families, and the steps and processes through which dying people realize their mortality. Social work literature can give you insights into client interventions on the issue, and your instructor can refer you to these sources.

Second, though you know the doctor's stand on the problem, you have not yet spoken with Mrs. Andrews. Gathering information on her and her family is a first priority. Of course you cannot yet inform Mrs. Andrews of her status, but an interview will provide much information while, at the same time, you provide emotional support for her because she is ill.

Third, you need to talk to the family and give them support.

Instruction 7.9.G   Generating Possible Solutions

From the information you gathered, you see several solutions. Feel free to brainstorm any number of solutions now, for very often such creative activity produces innovative new solutions. Remember, at this point you are working with a single family in crisis; however, solutions that go beyond this single family may arise. List them for possible future work with the same kind of problem. At this point, *brainstorm to find as many solutions as possible*. List them below.

STOP! Wait for instructor's feedback on brainstorming before you proceed.

Feedback 7.9.G

Several solutions lead the way to attaining the goal of informing Mrs. Andrews. Among them are

1. Go to the doctor and explain to him that telling Mrs. Andrews is essential for her family's happiness. Take along some literature for him to become better informed about the needs of the dying and their families.

2. Set up a patient advocacy service for patients so that information on death and dying can be offered regularly. A group of dying patients, perhaps, or their families, could offer solace and support to others.

3. Explain the situation to the hospital administrator and ask him to allow you to inform Mrs. Andrews despite the doctor's prohibition.

4. Have a group session with Mr. Andrews and the two children. In the course of the discussion, lay out all the alternatives that they have, including informing Mrs. Andrews.

5. Go to the hospital personnel office and offer them a course on caring for the dying.

6. Decide, given the constraints under which you operate, that nothing can be done, either at present or in the future.

7. Inform the family members that they have the right to tell the doctor to inform Mrs. Andrews.

Instruction 7.9.H   Preliminary Analysis

Consider the alternatives you have brainstormed to decide which is best. Look at possible consequences of implementing each alternative before you make a decision. First, *prioritize your alternatives*. Second, *list the consequences of each*. Finally, *choose the alternative you consider best* to pursue your goal.

Prioritize Alternatives   ***List Possible Consequences of Each***

Write your choice here:_____

STOP! Do not proceed until the instructor has looked at your choice.

Feedback 7.9.H

Having prioritized the alternatives, you decide that the family can best decide when to tell their mother, regardless of the doctor's wishes.

Instruction 7.9.I   Analysis and Synthesis: Solution and Feedback

Group members now role-play, taking the roles of the social worker and members of the Andrews family.

Role Play 1. With all members of the Andrews family except Mrs. Andrews, the social worker gives information, deals with the issues of death and dying, discusses fears, and models how to inform Mrs. Andrews.

Role Play 2. Family members and social worker tell Mrs. Andrews, and the social worker deals with the relationships.

Instruction 7.9.J   Evaluation and Discussion

How has this worked out? How is Mrs. Andrews? Her family? The hospital staff? What might be your next steps? Discuss and write them below. Write a short statement about your reaction to the role plays and the exercise as a whole.

1. Your reaction to the role plays and the exercise.

2. Next steps.

Discussion of Death and Dying Exercise

As with the "Teenage Pregnancy" exercise, we considered all the systems involved but did not become too deeply involved in therapeutic practice—counseling on death and dying would be interventive in a different manner. We noted that systems outside the direct worker–client dyad had to be involved. Though planning for wider systems was not undertaken, the work already accomplished had strong ramifications both to help hospital personnel and to change policies regarding death and dying for the whole system.

The tasks were difficult. To begin with, the primary client was, for all intents and purposes, unaware of the problem. To this extent, she was an involuntary client, and we needed to relate positively to her and help her deal with a difficult situation while keeping vital information from her. Though our values insisted she be told, we could not let them rule the situation—other values with power behind them were at stake. Though we could have chosen to pursue our values, that might have had unpleasant and unnecessary consequences for all concerned. Proceeding slowly meant that we took the appropriate course, ensuring that our values were served in the long run.

On the cognitive level, we had to evaluate and assess the possible results of several courses of action, their constraints, and their outcomes. At the point of synthesis, any one of several alternatives might have been chosen. However, awareness of the emotional relationships in the problem influenced us correctly to choose to center our work on the needs of the one client who had priority—the dying patient. Of course, as with so many social work problems, we could not limit our work to the individual client. The dying patient's problem immediately affected other systems—the family, the doctor, the hospital staff, and so on, and their needs also had to be considered.

This exercise could easily become the beginning of cross-level work. It has elements not only of direct practice but issues of indirect practice such as setting up a group support program for families of dying patients,[7] a training program for hospital personnel to deal with their own issues surrounding death and dying, and even policy change at the hospital level. One person's pain or problem is often the genesis of major changes in a system—policy, programs, ways of thinking, attitudes, and so forth.

Exercise 7.10 Establishing a Training Program on Death and Dying

Still in the "Mrs. Andrews" scenario, consider what needs to be done for others in the same situation. Because of your work with Mrs. Andrews, many physicians with dying patients ask you for advice on how to help them and their families. The hospital administration is now willing to change its policies if an adequate personnel training program is established. You are the logical person to do this, and the hospital administrator has asked you to set up the program.

You are not sure how to do it. Rather than just beginning a program that might not be appropriate, you need to get more information. List below the resources available in your social work program's community for such a training program, and discuss them in class.

1.

2.

3.

4.

5.

6.

7.

8.

Now, using the problem-solving model, describe the best way to set up your new program (under what auspices, what format, what trainer, etc.).

Step 1.

Step 2.

Step 3.

Step 4.

Step 5.

Step 6.

Step 7.

Step 8.

Step 9.

Step 10.

If your instructor wishes, develop an annotated bibliography and a resource guide for training on death and dying to be used in your local community.

The Power of Communication

While structure, or the "static" picture of an organization, is easily examined, mapped, and understood, an organization's dynamic processes are much more fluid and difficult to grasp. They include such aspects as informal relationships, formal and informal leadership, informal customs, communication, and power. We have already looked at some of these ideas; however, one of the most important concepts needs closer attention.

Information flow and its power, and communication in general, are what makes organizations into dynamic and growing entities. Whether formal or informal, communication exists, and freeing it to flow to all organizational members, or blocking it so that only specific members become aware of it, is power in action. An example might be the power a receptionist has to accept or reject clients, thus making an initial diagnosis; or the power a secretary has to route clients to particular workers, for negative or positive reasons. Another is the gate-keeping function of programs such as TANF or the Area Agencies on Aging, in which workers have discretion to refer clients to particular programs. Any person at a point of information flow has power.

Communication is a tool that, if not accurately assessed, can be used effectively against you, your work, and the organization. Removing blocks in channels of communication is essential, and writing—programs, plans, grant applications—is a tool fundamental to generalist practice. Agency planning takes place through communication, usually in small groups, and uses both oral and written communication.

Professional writing is basic to social work practice: when we are not seeing individual clients, our most effective tool is the way in which we can present our plans and programs in writing. Naturally, correct spelling and punctuation are required, but other elements are also needed: the goal statement, format, consideration of the audience, use of data, length of report, and the writer's conclusions. Reports should be succinct and to the point, with a maximum of four or five pages. Say what is necessary and leave the rest for discussion. Remember and use the adage of "tell them what you are going to tell them (introduction), then tell them (body of paper), then tell them what you told them" (conclusions). The conclusions, which are your recommendations, should logically follow from what you have presented. Don't omit recommendations: even though your audience may make the final decisions, they look to you as the expert to guide their decisions.

The format for a professional paper follows an amended problem-solving outline. Headings for each topic are essential. *Your* problem identification is how to explain your topic and gain support for your recommendations.

I. Introduction (identification of problem and goals)
    A. *Problem Identification.* What is the gist of the problem with which you want to deal in one sentence?
    B. *Goal Statement.* Goals and objectives should be presented in the first paragraph. Be sure that these are goals—specific and relevant to the task at hand rather than general and idealistic. The questions you answer for yourself are "Why am I writing this report? What purposes will it accomplish? What do I want to persuade the audience to do?" Remember who your audience is: what are their characteristics, how much do they know about the topic, what values do they hold. You will write differently for your fellow workers from the way you write for your agency board, a funder, a newspaper article. Knowing that social work and social planning are value-laden, you would downplay certain possible results and amplify others. As an example, if your report is to ask for sex education funding, emphasize the result as fewer teenage pregnancies and deemphasize the issue that sex education belongs in the home.
    C. *Rationale* for your report (information). Tell why your issue is important, name the client and target group, speak to the time context or the current political or economic necessity.
    D. Give a *brief overview* of what you will tell them.
II. Brief History of Problem (information gathering)
    A. *What is the problem with which your report deals?* Do not assume that your audience is expert on the topic, and give enough information so that the least informed of the audience will understand both the problem and the solution you propose. Always have more information than is in the report, and anticipate questions that will be asked.
    B. *Why is it a problem, and to whom?* Give basic information on who will be affected, what services are needed, and why your recommendations should be considered.
    C. *Statistical and theoretical information.* Be prepared with the appropriate data and background knowledge, and be honest. Though you emphasize statistics that support your position,

don't neglect negative data. Graphs, charts, percentages, and flowcharts work well. Don't be too complex.

III. Your Proposal (Synthesizing and Proposing Implementation)

    A. *Describe* your project and why it will solve the problem. Make a compelling argument.

    B. *Details of the proposal*

        1. Timeline: how long, in what time frame?

        2. Finances: how will it be paid for, by whom, and how much will it cost?

        3. Personnel: what new people or revision of present personnel structure is needed?

        4. Legitimation: who will support it, either financially or with value orientations, locally, statewide, nationally?

IV. Conclusions: Tell them what you told them (Evaluation and Discussion) in no more than one or two paragraphs.

    A. Restatement of purpose

    B. Summary of reasons for project

    C. Why you think it will work

    D. Reiterate the recommendations

Exercise 7.11 The Program Proposal

In groups of three, on separate sheets of paper, use the above format to write a funding proposal for a summer training program that will take inner city kids out of gangs. Your proposal is based on a conflict mediation model. Each group member should take separate tasks, but the entire group should develop formatting, discussion of content of the grant, and final editing.

Problem Situation

Four neighborhood churches and a community organizer have formed a partnership to reduce inappropriate and violent behavior among youth who might be drawn to gang involvement. Evidence of this occurring is delinquency, substance abuse, gang activity, and crimes of violence. The coalition's goal is to teach the young people self-advocacy, self-determination, and self-esteem skills through conflict mediation training. Initially funded by a local seminary, they have been joined by the Neighborhood Youth Outreach Program, the city's Gang Task Force, and the County Health Department. Their board includes members from each of the above agencies, other community leaders, and youth participants. You have comprehensive knowledge of assisting at-risk youth and their families in varied settings: alternative schools, substance abuse counseling, support groups, family-based intervention training, work with gangs, jail ministry, and ministry.

In the space below, write a very brief proposal for the Youth Mediation Project which, when approved by the board, can be submitted to the Health Department for funding. Use the modified problem solving format on pages 228–229.

During the process of communication in agencies, information is often diluted or even misunderstood. Business writing requires a formal approach: when we need to make sure the right message goes to the right person, we write memos confirming the information. This is true whether or not we have spoken with the information recipient in person or by phone. It is always safer to follow up our communication with a memo, along with a request that the recipient respond. Memos include date, time sent, to whom, from whom, and concerning what. They help to lay a "paper trail" of responsibility for getting an organizational job done. The exercise below will help you to practice skills in memo writing.

Exercise 7.12 Writing a Memo

Three days ago, you met with a colleague at lunch to discuss setting up a conference for local members of NASW. The conference would give Continuing Education Units (CEUs) for participants. You agreed on date and times for the conference, who would speak, the number of CEUs and the costs, and set tasks for getting the conference underway. Your colleague was to contact NASW to set up CEU credits, contract for the conference setting, and set up a tentative agenda. Your tasks were to contact guest speakers, make refreshment arrangements, set the keynote topic, and notify the public. You want to make sure all goes well, so you follow up your meeting with a memo.

Memos include to whom they are sent, who sends them, the date, and a brief statement about the content. The body of the memo confirms recent conversations, letters, or previous memos about the subject; tasks and who performs them; times and dates; locations; and other information essential to the task. In addition, a good memo asks for acknowledgment of the memo and a response to it in writing. On a separate paper, draft a memo that is no more than half a page long with all necessary information. Use the following format and submit the memo to your instructor for feedback.

Memo: To

From:

Date:

Re:

(Body of Memo)

The ways communication can get botched up in the process is a major problem in organizations. Often it happens because formal communication channels are not used, and there is lack of knowledge about informal ones. Power is also an issue: information can be blocked or withheld at nexus points, and although this may happen by accident, purposeful use of information nexuses for power is not uncommon in organizations. The following is a guided problem-solving exercise on communication skills.

Exercise 7.13 Why Did She Answer "It's Harry's Fault" When I Asked If She Liked Blueberry Pie?

General Instructions

Divide the class into groups of four or five people, and follow the problem-solving steps. This exercise will take about two hours to complete, and the instructor should set time limits on each step.

Problem Situation

You are the newly hired assistant to the executive director. Having worked previously in a business where profit and loss were the major concerns, you now find yourself in a human services organization. The organization is divided into departments according to purpose (legal services, child care, substance abuse, and so on), and, because each department has its own goals, coordination is difficult and problems are exacerbated during this time of transition; therefore, accountability to the federal office that funds the program is difficult. Reports are seldom on time and often in different formats that require interpretation before being standardized for reporting purposes.

    The executive director thinks the major difficulty is in communication, particularly in the area of standardized reports. She sends requests for information through memos to all departments, but her memos do not result in more timely or more usable data. Being new to the job herself, she has not had time to analyze channels of communication, where those channels break down, or what changes might be made. She wants you to do this. You know that she is a capable administrator, and you are willing to trust her instincts as to the location of the problem. You also know that if you can provide a solution before the next reporting deadline, four months away, it will reflect very creditably on your career.

Instruction 7.13.A   Problem Identification

While there are many organizational problems here with which to deal, you have been assigned only one, and you must not get carried away with the chaos in the organization's transition stage. *State, in clear behavioral terms, the problem to which you have been assigned.*

STOP! Wait for feedback from your instructor before proceeding.

Feedback 7.13.A

Because you know that efficient planning cannot happen without specifying objectives, you develop a general goal and specific objectives to attain the goal. The general goal is to provide an effective communications system for the agency. Specific objectives are to

1. Analyze present communication channels
2. Locate areas leading to ineffectiveness
3. Plan a communications model to provide adequate reporting feedback.

Instruction 7.13.B   State the Goals of Your Work

As you reflect on the problem, you become aware that there is a general goal that has three specifiable objectives. *What is the general goal? What are the specific objectives with which you must deal?*

*General Goal*_____

Objectives

1.

2.

3.

STOP! Do not proceed until the instructor has heard your goals.

Feedback 7.13.B

You need several categories of information, some of which you can find in texts and some you need from your boss. For *background information* you need to know

1. Review of organization theories and administrative functions
2. Steps in planning projects
3. Models of communications systems.

For *agency information,* you need to know

1. Structure of the organization
2. Processes, including power and information flow
3. Present system of communication
4. To what extent structure and process facilitate or hinder communication
5. How workers feel about the organization, its goals, structure, and so on, and how this relates to communications problems.

This is not an exhaustive list. Probably you have come up with more ideas, so please compare your list with ours. Do not hesitate to include your own questions in further considerations. For help, please consult the instructor.

Instruction 7.13.C   Gather Information

In reviewing your objectives, you realize that there are several general areas of information you need to proceed. One problem is that you come from outside the human service orientation; another is that you are rather unfamiliar with communications models, information flow, structures, and so forth. You need background information, so you go to the library to find it. Before you review the information, however, it makes sense to you to categorize it into background information and agency-relevant information. Categorized in this way, *what information do you need? Where can you find it?*

Agency Information		*Communications Information*	
What	Where?	What?	Where?
1.		1.	
2.		2.	
3.		3.	

STOP! Wait for instructor feedback before you proceed.

Feedback 7.13.C

Your boss gives the organization chart (Figure 7.2).

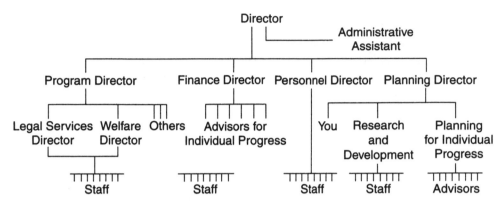

FIGURE 7.2 Formal Organization Chart

However, in explaining how the organization really works, a new configuration of power and information comes to your mind (Figure 7.3).

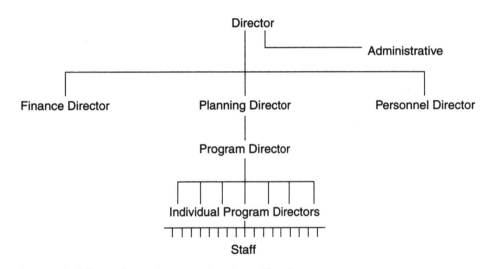

FIGURE 7.3 Informal Organization Chart

She says that when she needs information, she calls or memos the finance director (or tells her secretary to tell the finance director's secretary). She assumes that the information is then sent to the appropriate people.

Finally, the boss states she is continually frustrated by reports "via the grapevine" of worker dissatisfaction. She complains that the individual project directors seem completely wrapped up in their own project goals and care little for overall agency goals. A great deal of infighting occurs about the importance of each project and the resources available to it. Program directors also complain that they get information too late to prepare reports and that they can't be held responsible if their information cannot be immediately translated into the director's format. That, they say, is the responsibility of the "higher-ups," since they follow the their own program's strategy and goals.

Instruction 7.13.D   Initial Analysis

Now assess your information concerning the agency and the communications problem. You know the program goals, along with the mission, values, power, and organizational culture and structure. While you can't make final conclusions about "what to do" at this point, you can assess the information you have. Based on what you know from this and from other experiences (including past exercises), *what are the most apparent problems with the communications system in the organization?* List them below.

STOP! Do not proceed until so instructed.

Feedback 7.13.D

1. *Power relationships,* or *"who gets the biggest piece of the pie?"* As you see from the charts of the formal and informal organizations, individual program directors and workers are far down the line in terms of power. In fact, those who know most about the problems in individual programs have very little power in decision making.

Even the program director is subject to those who control vital functions, but does have immense power in allocating resources to the individual programs, for she can withhold or send out information at her discretion. If she has a favorite program or subordinate, those may be favored over others.

In addition, the executive director is removed several times from actual agency projects; therefore, programs have several reviews before they reach her office. This removes *project goal decisions* from *organizational goal decisions.* Central coordination, however, needs mechanisms other than those based on discretionary power, and this does not seem to be the case here.

2. *The communications system, or "It's his fault; nobody told me he dropped it."* Aside from the structure's informational bottlenecks, the major problem is a lack of a regularized system of communications. The director asks for information, perhaps from inappropriate people, perhaps not explaining clearly what she needs. Sometimes she sends memos, sometimes she phones, and sometimes she goes in person to get information (no regular process for sending). Further, no mechanism exists to insure that messages are received and understood (no receptor process), and there is no regular feedback as to who gets them or how complete the information is (no feedback process, no quality control process). Moreover, this bureaucracy works against communication: Because program directors are so far down the line, they are excluded from regular sources of information such as staff meetings. This gives them little opportunity for sharing ideas and needs with the director and no chance to explain and discuss the importance of their own programs.

3. *Worker relationships: "Who wants blueberry anyway?"* Obviously a great deal more hinges on your work than developing a communications system. Along with the formal structure, the informal structure, based on bad relationships among departments, must be considered.

Instruction 7.13.E   Generate Possible Solutions

Now you have a picture of the overall problem, so you can brainstorm alternative solutions. It's always a good idea to be free-wheeling when you're looking for possible solutions, because some that look unacceptable at first may prove really valuable when you investigate them. Feel free to look at solutions that range far and wide, because any ideas you have may lead to the perfect solution. *Generate and list possible alternative solutions,* and discuss their applicability to the problem you have identified.

1.

2.

3.

4.

5.

6.

7.

STOP! Do not proceed until the instructor has looked at your work.

Feedback 7.13.E

Possible solutions you may have generated are

1. Reorganize the whole structure to give better information flow;
2. Provide for a more democratic structure;
3. Set up a staff development program on the importance of adequate reporting;
4. Develop standardized forms for all programs and insist that they be submitted for monitoring one month before the federal reporting date;
5. Develop new memo pads with tear-off sheets for feedback;
6. Insist that all communications be written rather than phoned;
7. Get a grant for a data-processing system and set up an intercom system;
8. Make jobs or promotions of personnel dependent on timely reports;
9. Set up a staff training program in communications skills.

If you have other ideas, be sure to include them and to inform the instructor. Remember, your ideas may be more creative and innovative than any of those listed.

Instruction 7.13.F   Specify the Constraints and Identify Strengths

Now that you have prioritized all possible alternative solutions, you notice that some will not work as well as others. Some have critical constraints that make them unfeasible. Others have positive strengths that make them more feasible. *List below both the critical constraints and the strengths for each solution.*

Constraints	*Strengths*
1.	
2.	
3.	
4.	

5.

6.

7.

8.

9.

STOP! Wait for the instructor to give you feedback before you proceed.

Feedback 7.13.F

Among the critical constraints you may have listed are

1. Time. You want this done within four months.

2. Effectiveness. When this plan is developed, the communications system must work effectively. Halfway measures will not do.

3. Money. Aside from your salary, there is no indication that you have a great deal of money to develop your plan. In fact, it is unlikely that your boss is thinking in terms of massive change. She just wants things smoothed out so that the reports come in on time and in usable form.

4. Structure as a major constraint. For this job, it is unlikely that you can change the whole structure. As it stands, there is a status quo involving power that makes radical change problematic.

5. Attitudes of personnel. In the individual program divisions, workers probably enjoy the autonomy they have with the decentralized system, and a formalized set of central controls may be met with resistance.

6. Your own power. Though you have a legitimate planning job, you probably have little direct power over program personnel.

7. Values connected to the organization. Although its formal structure is bureaucratic, program values are still oriented more to professional expertise, and there is a feeling that there "ought to be" a more democratic structure.

What other critical constraints have you discovered? Please inform the instructor, and discuss them along with those listed.

Instruction 7.13.G   Assessment and Choice of Solution

Now compare the alternatives. Be sure to include those that you thought of, even if they were not in the written instructions. *Rank the alternatives* in order of feasibility, and *choose the best alternative.*

1.

2.

3.

4.

5.

6.

7.

What alternative did you choose?_____

STOP! Wait for the instructor to look over your work before you proceed.

Feedback 7.13.G

The solutions are not ranked here but presented in the order in which possible solutions were given in Feedback D.

1. Reorganize structure. It needs doing, but not by you, not now. There are time and money considerations, but mostly this is not your assignment. You should, however, certainly bring structure problems to the attention of your boss for later consideration.

2. More democratic and organic structure. The same constraints apply.

3. An idea for forms that will allow clear reporting procedure regardless of program reporting.

4. A description of new channels of communication: that is, to whom are memos sent, who is responsible for dealing with them, what questions should be asked, how should feedback flow back to the person sending the memos?

Instruction 7.13.H   Synthesis and Implementation

For your chosen method, list the necessary steps to implementation of a logical communications system. How will you put the plan into effect? What methods will you use? *Answer the following questions as a synthesis of your plan.*

1. What is the goal of your new plan? What will you accomplish?
2. What resources do you need to accomplish the new system?
3. What procedures or methods will you use?
4. Who will be responsible for each necessary task?
5. What evaluation methods will you set up for feedback to change the system if it does not work?

STOP! Do not proceed until so instructed.

Feedback 7.13.H

Goal of the plan. To develop an effective system of communication via a staff development program. This will

1. Speed accurate information to the proper people in understandable form;
2. Result in the necessary feedback, such as reports;
3. Be responsive to the values of the human service organization in terms of a more democratic approach to input and power;
4. Open new channels for communication, which may result in a democratic rearrangement structure.

How to do it. The resources fall into two categories—personnel and material. In this case, personnel is far greater in importance.

1. Develop workshop materials for a communications system lesson.
2. Develop information on the importance of good communication, using worker input to stress the values you want to follow.
3. Arrange a specified number of staff development sessions.
4. Gain legitimation from the director so that people will attend.
5. Do some background personnel persuasion in the form of personal contact to listen to gripes, explain what you hope to accomplish, and so forth.
6. Tentatively design new forms on which you will ask for worker input at your staff sessions.

Who is Responsible? You have been assigned the task, so it is your immediate responsibility. However, remember that the boss bears ultimate responsibility not only for benefits reaped through your plan but for its failures and errors. Be sure that you are aware of your responsibility to her in this matter.

Evaluation. One of the most important facets of any plan is to devise a means to measure its effectiveness. A six-month review, which could also serve as a review meeting for staff development, would evaluate it. A short questionnaire to spark ideas sent out before the meeting, with staff feedback used in plan revision, would allow for revision acceptable to all.

Future. Consider what the organization is now, and how effective the plan will be if the organization remains the same. Then anticipate the possibility of its change to a more democratic organization, which your meetings should help bring about. If your plan will be as effective in that setting as the one in which it is now, or even one more restrictive, you can be satisfied that it is a good plan. This is particularly true because you now have a mechanism for feedback and change.

Instruction 7.13.I   Making It Work

Now that you have solved the problem of communications, you need to put the plan down in writing. Develop the plan as a memo to your director, and write it on separate pages for instructor's feedback. Be sure it is a professional memo. Your feedback will be the grade you receive.

Exercise 7.14 The Classroom as Organization: The Executive Search[17]

A good way to put all this theory and exercise into practice is to look at the class itself as an organization to teach theory by practice. Through structuring, a variety of aspects of organizational life can be demonstrated: division of labor, coordination, leadership, group processes, performance appraisal, and formal and informal communication.

Let's make our class a women's organization that must hire a new administrator. First, choose a name for the organization. Then, through discussion, decide on the agency's history, purpose, tentative budget (revenue only), reputation in the community, and basic programs. Your instructor will act as consultant on all aspects of organizational theory and practice. To make your classroom an organization, take the following steps:

1. Students volunteer to be the board of directors, and the board elects its own officers and committee chairs.

2. The remaining students volunteer to serve as staff, clients, and members of the community. Each group appoints a recorder to note aspects of organizational behavior, such as leadership, group process, and communication.

3. Clients meet to determine what their primary needs are for the organization to meet. They inform the staff of this.

4. Staff meets to determine the kind and extent of services they provide clients.

5. The board meets to write the agency's mission statement and bylaws.

6. The board selects, from its members, a chair of the search and screen committee and then appoints one representative each from staff, clients, and community members to search for a new director, who must have experience in supervision, community work, budgeting, proposal writing, and program development.

7. Students interested in being the administrator write and submit a resume to the search and screen committee. The committee discusses interview processes and develops interview questions.

8. Candidates are interviewed by the committee through role play scenarios. All others observe from their roles.

9. The director is chosen. A role play is enacted to negotiate salary.

10. Group recorders report their findings to the class. How was the selection process observed from the clients' viewpoint? How did the community comprehend the new hire? What is the staff's opinion?

Exercise 7.15 The Classroom as Organization: The Audit

General Instructions

Using the organization above, form work groups of four to six students each. Each group will be the newly hired executive director.

Problem Situation

Your first job as the new administrator is to perform an organizational audit. Though you have the general mission statement and other documents that will help you with the audit, you really want to know what the relevant members of your agency think. While members of the class remain in their identities as board, staff, clients, and community members, discuss the following and set up a good human service organization. (This framework is adapted from Netting et al. and can be used for organizational functions such as time audits and volunteer audits.)[18]

1. What should be the agency's resources: funding, noncash resources, volunteers?

2. What should be the agency's constituency base? Who are they, what do they need, how well can they be served?

a. What are the constituencies?

b. What are the limits?

c. Who is the competition?

d. Who are the clients?

3. How should the agency relate to its clients, from both staff and client perspectives? Should clients serve on the board?

4. How might the agency relate with funders from the board's perspective? With competitors? With the community as a whole? What is attractive to donors?

5. Define the agency's mission, purpose, function, and principles.

6. Describe the agency's structure, its values, and its formal and informal leadership. How will the organization gain power?

7. Who will fund the agency? What will this have to do with its structure? Its purpose?

8. What sacrifices and compromises may be necessary politically?

Portfolio Building

1. What have you learned about the structure and processes of organizations?

2. What are organizational goals, and what purpose do they serve for organization and administration?

3. What are the differences among mission statements, goals, means, and outcomes?

4. What is the interconnectedness of agencies within a community?

5. How do organizational theories apply to social work practice?

6. How do information and power relate in an organization?

7. What more do you need to know about organizations?

Moving On Up: What's Next?

Our next level of practice is the community. Particularly today, when the safety net for the poor has been ripped apart, we must consider that much of what we do will be community-based. Any kinds of action to make a difference in helping others will have to be from community support at the grass roots level. So, fulfilling our professional mission must entail an understanding of and the ability to use local neighborhood and community systems.

Notes

1. Netting, F. Ellen, Peter M. Kettner, and Steven L. McMurty (1993). *Social Work Macro Practice,* 2nd ed. White Plains, NY: Longman Press, p. 123.
2. Schermerhorn, John R. Jr. (1993). *Management for Productivity,* 4th ed. NY: John Wiley & Sons.
3. Ibid., p. 231.

4. Excerpted from Netting et al. (1993). op. cit. Chapter 6 "Understanding and Analyzing Organizations," pp. 121–152.

5. Weber, Max (1947). *The Theory of Social and Economic Organization*. Ed. T. Parsons, Trans. A.M. Henderson and T. Parsons. Glencoe, IL: Free Press.

6. A compilation of theory by Netting et al. from Taylor, F.W. (1911). *The Principles of Scientific Management*. New York: Harpers; and Fayol, H. (1949). Trans. From French ed. (Durod) by Constance Stours, *General and Industrial Management*. London: Pitman.

7. Mayo, E. (1945). *The Social Problems of an Industrial Civilization*. Boston: Harvard University Graduate School of Business Administration, Division of Research.

8. Drucker, Peter (1954). *The Practice of Management*. New York: Harpers.

9. A compilation of theory by Netting et al. from Michels, R. (1949). *Political Parties*. Glencoe, IL: Free Press; and Peter Selznick (1951). *Leadership in Administration*. Evanston, IL: Row, Peterson.

10. March, James G. and H.A. Simon (1958). *Organizations*. New York: Wiley.

11. Burns, T. and G.M. Stalker (1961). *The Management of Innovation*. London: Tavistock Press.

12. Morse, J.J. and J.W. Lorsch (1970). "Beyond Theory Y." Harvard Business Review 45: 61–68.

13. Thomas, R.R. Jr. (1991). *Beyond Race and Gender: Unleashing the Power of Your Total Workforce by Managing Diversity*. New York AMACOM.

14. For further discussion on missions, goals, and means, please refer to Blau, Peter, and Richard Scott (1962). *Formal Organizations: A Comparative Approach*. San Francisco: Chandler Publishing Co.; Etzioni, Amitai (1964). *Modern Organizations*. Englewood Cliffs, NJ: Prentice Hall; or John R. Schermerhorn, Jr. (1993). *Management for Productivity*. NY: John Wiley & Sons.

15. Netting et al., op. cit., p. 122.

16. See Elisabeth Kubler-Ross (1969). *On Death and Dying*. NY: MacMillan; and Richard A. Kalish (1981). *Death, Grief, and Caring Relationships*. Monterey, CA: Brooks/Cole.

17. The "Classroom as Organization" idea is a modified exercise from an early edition of Schermerhorn, John R. Jr. (1993). *Management for Productivity*, NY: John Wiley and Sons.

18. Netting et al., op. cit.

ChapterEIGHT

Mobilizing Resources:
The Community

Community Practice

Community practice offers a variety of opportunities for using problem-solving skills: community needs assessment, grass roots organizing, coalition-building, and advocacy are only a few. Most importantly, community practice relies on the strengths of clients and client groups—populations-at-risk, people with common problems and a common target or goal, and those working to change inequitable systems or to insure social justice. Using their strengths in their own behalf, people not generally so involved in the forces that control their own lives can accomplish their goals while they learn how to take power through individual and group action

As a social work method, community practice is ideally suited to the strengths perspective and the empowerment model. Basically, the practitioner's role is to be an enabler, an educator, often a motivator and sometimes an expert in tactics, while people-at-risk lead and mobilize to solve their community problems. Effective management of problem-solving skills are an essential task of the community practitioner for working with the mobilization group at each step.

What Is Community?

A "community" is a *combination of social units and systems that perform the major social functions* for meeting people's needs on a local level. Communities may be geographical, but they also may have no specific boundaries, and communities are also groups of people joined together for common purposes, such as religion or ethnicity. In any case, a community takes care of the organization of social activities that people need for day-to-day living.[1] Communities have five important functions: (1) economic functions—production, distribution, and consumption of goods and services; (2) socialization, or the training required to become a community member; (3) social control, which encompasses all aspects of polity, including legislation, the judiciary, the executive offices, laws, rules, and regulations intended to enable people to live together and to correct deviance from social norms; (4) social participation, or the ways people interact in the community; and (5) mutual support to help one another with problems.

Exercise 8.1 The Functions of Community

For each kind of community listed, define what it is and then explain its functions and give an example. You may use your own communities if you like. After you have defined the communities, the class should discuss the differences found.

Community or Town: In the space provided, define "geographic community."

Now, for your geographic community, explain the functions and give an example.

	Definition	*Example*
1. Economic function		
2. Socialization		
3. Social control		
4. Social participation		
5. Mutual support		

Religious community: What is a religious community? Give an example.

Now define its functions, with an example:

	Definition	**Example**
1. Economic		
2. Socialization		
3. Social control		
4. Social participation		
5. Mutual support		

Ethnic or cultural community: Define these and give an example of each.

Explain its functions.

	Definition	**Example**
1. Economic		
2. Socialization		
3. Social control		
4. Social participation		
5. Mutual support		

Every geographic community has an ecological net of social services. All social service agencies are networked simply because they are all in the business of helping people, but there are also more formal ties based specifically on clients in common. Case management provides the use of networks for client services, but often only the agencies concerned with a particular client meet with any regularity. For example, a case manager for the local Department of Children's Services may call together an abused child's school social worker and teacher, mental health practitioner, public health nurse, juvenile justice worker, home preservation workers, and so on. Whether formal or informal, knowing the network of services in your community is essential for good social work practice.

Just as we consider the individual within the educational community, the political community, the religious community, the workplace, or people's systems of family and friends on a micro level, we explore a community's dimensions from the perspective of the population in need. Forces that shape the community environment, including changing needs, shifting demographics, interest group politics, legislative influences, funding patterns, and so on provide us with information necessary to client services.[2] The community where our organization operates and policies that affect our community service delivery system also shape our ability to fill clients' needs.[3]

Exercise 8.2 The Ecology of Public Assistance

Look at your county public assistance (TANF) office as a unit in the social service delivery system of the county. On a separate sheet of paper, design an eco-map symbolizing allied organizations—those agencies that serve the same client populations—as subsystems in the community system. Show the relevant referral systems to and from the office in terms *only* of client population.

Write below and then discuss in class:

1. Name the community subsystems on which TANF has *direct influence*. Explain what that influence is.

Subsystem   *How does TANF affect the subsystem?*

a.

b.

c.

d.

e. Others?

2. Name the subsystems on which TANF has indirect influence? How?

Subsystem	*How does TANF affect the subsystem?*
a.	
b.	
c.	
d.	
e. Others?	

Exercise 8.3 Your Field Agency Network

On a separate paper, draw a chart showing the relationship of your placement agency to five of the most relevant subsystems in the community that serve the same or similar populations in the community. This is your "network of sister agencies."

As we know, there are *manifest,* or obvious, connections and *latent* ones. Discover them and then, in small groups, discuss the questions below.

1. What are the *manifest* connections, such as referral, supply, information, or others your instructor may request?
2. What are the *latent* connections; that is, how does your agency provide services to other agencies?
3. What is the *ecological importance* of your agency to the community?
4. How will this knowledge help you in social work practice?

Exercise 8.4 Coordination of Resources

Divide into groups of four or five students. In your community several agencies do emergency counseling. These include a hot line connected to the YMCA aimed at young people who are runaways or drug abusers; a twenty-four-hour crisis center for call-in problems of any sort; a local hospital's drug abuse line; and the United Way's Information Center. While such duplication of services may be positive because it provides a variety of services, such an array of crisis services may either confuse clients about whom to call or may lose clients in the shuffle as they call an inappropriate service and then are advised to call another.

You are a group of social work students assigned to United Way for field placement. Looking at this array of emergency counseling services, and having talked with many clients who have not been well-served in an emergency, you take on the assignment of trying to coordinate the services. Your goal is a twenty-four-hour number that handles all calls, referring them to the proper service by a phone-switching operation rather than a referral system. You have already talked with the telephone company and know that this is a feasible plan. While you have not worked out all the problems of finance and staffing, your greater concern is problems of organizational "turf." Discuss

1. The steps you need to take to begin the coordination efforts (three minutes)
2. The information you need (three minutes)
3. The problems of "turf" and how that will set constraints on your success (five minutes)
4. The power and influences you exert for such coordination (three minutes)

Report on your discussion to the class as a whole.

Needs Assessments

In any community, assessing the whole of the social services network would be difficult. Therefore, we can best assess the community, or do a needs assessment, by looking at a particular target population and the extent to which the community's human services system meets the needs of that population. Moreover, we have a dual focus in community practice: the needs of the client population *and* what these needs and their possible solutions mean in terms of the collective community.[4] Needs assessments insure that programs target *client* needs rather than what board, staff, or workers *think* are their needs.

All needs assessments contain the elements listed below, but let us look at a specific client group—HIV/AIDS patients. Our purpose might be to expand services to their families.

A. *Purpose of survey:* a behaviorally specific statement of what is to be accomplished in the needs assessment. This includes
  1. *Why,* or the reason for the needs assessment survey;
  2. *What,* the survey method;
  3. *Who,* a specific statement of the client population system;
  4. *Where,* or the target area to be assessed;
  5. *When:* the time period the survey will cover.

For example, in assessing the need for expanded services among the families (of choice or origin) of our client group, you might conduct a questionnaire survey of all people in your community who have had contact with the local AIDS task force or health department within the past six months.

B. *Assessment dimensions*
  1. *System composition*—the system in which the client system is embedded. For example, we would ask our HIV/AIDS clients

who comprise their family systems and what is the relationship of each member to them? To what degree have they disclosed their HIV/AIDS status to their defined family systems?

2. *Strengths, resources, and stressors*—an assessment of what can be depended upon in the client system and what major problems there will be for it. In our HIV/AIDS case, we would assess family-related stressors, along with perceived strengths and coping resources.

3. *Support network*—the quality of resources in systems outside the client, and how it furthers well-being. HIV/AIDS clients would evaluate the quality of their social support network and the extent to which it furthers their physical, emotional, and economic well-being.

4. *Organizational support*—what agencies or organizations serve the client system or the relevant population at risk. What organizations could be involved?

5. *Service needs*—what the client system perceives is needed, along with client interest in accessing available services. In the HIV/AIDS case, this would be interest in accessing specific types of family-oriented services, including psychoeducation and support groups; family, couples, and children's counseling; family case management; and advocacy training for family members.

Exercise 8.5 Assessing Client Needs in Your Community

Pick a client population in your community that you believe needs expanded services. Using the aforementioned needs assessment format, write a needs assessment proposal on a separate paper, with a time frame of a semester in field placement.

A. Purpose of survey

B. Assessment dimensions

1. System composition
2. Strengths and stressors
3. Support network
4. Organizational support
5. Service needs

A needs assessment is often required before any new program, or an extension of a present program, will be given legitimacy by a funding body. Obtaining adequate funds to support programs is an ongoing process. Securing "new" or "seed" money to develop programs is extremely difficult.

Exercise 8.6 Preparing a Needs Assessment: Why Another Program?

Break into groups of four or five students each. Working on the problem of homelessness in your community, you have just discovered that there is no shelter that will accept teenage boys. They are not allowed in men's shelters because of perceived danger to the boys, and they cannot be accepted in family shelters because they are seen as disruptive and even dangerous. Yet you know that there are many runaway boys coming into your community and being picked up by the police. The law says that they should be returned to families or responsible guardians, but many have run away because of abuse and cannot be returned to their homes. Many of their own families or foster families simply do not want them. They cannot be jailed, no place can be found for them, and so, within twenty-four hours, they are back on the streets to dangerous situations, lack of food and shelter, and possible delinquent acts as they try to survive.

You have determined that a shelter for these boys must be established; however, before you can begin you must discover the extent of the problem, social service agencies that are or should be involved, where such a shelter might be placed, and how it could be structured and funded. In other words, you must do a needs assessment.

A. Discuss the problem and partialize it, looking at the systems in your community that the problem affects.

1. On a separate sheet, draw an eco-map of community systems that might be affected.

2. From the perspective of this population-at-risk, (a) why is the lack of shelter a problem? (b) to whom? and (c) what might occur (to whom and with what results) if the problem is not solved? Write your answers below and discuss them in your group.

a.

b.

c.

d. Other ramifications?

e. Other ramifications?

B. Where would you find information on the extent of the problem? List community resources that might have that information, and discuss their present and/or possible involvement (what they do now and what they might do).

Agency	*Present Activity*	*Possible Activity*
1.		
2.		
3.		
4.		
5.		
6.		

7. Others?

C. Explain and discuss the logistics of obtaining a boys' shelter in your town.
   1. What would you have to do on the political level?
   2. What economic problems do you foresee?
   3. What would the structure look like? Would it be free-standing, or is there already an organization into which it would fit?
   4. What kind of staffing would be involved?
   5. What rules and regulations do you see as necessary?
   6. What would be the agency mission?

D. How can you involve the client population so that you can insure the social service delivery system will meet *their needs* rather than those of others?

E. How would you mobilize the community to begin such a program?

1. Who would be your allies, and why?

2. Who would oppose the program? Why? What arguments would you use to win them over?

F. On a separate page, list possible funding sources for the program. To whom would you apply? How would you convince funders to support the program?

G. On a separate paper, have your group develop a plan to present to the class.

Fund Raising

While resource mobilization includes mobilizing influence, power, and people on the neighborhood or community level, it also occurs in organizations to develop programs and secure funds. Because such resources are limited, securing additional support means a reallocation process—taking funds that could be used for one purpose and using them for the unmet needs. In addition, social needs are relative in nature: Communities fund programs that address both survival and quality of life needs where those needs are most critical. Securing additional support for new or expanded services, therefore, is both a political and a technical process.

According to Seiler,[5] all fund raising must stem from the mission of the agency. His "Five Principles of Successful Fund Raising" say that to be successful, you must have

1. A marketable product, identifying the needs to which donors will respond and communicating shared mutual values;

2. Informed constituencies and a diversity of funders, to demonstrate visibility, credibility, and accountability;

3. Unqualified, dedicated leadership to attract high profile volunteers;

4. A workable plan projected out for one, three, and five years;

5. A willingness to ask people to give money. Informed, interested people will make an investment if you persuade them that your plan *is* an investment.[6] Use these ideas in your next exercise.

Exercise 8.7 Funding Sources

Maintaining the funding for program services is a complex, difficult job requiring constant effort. Practitioners working directly with people and their problems lose sight of this vital aspect of the agency.

A. List five social service agencies and identify the sources of funding for each.

Agency   *Funding Source*

1.

2.

3.

4.

5.

B. Identify the names of funding organizations for social services in your community.

C. What is the process by which a social agency seeks funds?
  1.
  2.
  3.
  4.
  5.
  6.
  7.

D. Identify five factors that directly affect the amount of funds available for social services in your community.
  1.

  2.

  3.

  4.

5.

E. On a separate sheet, write the impact of budget cuts and discuss in class.

Social workers need a basic understanding of the funding base of their agencies and of the procedures for funding. Although the intricacies of fiscal management are the administrator's responsibility, because funding directly affects programs and practice options, we should know the procedures to obtain additional resources to more adequately meet client needs. A major task is proposal writing: a proposal is the complete explanation of a project, concisely or logically written to explain its costs, goals, and benefits. Our next exercise, which continues our saga of Sloan House (see Chapter Six), develops a proposal to a funding agency for the financial support of an expanding Independent Living Program (ILP) for girls who must leave Sloan House at age eighteen to live independently.

Exercise 8.8 The Search for Funds

General Instructions

Break into groups of four or five people for this guided problem-solving exercise. There are four committee members in each group, so the fifth person serves as observer and reporter. Each group is a subcommittee of the Program Evaluation Committee (PEC) in our previous Sloan House problem-solving exercise. This is the initial committee meeting, at which the executive director presents a program overview and long-range planning goals of Sloan House and its relationship with allied agencies. The committee members are

> Lois White, chair;
>
> Jay Martin, a local attorney who is also vice president of Sloan House's board of directors;
>
> Mary Edwards, ACSW, mental health counselor at Sloan House for more than fourteen years; and
>
> John Blake, ACSW, an administrative supervisor at another agency.

You are members of PEC and are enthusiastic about the potential of increasing the effectiveness of the ILP.

Problem Situation

One of PEC's recommendations was an extension of the present Independent Living Program (ILP) for girls leaving the group home for independent living. Therefore, the subcommittee had to draft a proposal for creating an expanded type of transitional living arrangement to assist residents in moving from residential group living to independent living. The proposal would be included with the PEC recommendations, and if support existed among the board of directors, the proposal would be submitted to a funding source.

The director of Sloan House, along with her executive committee, has had two meetings with staff officials of Stand Foundation, a community funding agency. As a result of the exploratory talks, the Foundation has invited Sloan House to submit a proposal for funding consideration during the next twelve months.

Instruction 8.8.A   *Defining the Primary Task*

Following a reintroduction of yourselves and an exchange of some small talk, the chair suggests that as a small work committee your first task should be to agree on the purpose of your work. You review the assignment given to the subcommittee by Sloan House's director. Your specific assignment was to draft a program proposal to create a halfway house to provide a time-limited living arrangement for girls terminating placements. You also consider the outcomes of the meeting between the executive committee and staff officials of Stand Foundation. The benefits of these meetings, you believe, are

1. Funders feel they are involved in the project from the beginning;
2. Sloan House as a social service organization is now familiar to the funders;
3. The executive director had an opportunity to present the program overview and long-range planning goals of Sloan House and its relationship with allied agencies.

You begin to generally discuss where to start and discover that no one has recently written a completed proposal of the type that the board is likely to expect. You agree that it would be very helpful to identify the steps the subcommittee must take in completing a proposal, and then to gather specific information needed to complete each step. Some of the preliminary writing could be done by specific individuals with copies made for the whole committee to review. *What are the steps to complete a proposal? What information needs to be gathered for each step?*

Steps	*Information Needed*
1.	
2.	
3.	

4.

5.

6.

STOP! Do not proceed until your instructor has looked at your work.

Feedback 8.8.A

The proposal must reflect careful program planning as Sloan House seeks funds from a grant-making organization. A proposal is a selling device that will be read only once by the grant review committee. Repetition of key program concepts must be skillfully integrated into the proposal. Basically, the format would evolve from three principles:

> **1.** This is what will be presented
>
> **2.** This is what is being presented
>
> **3.** This is what has been presented

The place to begin the selling process is *the proposal summary*. Even though it will serve as introduction to the proposal, it is written after completing the total proposal, because some portions of the proposal (e.g., evaluation) will not be finalized at this point. The summary must be relevant to the grant guidelines, be internally consistent in logic, and present content concisely and clearly written. The summary must tell the reviewers (1) what will be presented in the proposal, (2) what ideas should be the focus during the reading, and (3) what are the distinguishing features of the proposal.

Instruction 8.8.B   Preliminary Questions

Jay says, "Now that we know generally where to begin, it seems that our summary represents a composite overview of the total concept. It might be helpful to the committee to *list the types of information needed for the proposal summary.*"

1.

2.

3.

4.

5.

6.

   STOP! Do not proceed until your instructor has looked at your work.

Feedback 8.8.B

The committee needs to answer these questions to get started:

1. Reason for the grant request
2. Definition of the problem within the ILP and the necessary resources to remedy the situation
3. What objectives will be achieved through this funding
4. What activities/methods will be undertaken to accomplish these objectives
5. Identification of the applicant (personal and organization), including summary-type statements about the applicant's credibility and capability related to the proposal objectives
6. Approximate cost of the project, including the amount requested, the amount of funds already committed, and the source of these.

Because this proposal will be competing with many others seeking the limited funds, the summary section is essential because it is the first part read by reviewers, so it must interest them as it defines the proposal as realistic. Because reviewers read many proposals, this may be the only section they read, so it begins the rating and evaluation process. The summary provides the proposal's framework, providing a context for the problem, proposed approaches, and resources needed.

Instruction 8.8.C   Next Steps

You all agree that the summary will force you to clarify your thinking about the needs of ILP and provide a summary of the entire proposal. Jay asks, *"What is the next step in writing a proposal, and what type of information should be included? Should we determine how much a halfway house is needed?"*

1. Next step

2. Information needed

3. Extent of need

STOP! Do not proceed until the instructor has looked at your work.

Feedback 8.8.C

The introduction of a proposal establishes the organization's qualifications as an applicant for grant funds in the reviewers' minds. Because Sloan House is not a nationally known facility, the proposal must prove that it can provide the program for which support is sought. Useful information includes

1. Summary statements of the goals and philosophy of the organization;
2. Brief historical summary of the beginning and development of Sloan House, including the identification of significant events during the twenty-two years the organization has existed;
3. Overview of programs and services offered, including the number and characteristics of clients served, professional and administrative staff, and scope of the organization within the field of residential care;
4. Description of organization and evaluation efforts, including a report on current accreditation by the regional and national child welfare organizations and the state licensing bureau;
5. Statistical data;
6. Letters of support by allied community social service organizations describing benefits of a transitional living center.

Instruction 8.8.D Focusing the Problem Area

Now that the proposal summary and project introduction have been discussed, the next step needs to be defined. *What would be the next section of the proposal, and what type of content would be included in this section?*

STOP! Do not proceed until instructed to do so.

Feedback 8.8.D

The next section of the proposal is the *problem statement and statement of need*. It is a comprehensive description of the existing problem situation and a listing of proposed outcomes focusing on the unmet needs of girls transitioning to independent living. The problem statement is the *most important* part of the proposal. It must

1. Clearly state the problem or need and its relation to Sloan House's purposes and program goals, based on realistic expectations of what could be accomplished with resources, time, and specific methods demonstrating understanding of the client's needs.

2. Factually document the need for the project within the community and service delivery system, citing statistics related to the incidence of abuse and neglect, community economic indicators, the availability of various service components, current procedures in use, or other factors that demonstrate the need for the proposed project.

Program objectives and measurable benefits or outcome results flow from a well-defined problem statement. These are the criteria to be used in evaluating the effectiveness of the proposed program. This section is used also to provide (1) a summary of specific goals and objectives and (2) a summary of the results and benefits expected, including who will provide what to which population in what time frame and quantity with what expected results measured.

Instruction 8.8.E   Addressing the Problem Area

Once the problem situation has been clearly defined and the proposed outcomes have been listed, *what would be the next logical step in constructing the proposal? What is the work plan?*

STOP! Do not proceed until instructor has given you feedback.

Feedback 8.8.E

The next section is the work plan—a description of what will be done to achieve the objectives. The methodologies should be clearly described, showing support for the choice of those methods. A review of similar projects and their methods would be helpful in justifying the approach you want to take.

Methods may be broken into subunits to convey more clearly, a clear understanding of the nature and scope of the proposed project. This helps identify the subprojects to be completed and keeps the project on a time track. The work plan should include

1. A narrative explanation of scheduling for project start-up and implementation and a timetable;
2. Information about personnel, such as who will manage and implement the proposed services, including brief job descriptions;
3. Collaboration with other organizations, if any.

Instruction 8.8.F   Assessment

Your subcommittee, at this point, has identified the successive steps in constructing the program proposal. In general discussion, you agree that this has been a good approach to force you to think critically about the client group's needs and whether the ILP fits into the continuum of care. Now you must evaluate the project including whether or not this change is needed on behalf of the Sloan House girls. In the final determination of evaluating adequacy of resources for this population in the community, *What should be considered in developing the evaluation? Who should be involved?*

STOP! Do not proceed to Feedback 8.8.F until so instructed.

Feedback 8.8.F

A well-defined problem statement and program objective will raise questions that determine the program's effectiveness in meeting its objectives. Considerations in designing the evaluation section include

1. The criteria to be used in evaluating the program;
2. The targeted audience for the evaluation (specific approaches will be influenced by whoever is looking at the evaluation);
3. Inclusion of evaluation of expected outcomes and the implementation of the program. The former determines the extent to which the program will achieve its objectives, while the latter determines how the program is to be conducted;
4. Inclusion of a unit costing, accountancy-based method of assessing costs and evaluating outcomes and a cost-benefit analysis-assessment of long-term benefits;
5. Means for collecting evaluative data and the analysis method for its analysis: because the project proposes need to evaluate outcomes (adjustment to independent living) over an extended period of time, a longitudinal method is necessary;
6. Method of reporting: its use for ongoing program improvement and who would be receiving the reports.
7. Who evaluates: an agent outside Sloan House can strengthen the proposal's credibility, while an inside evaluation would involve a staff person familiar with the overall program.

Instruction 8.8.G   Determining the Cost

You decide to explore the financial resources needed to fund the ILP and consider (1) the creation of an expanded ILP program with detailed cost of maintaining program and facilities and (2) a proposed budget detailing the estimated cost of the new halfway house. Help write these sections, on a seperate piece of paper, listing

1. Major categories of expenditures to support the proposal (detailed or unusual costs can be added once the narrative sections have been completed).
2. Possible sources of ongoing funding beyond the two-year budget period.

STOP! Do not proceed to Feedback 8.8.G until so instructed.

Feedback 8.8.G

Two major categories of expenditures in the budget of the proposal are (1) personnel costs and (2) nonpersonnel costs. Each of these can be broken down into small categories and identified item by item.

1. Personnel costs—professional and nonprofessional staff salaries and wages, including fringe benefits as a percentage of salaries; consultative and contract services, including explanation of basis of costs (hourly, daily); travel costs; etc.

2. Nonpersonnel costs—space costs; equipment and furnishing costs; consumable supplies such as stationery and envelopes; services such as printing and computer time; telephone; travel—how the total sum is determined; and other costs such as fire, liability, and theft insurance.

Depending on the specific nature of the final proposal, continuation of supplementary support can be addressed in two ways: (1) assumption of funding by other sources once the grant period is ended, for maintenance or possible expansion; and (2) supplementary or specific funding to pay for nonrecurring costs, such as those for specialized equipment. Possible sources of ongoing support include

1. A contractual fee-for-service with the public agencies currently paying for the primary service;

2. A fee-for-service based on client income;

3. Incorporation of the new program into an expanded ongoing budget of the organization once its validity is established and the funding request is justified;

4. Fund-raising events to purchase specific program items operated by various types of service organizations that assume ongoing sponsorship;

5. Operational grants from local, private foundations operated by area businesses;

6. Public monies earmarked for community development from the Community Development Office, Department of Housing and Urban Development, and so on.

Instruction 8.8.H   Concluding the Exercise

You have completed your discussion of the budget items and reviewed the five sections. Now you turn to writing the content for each section. For your conclusion to the exercise, write a brief proposal based on your problem-solving steps for funding a halfway house for six girls in your community. Your feedback will be your instructor's evaluation of the proposal.

Mobilizing Community Resources

A major function of community social work is to mobilize resources to fill an unmet need within the social service delivery system. Resources include money, people, and influence and power; and mobilization is most easily seen in building coalitions for cause advocacy (as opposed to case or single-client advocacy). Generally, such mobilization takes place on the neighborhood or community level. Mobilizing requires social work roles across all levels of practice, and many social action models are available to demonstrate these roles.[7] Depending on the positions generalist social workers hold, they may be called on to facilitate local movements, develop services at grassroots levels, advocate or lobby for particular groups, or organize neighborhoods, groups, or communities for social action. Whether speaking to the needs of local groups such as unwed mothers or lobbying on the state or national level for consumer rights, cause advocacy is an appropriate area of social work practice.

Whatever the level or area of service, the resources being mobilized are people and their resources in money, influence, and power. The generally accepted mobilization procedure[8] for social action is summarized in Figure 8.1.

FIGURE 8.1   *Practitioner Roles and Activities*

	Enabler	*Developer*	*Advocate*	*Organizer*
1. Problem identification	Seen as lack of communication and coordination	Limited access to opportunity	Failure of institutions	Structural failure in society
2. Analysis	Concerned with improving procedure and efficiency	"Natural" study	Intensive collection of data	Limited unsystematic action
3. Goal setting	More effective communication	Task-oriented to "better" one's lot	Set more adequate goals	Total rearrangement of system
4. Strategy	Consensus and persuasion	Through existing structures	Social reform, gain consensus	New forms, such as unions
5. Tasks	Ad hoc groups	Involve local citizens, systems	Key systems with change readiness	Choose or build new systems
6. Intervention role	Intermediary in structured situations	Local leader, expertise role	Speaks for group	Leader in fact, charismatic
7. Overall purpose	System maintenance and stability		Social change	

Exercise 8.9 Identifying Mobilization Roles

Below, identify three social movements you know of from your social policy classes (or other resources). (In some cases you may be able to identify particular people who led or enabled those changes.) For each social movement, identify how each social action role (identified in

Figure 8.1) aided the progress of the social movement. Write them below and discuss them in class. Then discuss the process by which resources were mobilized to make the changes.

A. *Social Movement 1.* _____ Leader? _____
   1. Enabler

   2. Developer

   3. Advocate

   4. Organizer

B. *Social Movement 2.* _____ Leader? _____
   1. Enabler

   2. Developer

   3. Advocate

   4. Organizer

C. *Social Movement 3.* _____ Leader? _____
   1. Enabler

   2. Developer

   3. Advocate

   4. Organizer

Exercise 8.10 Group Mobilization

Break into groups of four or five members. You are workers in a community action agency in a big city slum. A resident of the neighborhood has just come in to tell you that the heat in her building has been turned off. The reason given by the landlord is that he needs more rent to pay higher gas bills and will not pay the gas company until he can collect more rent from the tenants. There are fourteen families in this building, and the landlord owns three more buildings on the block. He has threatened to take the same action with them. The resident wants you to help her, and you see the problem as one for neighborhood rather than individual action. You discuss with her mobilizing the families on the block to institute a rent strike, and she agrees that it is a good idea. She agrees to work as a leader in the movement if you will serve as resource person(s).

1. What will be your role(s)?

2. What steps will you take to mobilize the families for their first meeting? List and explain them them below.

    a.

    b.

    c.

    d.

    e.

    f.

    g.

3. What information do you need before the meeting? Where can you get it?

    Information Needed   *Information Sources*

4. What community resources can you call upon for help?

Exercise 8.11 Developing a Community Service: Food for the City

Problem Situation

Because of recent cuts in funding for essential subsistence programs such as food stamps, WIC (Woman's, Infants', and Children's Nutrition Program), School Lunch and Breakfast Programs, and subsistence grants previously available in AFDC, many people go hungry. Though you know that major efforts must be directed at restoring funding to vital programs and lobbying for increased services, your first obligation is to insure that people eat. As concerned citizens with social work training, you want to establish an emergency food service; however, despite sporadic efforts such as a local soup kitchen, little is being done in your community. You determine to organize a task force to find food and bring it to the hungry people in your town.

General Instructions

Divide into groups of from four to seven, discuss the problem, and write out the following steps. After you have agreed on the steps, report to the class.

A. Problem identification

   1. In behavioral terms, state what you consider the problem to be.

   2. To whom is it a problem? What client groups? You? Identify as many groups as possible and tell why it is a problem to each.

B. Problem assessment
   1. What data is available in your community to show the extent of the problem? Find the data, report it to your group, and discuss it.

2. Are there theories or empirical research that can demonstrate the far-reaching effects of nutritional deprivation? What are they? Discuss them.

C. Constraints
  1. What are the conflicting values involved? Why do these represent constraints on your activities?

  2. What are other constraints?

  3. Who benefits and who loses from not having enough food available?

  4. Who will benefit and who will lose if there is enough food?

D. Forming a coalition
  1. Who are the relevant publics? On whom can you depend for support in your efforts, and who (or what groups) will be neutral? Who can you neutralize, and how? How can you insure the participation of the people at risk? What should be their roles?

  2. What benefits can you insure to the groups who support your coalition? What's in it for them?

3. Who should lead your coalition? You? A person influential in the community? A person from an established agency? Why? What should be our roles as social workers?

E. Organizing a meeting
   1. What are the meeting's goals?

   2. What is the general plan? Develop a tentative agenda.

   3. What must be accomplished before the meeting ends? What tasks should be assigned?

F. Informing the publics
   1. Which relevant publics should you inform about the meeting? About the results of the meeting? Why?

Relevant Publics	*Why Inform These?*
(1)	(1)
(2)	(2)
(3)	(3)
(4)	(4)

   2. What methods should you use to inform the general public? How will you go about that?

   3. What values will legitimate your actions to the public?

G. Taking action

    1. What kinds of actions will you take? Why?

    2. What are your areas of compromise, your "pull-back" stances?

    3. Where will you not compromise?

    4. What are your final goals? That is, what will your new program look like?

H. Report on each group's food program to the whole class. Discuss the similarities and differences, and vote on which one would work best.

Grass Roots Organizing

The personal is political. This feminist precept is the core of many community organizing efforts. It is about changing the world and changing how people act together. As union leaders organized to fight for workers' rights from the late 1800s, now we must organize to help those in distress because of present-day laws, institutions, and structures that disempower them. Many tactics can be used, but "however you do it, organizing begins with finding out what people want as individuals and then helping them find collective ways of getting it."[9]

Social agencies help individuals with their problems, but group mobilization works for large numbers of people who are populations-at-risk. Through this indirect method of practice, we help to give people a sense of their own power, for community organizing's main principle is that power relations be changed.[10] This means that we build a strong organization, elevate the issues that affect our constituency, and become a political force. Usually, social agencies delivering services to individuals do not engage in community organizing or advocacy. Mostly this is because funding would be threatened: often funding comes from the very sources against which we organize. In the following exercise, we organize against the state itself, to gain its funding for a new program.

Exercise 8.12 Mobilizing for Advocacy

Problem Situation

Mrs. Annabelle Watkins, 80 years old, fell and broke her hip. She was taken to a local hospital for treatment where you are the social worker. Although her presenting problem was the hip, you realize that she is poorly nourished and in fragile health. While at the hospital, she contracted a serious case of influenza. You know that she should not be released when the amount of time mandated by Medicare's Diagnostic Related Group (DRG) payment schedule ends. She is still sick with flu and her hip has not mended.

Because she was admitted for the broken hip, the hospital insists that she be released to a nursing home for further care. The privately owned nursing home, however, will not admit her because of fear of influenza contagion. Mrs. Watkins has no one at home to care for her; she is bedridden; and, although eligible for home meals and home nursing care, her illness means that someone should probably stay with her full time. You find a home care aid that she can afford, but you know that this is an ongoing problem for people with the same kinds of risks as Mrs. Watkins.

General Instructions

Break into groups of four or five people. You (collectively) are the hospital social worker. Use the problem-solving model to find help for populations-at-risk as exemplified by Mrs. Watkins.

Instruction 8.12.A   Problem Identification

Although many problems are obvious in Mrs. Watkins's situation, you are concerned with the plight of all persons with this set of problems. Medicare will pay only for time according to the DRG. People in Mrs. Watkins's position often do not qualify for Medicaid because of assets such as home, car, and pension. Private nursing homes cannot be forced to take patients if their rules state that people with contagious diseases cannot be admitted. What happens to people like Mrs. Watkins if no immediate care can be found?

You know that you cannot change DRG's regulations, nor can you change the policies of the hospital or private nursing homes. You are also aware that at least one other state has programs for elders called CHOICE, which enables people needing care to receive it in their homes rather than to give up all their assets to qualify for Medicaid or to be placed in nursing homes or long-term care facilities. The state legislature, however, has not accepted the idea of CHOICE (Community and Home Options to Institutional Care for the Elderly and Disabled) in the past. In other states, strong coalitions have influenced the legislature to enact CHOICE, and you want to see it here. You, therefore, must build a strong coalition to influence the legislature. *Identify the major problem you face* in getting the state legislature to enact CHOICE.

STOP! Do not proceed to Feedback 8.12.A until so instructed.

Feedback 8.12.A

The problem is that a coalition for CHOICE does not yet exist.

Instruction 8.12.B   Goals of the Work

Knowing that you need a strong coalition, you begin to consider others who might be interested in joining a coalition. You know that there is an immediate goal to consider, and if that is properly attained, you can reach your long-term goal. *What is your immediate goal? What is the long-term goal?*

STOP! Do not proceed to Feedback 8.12.B until so instructed.

Feedback 8.12.B

Your immediate goal is to get your coalition formed, and the long-term goal is to have CHOICE, or home-based services, enacted in your state. You know that the long-term goal must be presented to potential members of the coalition to persuade them to join with you in advocacy and social action.

Instruction 8.12.C   *Brainstorming the Coalition*

While you would like to brainstorm how to get CHOICE passed at this point, you must first attain your short-term goal, forming the coalition. To do this, you need to research state-wide resources for elders, because this is a state-level problem. *Who are the likely participants in your coalition? Why? What resources would they bring?*

Likely Participants	*Reasons for Participation*	*Resources*
1.		
2.		
3.		
4.		
5.		
6.		

STOP! Do not proceed to Feedback 8.12.C until so instructed.

Feedback 8.12.C

You should conduct a state-wide search for members of your coalition, because this is a state issue. Among your members might be Area Councils on Aging, state-wide church networks, the American Association for Retired Persons (AARP), United Senior Action, NASW, and, of course, groups of elders interested in action. There are many such groups in your state, and you should now know who they are. Your instructor is also a resource for this problem.

Instruction 8.12.D   Brainstorming for Action

Now that you have your coalition, you can begin to plan for action. *What is your long-term goal? What are your choices (alternatives) to accomplish it? List and prioritize them by what would work best in your state.*

Long term Goal_____

Alternatives:

  1.

  2.

  3.

  4.

  5.

  6.

STOP! Do not proceed until instructed.

Feedback 8.12.D

Among your choices are

1. Plan an advertising campaign
2. March on the state capitol and demonstrate
3. Begin a letter-writing campaign
4. Have each coalition member phone or email their local legislators
5. All of the above
6. Whatever other plans you may have brainstormed

Instruction 8.12.E   Choose Your Plan

When you have chosen your plan, list its elements below as an "Agenda for Action." Then develop a timeline with a six-month limit.

Agenda for Action

Timeline for Action

Your instructor will give you feedback on your plan and timeline. Evaluation will be whether or not CHOICE is instituted in your state.

Portfolio Building

This chapter's exercises have provided a very beginning look at some of the roles of community practitioners. As you have seen, they can work within agencies, within communities, or at higher levels. In any case, both relational and cognitive skills are needed, but, generally speaking, the cognitive or organizational skills are essential for effort in this area.

1. What are the elements of a community?

2. What is community practice, sometimes called community organization?

3. How do we use mobilization in agencies? In groups of agencies? Among a general populace?

4. What is the advantage of problem-solving in community practice?

5. What have you learned about leadership, power, and empowerment in this chapter?

6. What more do you need to know about communities and community practice?

Looking Ahead

In our final chapter we will not speak primarily to programs in action in the social work field but to the ways in which programs are conceived, formulated, and developed. That is, the final area of macro-systems practice is the understanding of the importance of policy to the generalist social worker. Policy occurs at all levels of social work practice, and our ability to identify policies, their reasons for being, and if they serve as intended, whether in latent or manifest functions, is part of the critical thinking that adds to our ability to be generalist workers.

Notes

1. See Netting, F. Ellen, Peter M. Kettner, and Steven L. McMurty (1993). *Social Work Macro-Practice,* 2nd ed. White Plains, NY: Longman Press, p. 47.

2. Netting, op. cit., p. 4.
3. Meenaghan (1987) in Netting, op. cit., p. 4.
4. Netting et al., op. cit., p. 94.
5. Tim Seiler (no date). "Successful Fundraising," Indiana University Center on Philanthropy, unpublished paper.
6. Ibid.
7. For example, Will Richan (1991). *Lobbying for Social Change.* New York: Hayworth Series in Social Administration, 1991; or Jack Rothman (1974). *Planning and Organizing for Social Change.* New York: Columbia University Press.
8. In Rothman, *Planning and Organizing for Social Change,* op. cit.
9. Bobo, Kim, Jackie Kendall, and Steven Max, Eds. (1996). *Organizing for Social Change: A Manual for Activists in the '90s.* Santa Ana, CA: 7 Locks Press, p. 7.
10. Ibid., p. 8.

ChapterNINE

Exercises in Social Policy

Concepts and Definitions

While as generalist social workers we are unlikely to begin our careers in the field called "policy as practice," we know that no action taken by a social worker is outside the field of policy. Working with clients in agency settings, we *formulate, implement, change, or destroy* policy with everything we do. We can and do change policies at small or large levels through policy tasks—problem identification, information gathering, formulation, implementation, analysis—all of which are inherent in our problem-solving model.

Continuum Policy

Social welfare policies and programs arise from society's agreement on defining a particular situation or behavior as deviant from current societal norms. We can look at this as a continuum.

Society defines current → Policies developed to → Program is implemented
   situation as deviant   solve problem   to carry out solution

Each element of our continuum requires definition.

1. A *social problem* is a situation or behavior that a majority of society's members, or a powerful group in society, defines as questionable, dangerous, or deviant in relation to current norms. *Personal* aberrations or problems do not become social problems until they reach this "critical mass" where societal definition takes place. Time and the current political, social, or economic context are also critical in definition: some of the situations we see as social problems today were not "social problems" until recently.

For example, until about the 1960s, abusing one's wife was considered either righteous action, if the rod being used was no thicker than a man's thumb, or a personal family problem. Not until the scope and cruelty of wife-beating was brought to the attention of society by the women's movement did society begin to devise solutions (pass laws, develop treatment) for the abused wife and her abuser. Even today, the situation of women who have killed their abusers in self-defense is unclear. On the other hand, men who kill their wives "for cause" are often still treated very leniently—while the wives "committed murder" many husbands committed "justifiable homicide."

2. A *social policy* is society's attempt to solve a defined social problem. An *agency policy* regulates activities toward agency goals through written procedures or unwritten custom. "Policy" is easier to understand if we cut out the jargon: a policy is simply a *solution* people came up with to solve a *problem* they identified at societal or organizational levels. Social policies are written into *legislation and judicial decisions, or organization and agency procedures; or* they may be unwritten *customary procedures*, many of which are based on deeply held values and traditions, including sexism, racism, classism, and heterosexism. Unwritten policies remain often specifically *not* written so that they can be used covertly to maintain an often unjust status quo (such as job discrimination against women).

    Examples of written policies (plans on how to deal with identified social problems) include a city curfew for children (legislative); a court decision that states cannot set different voter registration for diverse groups (judicial); or agency policy requiring affirmative action (organizational rules and regulations). Policies of customary procedure, until challenged, might include discrimination against gays through not allowing them family medical benefits or the "midnight raids" against welfare mothers that were so common in the 1960s.

3. A *social program* implements, or carries out, the policies on which it was based. Programs may require new settings, such as agencies or offices specifically oriented toward dealing with the problem, or they may be placed in agencies or organizations already established for a similar purpose. Examples of new agencies or offices include community action agencies in the 1960s for the war on poverty, or Selective Services Offices to draft soldiers in World War II. A newly established office in already existing organizations might be disability offices mandated in most universities for Americans with Disabilities Act (ADA) compliance, or community mental health agencies with programs for substance abuse established by legislation in the 1970s.

    Any policy or any program is based on societal values,[1] as are its goals and means. A solution (policy) may not be the best (or even very good), but *at the time it was created,* with *then-existing values in an historical context,* people thought it would work. So they enacted the policy or it became custom: at the societal level as *legislation* or *judicial decision;* at the agency level, *rules and regulations.* Every policy and every program has manifest functions—those uses that are obvious—and latent functions—uses that are hidden.[2]

In terms of our timeline, then, first comes the awareness and identification of a *problem,* then the *policy* that hopefully will solve it, and finally the *program* that develops from the policy (Figure 9.1).

To compound the jargon problem, we often confuse concepts of *policy* and *program* and refer to them interchangeably. Remember that policy sets up the solution to a problem, including goals, means, and rules, in writing (usually). Then program puts the policy into effect in an activity set up to deal with the problem, through an agency or a procedure. In addition, all three—problem, policy, and program—have historical contexts based first on politics, economics, and belief systems, and second on sets of values that may or may not be the same for all three.

FIGURE 9.1. *The Policy Continuum Revisited*

PROBLEM	*POLICY*	*PROGRAM*
A lot of people think something is a problem	They develop and enact a solution for the problem	They set up methods to carry out the solution (policy).
Each problem has a context and a set of values that may be different from those of policy or program	Each policy has a context and a set of values that may be different from those of problem or program	Each program has a context and a set of values that may be different from those of problem or policy
Example: mothers on welfare	Example: TANF law	Example: Workfare
Context: What social, economic, political factors happened in our past that we consider mothers on welfare a problem?	*Context:* What political, social, economic factors influenced passage of TANF?	*Context:* Why is TANF politically feasible today? What manifest and latent functions does it have for society?
Discrimination against women; need for more jobs for men; end of war. Values: What societal value most accurately applies to this problem? *Patriarchy.*	*Republican majority in congress; conservative values against women and workers. Values:* What values were incorporated in TANF? *Protestant work ethic, patriarchy.*	*Fewer workers are needed because of computers and robotics. Workers cut into net profit. TANF does not train them for work but will get rid of their expense.*
		Values: Protestant work ethic favored over Judaeo-Christian charity values.

Exercise 9.1 Following the Policy Continuum

The following excerpt comes from a recent newspaper article:

> Capping a major Republican campaign to tighten Michigan's welfare rules, the state Senate on Wednesday approved a bill calling for drug testing of welfare recipients. . . . Democrats accused the GOP of playing election-year politics with the issue. . . . Under the bill, a person who tests positive for drugs would have to enroll in substance abuse treatment. . . . [3]

Using Figure 9.1 as your model, write your answers to the following questions:

1. What is the problem the senators have identified?

2. What policy (proposal) have they established?

3. What program (procedure) will the bill require?

4. What political/economic/social context is involved?

5. What major societal values are involved?

6. What are the manifest functions of the proposed policy?

7. What are the latent functions (hidden purposes) of the proposed policy?

Identifying Problems for Policy Practice

Any social work begins with clear and concise definitions of problems, and this includes work with policy. To do good social work, we focus clearly on specific problems: we *behaviorally specify* the problem to avoid assumptions, our own and those of others, that send us off on tangents wasting time, energy, and even money on the wrong solutions. For example, in Exercise 9.1, the senators identified drug abuse as a problem among all welfare recipients and proposed wholesale testing. However, we know that a majority of welfare recipients are not drug abusers. We would find data about the extent of the problem and direct our efforts toward a different solution. Or we might identify the real problem as "the senators' lack of knowledge about drug abuse among welfare recipients," and our solution would be to educate the senators.

When identifying a problem (or a policy), to be "behaviorally specific" means to specify the actions (how or what is happening), along with saying who is doing it (define the people, including numbers or percentages); where (geographically specific) and when (time specific). Avoid generalities and idealism and bring the definitions down to facts. For example, solving elder abuse by juvenile delinquents is impossible if we say that "such behaviors are bad for kids," or that "they disrupt society" or "harm the elderly." Our behavioral specification would say that, in a particular area (town, city, etc.) there has been a 20 percent (or whatever) increase in muggings of the elderly by persons age eighteen and under. Our solution would be based on those specifications.

Another ramification is that *most personal problems have political implications*—people do have crises and troubles, but often the genesis of the problems is in societal institutions where only political action can make change. For example, when families become poor as the breadwinner loses employment, abuse and even suicide may occur. Those are personal problems, but the local or national political economy is their source. To deal with this, partialize the problems as personal *and* political, so that you can work at different levels with appropriate action at each.

Exercise 9.2 Specifying the Problems

Look at the following newspaper excerpt, and consider problem specification and political implications:

From his cramped living room . . . 75-year-old Herman Walker wonders what he will do if he is thrown out of his public housing apartment. Walker is one of millions of tenants subject to a federal "one-strike" drug law that can result in eviction for the wrongdoing of visitors or relatives. Officials say they found crack cocaine or crack pipes on three visits to Walker's apartment. His caretaker and a friend were arrested on drug charges. . . . The one-strike-and-you're-out policy under which tenants can be evicted if they or their guests are arrested—no conviction required—[meant that] . . . [n]ationwide, 3,847 public housing tenants were ousted in the policy's first six months. That was an 84 percent increase over the number evicted for drugs and other crimes in the previous six months. . . .[4]

1. In behaviorally specific terms, define first the personal problem and second the political problem.

a. Mr. Walker's personal problem is

b. The political problem is

2. Problems are suffused with values that define them, so before we can work on a problem we need to understand its underlying values. What values are involved in the personal problem? In the political problem?

a. Personal

b. Political

Identifying Policies for Policy Practice

Like problems, policies must be identified in behaviorally specific terms. Although legislation, judicial decisions, and agency manuals often elaborate their policies in many paragraphs, a skill for policy practitioners is to find the gist of the policy and write it in clear, concise, and behaviorally specific terms. When working with policies, cite the source of the policy and then reduce it to one sentence for clarity. A policy can usually be stated in a single sentence; everything else is elaboration, explanation, or "running off at the mouth."

Exercise 9.3 Stating a Policy

General Instructions

Divide into groups of four or five people. Your instructor will provide for each person in each group a current newspaper article having within it a policy. It may be a piece of legislation, a judicial decision, or an organizational policy. The group task is to read through the article and pick out *one* policy statement, although there may be several. You may call on your instructor at any time for feedback on your progress.

1. Write down the policy statement as it appears in your copy.

2. Discuss and define the gist of the policy statement. Write it below.

3. What is the problem the policy was established to solve?

4. What values underlie the policy?

5. What are the manifest and latent functions of the policy?

6. Write the policy in clear, concise, behaviorally specific terms in one sentence.

7. Submit the policy to your instructor.

At times, established social welfare policies can be detrimental to the people the social work profession is dedicated to serve. One such policy is Temporary Assistance to Needy Families (TANF), signed into law in 1996 by President Clinton. While its creators say it is to help poor people to get out of poverty, its net effect is to punish women, along with their dependent children, for perceived laziness and promiscuity. To change *that* policy is beyond our scope today, but we can change oppressive agency policies.

The process of change is to identify the policy, identify the problem it claimed to solve, identify the problem with the policy (why it does not solve its claimed policy), state your new goals for the policy, and finally reformulate the old policy. The following newspaper clipping demonstrates how a nursing home's policy discriminated against a group of elderly patients.

> State health-care investigators . . . recommended fining a nursing home $360,000 for telling 52 Medicaid patients they would have to leave for a renovation project with no promise they would be allowed to return. . . . Company officials at first said it was a coincidence that all the patients were on Medicaid. . . .[5]

Exercise 9.4 Reformulating a Policy

1. Identify the agency policy in question. Be specific. What values are behind the agency policy?

2. What manifest problem was the policy designed to serve? What latent function?

Manifest function

Latent function

3. What is the problem with the policy as it is formulated? In what ways is it peripheral to the manifest function it stated it would serve?

4. What are your goals concerning the problem? What do you want the new policy to accomplish?

5. Restate the policy so that it meets your goals. Be behaviorally specific with your new formulation.

Policies and Politics

In working with policies, we often jump from our initial identification of the problem to the quickest or most "in" policy solution we can think of (this is the sociological phenomenon known as the Iron Law of Specificity). In other words, we don't *think* about other possibilities but accept the first idea we think will work. We don't use our problem-solving abilities to find the best solution, we merely take the first, or one that other organizations have used whether it worked or not.

Also, we jump into policy formulation from our value perspectives rather than feasibility, or base policies on political, rather than reasoned, information. Before we propose a policy, we should be aware of three caveats.

1. Social welfare policies are rarely solely altruistic, even though they may have altruistic elements, reasoning, and applications. They develop from a set of perceived needs which arise from political concerns. For example, many policies and programs developed after World War II to deal with the growing number of delinquent children who came, presumably, from homes unsupervised because

their mothers worked. Aside from the delinquency, the policies were used politically to persuade women to leave their jobs so that returning veterans could have them, which in turn persuaded men to return to work and family support roles. In fact, then, policies are *political artifacts* based on political agreements or compromises.

2. The elements *not* written into a policy are as important as those that are and should be considered policies by omission. For example, legislation for jails or prisons that do not specify provision of education, recreation, or rehabilitation leaves wardens discretion to include such services or not. This is a policy by omission.

3. The *implementation* of a policy, no matter what the guidelines, proves what the policy really is. For example, most public assistance laws state their major purpose as providing for the needy. Yet legislation rarely provides enough money to eliminate poverty, though it may keep recipients from outright starvation. The real goal, then, appears to be to maintain people dependent on public assistance, which can then control their lives in such areas as economic behavior, work behavior, surveillance of their children, and women's sexual behavior (at times, even dating has led to cutbacks in public assistance grants).

Policy is hard to hold on to—the product of strange bedfellows, none of whom is altogether sure of what they created. No wonder social policy students are confused. However, if you remember that any policy is based on politics that show up in strange ways, and you can identify the politics behind policy, you have a very good grasp of the process of social policy.

The following exercise will give you a new way to look at an old problem, that of providing for dependent children, along with a new awareness of the extent and power of the values that go into policy.

Exercise 9.5 Mothers' Wages[6]

General Instructions

The instructor will assign your roles. In groups of no more than seven, play the roles as if you were those people, using your own stereotypes about their attitudes and capabilities. Each group should have an observer of the group process who notes leadership, peer influence, group think, and so forth. After about twenty minutes, observers report to the class on their process.

Roles

1. *Social work professor*—believes that public assistance is a right of members of society. A noted welfarist, he has served as an advocate for the poor at all levels of practice. He knows the welfare system thoroughly.

2. *Steel worker*—in his early forties, he has worked in the steel mills all his adult life. A hard worker and dedicated father and husband, he knows what it means to labor, bring home a good income, and provide not only the necessities but a few luxuries for his family. He believes in individualism and the work ethic and has no patience with "welfare handouts."

3. *AFDC mother*—in her mid-twenties, she has four children ages 4, 6, 8, and 10. She married her high school sweetheart, who deserted her a year ago. She has no special abilities or training, and is in rather poor physical and emotional health. She has never worked outside the home.

4. *Middle-class housewife*—in her mid-thirties, she has three children, ages 12, 14, and 16. She is happy with her role as wife and mother, has never worked outside the home, and has no desire to do so. Her husband, a high school teacher, makes an adequate salary.

5. *Priest*—while believing that society must support its unfortunates, this man has stereotypical views about the roles of men and women. A loving man with a great deal of tolerance and patience, he believes in the uniqueness and beauty of each human being.

6. *Restaurant owner*—deserted by her husband, with whom she had established the business that was only beginning to be profitable when he left. Her children were ages 10 and 12 when he left. She was determined to make the restaurant thrive and has no use for women who "hide behind their children to keep from working." She has hired some mothers through TANF who quit shortly after being hired because of transportation and day care problems.

7. *President of a local canning factory*—having inherited the factory from his family, he is well educated, works hard, and gives much time to community projects. He believes in the work ethic and takes a firm stand on work as the way to get ahead. He has a TANF contract to train clients to plant and pick in season and does not understand their objections to working for him.

General Instructions

The federal government is conducting a long-term research project on alternatives to public assistance. Your community has been one of those selected for a demonstration grant; however, implementation of the new program, called *Mothers' Wages*, depends on the local community's acceptance. You have been appointed as a task force by the County Council to determine whether the program should be implemented in your community.

1. Do a role play discussing the issue of mothers' wages (ten minutes).

2. Discuss whether or not to institute mothers' wages in your community (ten minutes). Vote on the issue.

3. Report on the following:

   a. What were the major values brought forth in your discussion?

b. How do these fit in with your own values?

c. What are the cost effectiveness versus social effectiveness issues of the program?

d. Would your group institute the policy? Why or why not?

Why Social Welfare Policy?

Aside from their places as solutions to social problems, social welfare policies are created to socialize society's members to certain societal norms or to control those who deviate from them. There are two perspectives on the "oughtness" of social welfare, and they form a continuum of "intention to policy." At one end is *residual* social welfare, which says that society should provide support only when there is a complete breakdown of "natural" support systems such as the family and only then for short-term emergencies. Usually need is means-tested before any help is given. At the other end of the continuum is the *institutional* perspective, in which society provides certain goods and services simply because, as members of society, people have a "right" to them.

Remember, these are perspectives, or viewpoints, rather than program descriptions. Also, most social welfare programs have a mixture of residual and institutional services. For example, in the most residual of programs, such as prison incarceration, educational programs can be found (institutional) and in the most institutional, for example, grade school education, residual programs such as truancy programs (residual) exist. Programs fall along a continuum from institutional to residual (Figure 9.2).

FIGURE 9.2 *Continuum of Welfare Perspectives*

Residual ── >*Institutional*				
TANF	Hospital emergency rooms	Community mental health	Veterans' benefits	Social insurance
Prisons	Mental hospitals	Probation offices	School social work	K–12 education

The perspectives of policy developers, whether residual or institutional, have a major effect on the kinds of policies and programs that develop. For example, public assistance is mostly residual in nature. In general, we feel that mothers not working outside their homes and their children do not have a "right" to societal support. On the other hand, education, at least through age sixteen, is considered the right of children regardless of any means-testing. Therefore, public assistance is begrudged, stigmatized, and meager while education is encouraged and even enforceable by law until age sixteen.

Exercise 9.6 The Context of Policy Development

The directions and goals of social welfare policy are neither accidental nor aimless; they develop because people make choices. This exercise looks at the context in which choices about solutions to problems are made.

General Instructions

Form groups of from four to seven people. A set of programs developed to deal with specific needs or problems follows.

Program List. Each of these programs still exists somewhere in our nation.

1. Food stamps
2. A tax-supported public school system available to all
3. Psychotropic therapy for the emotionally distressed
4. Jailing alcoholics
5. Protective services (in welfare departments) for children who are abused
6. Federally subsidized housing for people falling below certain income levels
7. Medicare "buying-in" system, in which clients must pay a premium to be covered

Pick one policy to discuss by answering these questions.

1. What was the range of choices? That is, what might have been some alternatives to the solution actually chosen?

2. What values were implied in the solution chosen?

3. What was the historical framework (social, political, economic) at the time the choice was made?

4. How did a residual or institutional perspective influence the decision?

5. What societal values influenced the decision and in what way?

6. Place each on the residual-institutional continuum.

Program most residual <<————————|————————|————————|————————>>Most institutional

---

Exercise 9.7 The Policy Formulation Process

Here is a *list of policies* that exist somewhere in the United States.

1. Runaways who cannot be placed in one of the available county shelter homes or returned to their families are sent to jail.

2. At a residential home for care of girls aged ten through seventeen, all entering girls regardless of age are given a vaginal exam, pregnancy test, and a venereal disease test.

3. In cases of wardship for children, where the court or state can take children from their parents, an attorney is appointed for the child but the parents are not informed that they have a right to counsel to protect their rights.

4. Adjudicated delinquent children, regardless of age or offense, are placed in institutions for indeterminate sentences; that is, a child adjudicated incorrigible because of truancy can be institutionalized until age eighteen.

General Instructions

Form groups of from four to seven persons, and, from the list above, choose a policy with which you have a problem, that is, one that you believe does not solve the problem it was meant to solve, or is inadequate, inaccurate, or in error. Use behavioral specification in all three steps. Consult with your instructor to make sure you are on the right track for each new step. When you decide what is wrong with the policy as it stands

1. *Write clearly and in one sentence the problem the policy was first intended to solve.* What are the politics behind its inception and continuation?

2. Write clearly the problem you *perceive with the policy.* Why do you think the policy is inadequate, inaccurate, or in error? What human service values are involved? Why is this a problem? To you? To the client?

3. What are your goals in changing the policy? Write a general statement of broad-based objectives or goals to be achieved through your new policy.

4. *Formulate a new policy* to better solve the original problem, stating it just as clearly. What societal values are involved in your reformulation? What professional ethics are you using?

5. *Report your process* to the class and discuss the process, the identifications you have made, and your goals and reformulated policy.

Policy as Practice

Policy practice takes place at every level of generalist practice. Policy as practice can be used at community levels in city or county planning; often the staff of senators and representatives are social workers who can write policy that includes social justice elements. Social workers at community, state, and national levels can join together (often with their clients) to produce legislation through speaking as experts, lobbying, or building local coalitions for action. The best way to formulate your new policy or plan is to use the problem-solving model. Generally, you need to identify in specific and behavioral terms one of two problems: either there is a lack of a needed service in the target system, or there is a policy to implement an existing policy that is oppressive or inadequate. Using problem solving insures that you have covered all the problem's details and provides a format for writing your new policy for presentation to agency boards of directors, legislators, or social activists who will carry forward your policies.

Exercise 9.8 Permanent Housing

General Instructions

Divide into groups of three or four. You are community practice workers from one of three local homeless shelters, the YMCA that runs a hotline for teen runaways, the community action agency, and an interfaith group for social action against poverty.

Problem Situation

In a midwest community of about half a million people, the mayor and city council are concerned about the growing number of homeless families with children. While several shelters are available, they are inadequate to meet the need, and although the policy states that new shelters can be opened, money has dried up because of federal cutbacks. The city's policy is solely to develop temporary shelters, as in this conservative community people believe that the homeless should move on after they have been "helped." The help they receive is time-limited, from thirty days to six months depending on the shelters' goals and target populations. There are no transitional housing programs in your area, even though you know that best practice models provide housing options on a continuum, from temporary to transitional (up to two years) to permanent low-cost homes.

You believe that the policy should be reformulated to allow for permanent homes at low cost. You are aware that a recently closed military facility nearby has been donated to the city, with good houses, just at the city's edge and within easy walking distance to stores, offices, groceries, and other necessities. However, the city's "temporary shelter only" policy means that the facility cannot consider these properties as homesites for the homeless. You want to change that policy, even though you know a great many people will object to "giving" these homes away to the poor. You begin a local campaign to influence policy change that will allow the homeless to buy these homes at minimal cost through city processes.

A. Identify your problem (five minutes)

B. Set your goals (three minutes)

C. Reformulate the policy—write it below as you want to see it enacted in legislation, in clear, concise, behavioral terms (five minutes)

D. Build a coalition (fifteen minutes)
   1. Which publics are relevant to the problem? The concerned public depends on the nature of the problem. What are the most likely groups, and what do you need to know about them to interest them?

   2. How would you interest the public in your problem?

   3. How do you get your information out to the relevant publics? What other kinds of organized methods would you need?

E. Build legitimation (five minutes)
   1. What influences could you bring to bear to form a supporting coalition?

   2. How would you cultivate leadership? What kind of coalition would you develop, and how would you bring that about? How would you negotiate consensus among your relevant supporting publics? What compromises would you make, and what compromises would you refuse to make? How would you handle those refusals?

F. As a group, rewrite your policy proposal on separate pages with the above considerations. Use the professional paper format given in Chapter 7. Make sure the proposal says what you want it to say and that it meets arguments you have come up against in your discussions above. Include a tentative plan that demonstrates the feasibility of the new policy and how it might be implemented.

G. Evaluation and assessment (five minutes)
  1. Why do you think the reformulated policy will do what you want it to do?

  2. What are possible pitfalls to its success?

  3. What unanticipated consequences can you foresee? How will you counteract them?

  4. What compromises might you be forced to consider?

Social Working Synthesis

In the preceding chapters, we worked with exercises from micro- to macro-levels, indicating the importance of policy but not specifying it directly. We looked at levels of practice, systems perspectives, and the simultaneous nature of all the elements of social work practice. Our last exercise, the Serendipity Project, emphasizes all these levels of social working. In much the same way that you have learned to synthesize your work in the problem-solving model, we hope Serendipity will synthesize our goals in this book. Have fun. Good luck.

Exercise 9.9 Serendipity, Incorporated

General Instructions

This exercise helps to tie together most of the concepts presented in the workbook. Although it is primarily a policy practice exercise, it requires an understanding of interactional skills and a careful assessment of values and biases. Moreover, it requires that policy practitioners develop both a realistic plan for service and a strategy for plan implementation. The exercise may take two weeks to accomplish and requires outside research work, a knowledge of organizations in the community, and an awareness of the availability of resources. Moreover, the assignment of carrying out tasks for the group purpose is an important part of the exercise.

Break into groups of from four to seven people. Consider the group as one individual, a planner for the Health Service Board of your own local community. Do not proceed along the steps of the exercise until your instructor has given your group the signal to do so.

A general guide to the process follows:

Study Guide: an outline of your process (note that this is the problem-solving model).

1. Identify the problem in clear behavioral terms.
2. State the goals you want to accomplish.
3. Gather information from your board members, your instructor, local planning organizations and local agencies, census data, and library and Internet resources if your instructor so directs.
4. Generate possible solutions for payment for services.
5. Specify the constraints you might face on target populations, kinds of services, and so on.
6. Perform a preliminary evaluation to select possible payment models.
7. Analyze one kind of payment model in detail.
8. Synthesize the design as a whole.
9. Prepare a report, including a means to evaluate the program.

Take the steps that follow on next pages one at a time, reach consensus on answers to each step, and do not proceed to the next step until your instructor has heard your work and given you feedback on it.

Problem Situation

The Serendipity Foundation has just awarded the County Health Planning Services Board $10 million to establish a Health Services Center for the county. The purpose of the center will be to provide both preventive and remedial health care of all kinds to individuals and families whose income is below United States Department of Agriculture (USDA) poverty standards. It will not exclude any people whose income is over that amount, but it *must* serve people with low income. The grant is contingent, however, upon the consensual agreement of the five-person board on the method by which users of the service will be charged for service (method of payment for services). A plan for payment agreed to by all members must be submitted within a six-month period or the grant will be withdrawn. Continued grants will be assured if the center is instituted, and these continuing grants will be based on needs created by method of payment plan. Board members are:

> **Mr. Andrews,** an attorney who is African American
>
> **Mr. Donaldson,** a member of the Board of County Supervisors (or like official for county government)
>
> **Dr. Boling,** a female physician
>
> **Mr. Edwards,** city commissioner
>
> **Mrs. Collins,** a TANF mother with four children

Instruction 9.9.A   Identify the Problem

You have just been promoted to assistant planner for the Health Services Board, where you have been a field worker for the past two years. Your supervisor wants to start you on this particular project because of your familiarity with the community. Also, you are familiar with the board members and know their values as well as the needs of the country for health care. Your own major value here is that health services are a human right rather than a privilege. Your job is to present a plan for client payment for health services that is acceptable to all members of the board. *In clear behavioral terms, identify your problem.*

STOP! Do not proceed to Feedback 9.9.A until instructed.

Feedback 9.9.A

Your problem is that you must develop a fee payment plan that is agreed to by all your board members within a six-month period.

Instruction 9.9.B   State the Goals

Now that you have identified the problem, your goals must be set to meet that problem and no other. *What is the goal of your work? What do you need to accomplish by this plan?*

STOP! Do not proceed until so instructed.

Feedback 9.9.B

Your major goal is to develop a plan for payment for medical services that will be acceptable to all board members, given their values. It also must be acceptable within your own set of values as a social worker. This breaks down into two major tasks: developing a "satisficing" plan; and using your professional expertise to insure an early compromise for people with quite diverse sets of values.

Instruction 9.9.C   Gather Information

Because goal attainment depends on two major tasks, you need to gather information relevant to each. What data are necessary before you can develop a plan for payment? *What information is required* on both board values and statistical information? *Where can you obtain the information you need* in each of these categories?

A major set of information here relates to the board members. You know the backgrounds and possible values of each.

- **Mr. Andrews** will be sympathetic to the needs of the members of the black community, who are generally poorer than are the majority of people, relatively speaking. Yet, he wishes to maintain his status in the middle-class referent group. This presents him with a dilemma, as he is also considered by the black community as its spokesperson.

- **Dr. Boling,** though she is a woman and, therefore, is perhaps more keyed to the needs of women and children in the county, probably takes as her major reference group the community of physicians. The proposed center threatens her practice and the practices of other medical personnel in the community. This is a severe constraint, because she must be the spokesperson for physicians in the community and, yet, because she is a woman, is peripheral to the medical association's power.

- **Mrs. Collins** knows her own needs for health services and those of other people in her situation. Nevertheless, she shares the majority values of middle-class America, as do most people in poverty. She believes that most are at fault for their own poverty and that they are lazy and unwilling to work for anything, including health care. She is not totally dedicated to the idea of free health service.

- **Mr. Donaldson** and **Mr. Edwards,** as elected representatives, must be responsive to the wishes of their constituencies as well as to the possible input of millions of dollars into the local economy via the health center. Mr. Donaldson, however, has strong feelings about welfare. He believes that it is morally wrong to be poor and is likely to be adamant in his views that everyone should pay for health services one way or another. Mr. Edwards is more likely to be impressed by the benefits to the community of the health center but is aware of its possible political backlashes. He is damned if he does approve (because of the power of the medical community and the conservative population, which holds strong anti-welfare views) and damned if he doesn't (because of money loss to the community).

A. What predictions can you make about board values?

B. What information do you need on the community? Where can you find it?

Community Information	*Information Location*

STOP! Do not proceed to feedback until so instructed.

Feedback 9.9.C

A. For the *values of the board,* you need to note
   1. What are the major values of each, and how much would he or she be willing to compromise?

   2. Politically speaking, what questions can you ask the board members? In what form?

   3. Given the problem, which board member has the most influence or power, and how can you utilize this for your purpose?

   4. What information can you locate on the costs of health care and the costs of not providing health care that you use to influence board members?

B. For *demographic data,* you need
   1. Information on other health care projects and the way they assess fees (models of programs, copies of payment plans, etc.);
   2. Statistical and demographic data on the extent of poverty in the county and its relationship to poverty levels;
   3. How great the actual need is (needs assessment);
   4. How this need has been met before this time or to what extent?;
   5. Relationships of health care systems to other service organizations in the community, particularly in terms of payment for medical services (e.g., Blue Cross, Medicaid, etc.).

Your instructor may assign you to research the information you need.

Instruction 9.9.D   Specify the Constraints

Several constraints will limit your options in developing the plan. Some are quite obvious (manifest) and can be handled as a matter of course. Others, however, are political. These latent constraints are the more problematic because they require finesse and careful planning strategies.

Constraints are factors that limit your choice of options. They provide a steering mechanism when you begin to judge your possible solutions. Given all the information you have gathered, *what are the critical constraints, both latent and manifest, that you must consider in your plans?*

STOP! Do not go to Feedback 9.9.D until instructed to do so.

Feedback 9.9.D

Time is the first and most obvious constraint. If the plan is not developed within six months, the money is lost. The second major constraint is the consensus requirement. Your plan must convince each member of your board that they will not lose too much with your plan. Skills in communicating, including persuasion, are very important at this point. Because any plan will be harmful in some way to some member of the board or to his or her reference group, you must minimize costs and maximize results. Another constraint, and one with which each social worker must deal, is your own value orientation. You cannot impose your values on your immediate clients, who in this case are the board members. Yet, you cannot forget or compromise your wider values toward clients who will use the health services. Therefore, you must develop a plan as close to the institutional perspective as possible, given board members' values. Moreover, you must determine a strategy based on your expertise that will assure members that their values and wishes are being considered, given the consensus requirement.

Instruction 9.9.E   *Generate Possible Solutions*

We can always brainstorm possible solutions before considering constraints, a valuable method for opening new channels of thinking. However, to save time we will not brainstorm in the true sense—we will not generate ideas that fall beyond the limits of our constraints. Given the information you have gathered and the constraints that limit your options, you can now begin to *generate possible plans for client payment* for health care that, at least in part, satisfy the constraints. Possible plans include

1.

2.

3.

4.

5.

6.

7.

8.

9.

STOP! Do not proceed to Feedback 9.9.E until instructed to do so.

Feedback 9.9.E

Possible solutions range along the continuum from free services to all qualifying clients being charged the total fee and collecting overdue bills by established business methods. They include

1. Free provision of services
2. Partial payment on sliding fee basis, fees same as for private physician
3. Sliding fee scale developed by health center
4. Reduced fees for service, payable at time of service
5. An "insurance" system by which each eligible client buys annual coverage for a set small fee (can be purchased at first time of need)
6. Client billed for total service, grant money used for noncollectibles, billing either at reduced or full rate with collection procedures available for nonpayment
7. Share cost with other provider, as Medicaid, on fifty-fifty basis.
8. Refuse grant and establish no new health center
9. Other

Instruction 9.9.F   Preliminary Evaluation

Rank each possible solution in terms of your own (professional) preference. Define board member values and compare this list with your ordered preferences. Does any solution, or do several, fit rather closely? Decide which are the most *viable alternatives*. List their "selling points" in terms of board member values. *Decide how best to effect a compromise plan.*

1.

2.

3.

4.

5.

6.

7.

8.

9.

STOP! Do not proceed to next feedback until so instructed.

Feedback 9.9.F

1. Free provision of services, although it meets your primary values, would be unacceptable to most people on the board. Even Mrs. Collins believes that there should be some kind of payment for services.

2. Partial payment, sliding fee. This alternative is workable and is a standard fee method, so models are available. It requires that people pay something while recognizing that there are differences in situations. It would be particularly appealing to the medical community, and that is where the power lies on this board. It would also be palatable because the medical community would not be undercut by health center fees.

3. Sliding fee developed by center. Charges are based on ability to pay and can range from nothing to full fee for service. A commonly accepted plan for many kinds of services, there are models available that already have been legitimated. It is, however, a cumbersome method because eligibility is still based on income. It would still satisfy diverse interests and conservatism of board and community, though it is, in a way, stigmatizing. It is easier to explain than the insurance system and might be more acceptable because it has been tried before and because it is "precisely" tied to need rather than approaching the institutional level of service.

4. Reduced fees. This plan recognizes the patients' situations while still requiring some payment. While it would satisfy some board members, the medical community might not like it.

5. The "insurance" system. This is innovative and fits in with many already established values about health care. In the long run it would fill many of the needs of board, community, and clients. Also, because of the popularity of the insurance ideal, it would be appealing to potential clients in terms of their self-respect. It is nonstigmatizing in nature and does not seem cumbersome in terms of application or collection.

6. Clients billed for total fees. This recognizes that some people will be bad debtors and falls into our present model of dealing with bad debts. It entails much bookkeeping and is stigmatizing, but it is a traditional way of dealing with the problem and, therefore, easy to understand and explain; however, it creates a need for further policies on collection that may be detrimental to nonpayers. How does the center treat those who have not paid previous debts? This fits many board values and ties in closely with community values. It has distinct disadvantages concerning client treatment and credit processing.

7. Share the cost. This would be a good partial solution, and one that might be considered at a later time. It would work only for those clients on welfare. It does require working out policies with other agencies, and this means a loss of autonomy and time (a major constraint here).

8. Give up the grant. If health care services are now considered adequate, this could be a viable possibility, especially in view of board values. Still, that is a lot of money to throw away.

9. Other plans should be considered by your instructor.

Instruction 9.9.G   *Analysis*

Your goal to this point has been to develop an acceptable plan, along with consideration of consequences of each of the various alternatives. Now it is time to look at the feasibility of your alternatives. *What are some practical considerations in developing a health center? With what conflicting values will you deal? What political means will sway the board?*

1. Practical considerations: the logistics of setting up a health care center.

2. Conflicting values in use of your expertise.

3. Political considerations that might sway values.

STOP! Do not proceed to feedback until so instructed.

Feedback 9.9.G

A. Practical considerations
   1. Some of the alternatives are too costly in terms of time, money, or complexity of structure. Which are these, and to what extent do these roadblocks make the alternatives infeasible?

   2. The more complex a proposal, the more difficult it is to explain to the board. In this case it is not the complexity of the proposal to worry about but the competence of the presenter.

   3. What are the problems of putting any plan into operation? You have the money, but how will you get medical personnel from the community? How do you get clients? You must be ready to show that the plan you choose has an acceptable policy on these items also.

B. Conflicting values
   1. Your major value is to provide services as near to the institutional model as possible. Yet your values are not those of the board. What are the compromises you must make for the greater good? Do your own values become a major roadblock?

   2. Honesty is an absolute necessity in dealing with others at this level. How can you let board members know your own stance without jeopardizing your project? Can you? Is it necessary?

   3. What are the "hard core" values of the board members? That is, how far are they willing to compromise? What tactics can you use to effect such a compromise?

C. Political considerations. These can be used to sway values. If you know the particular social values of each member, you can also determine the politics of their values and how your expertise can draw out other values they have. Politics are roadblocks viewed one way, tools viewed another.

1. How would each member benefit the most from the health center? How much would it cost each member to have a health center? What plan would minimize costs and maximize benefits to each? To the whole board?

2. Consider the reference groups of each member. How would such groups benefit or lose? What power could be utilized to maximize benefits and minimize cost here? What plan is best for that?

3. Who on the board has the most power, and how can you utilize it? Regular fee schedules (present charges) of local physicians might be forced down by subsidized service, causing backlash and possible nonparticipation of local medical personnel. You need a political perspective—understanding and use of expertise, influence, and power.

There will be no way to get completely free service instituted. What would the loss of $10 million and more mean to the community? To the political elements responsible for the loss? Preventive care saves more money than does remedial care and will provide many nonmonetary benefits to society. How can a compelling case be made for this?

Instruction 9.9.H   Synthesis

The analysis step makes you aware that a great deal of planning expertise is necessary to make your project go. Your job now is to *synthesize your efforts, choosing a plan* best suited, developing it enough to answer board members' questions, *and planning the strategy to ensure consensus of the board* in accepting it. As a group, decide the "best" solution.

STOP! Do not proceed until so instructed.

Feedback 9.9.H

There are two "best" solutions, depending on the way you have analyzed board member values and the politics of implementation. The insurance plan has quite a few selling points: innovative, has not been tried elsewhere, and can be seen as a "bold new program." Appealing to conservatives, it is also innovative in the delivery of clinic services. The insurance model is basic to our social values, implying individuality, self-responsibility, and voluntary participation purchased in advance of need. Still, it takes into account society's responsibility and remediation in cases of poverty. Moreover, the insurance "fee" would not have to approach the real cost for services: The prospective member is not buying the services—he or she is buying membership.

The second solution is the sliding fee scale, which is used in a great many agencies today. It is common, well understood, and usually acceptable even to those who oppose "something for nothing" among the poor.

Instruction 9.9.I   Evaluation

Congratulations on working your way through this difficult process. Write a very short group report analyzing the situation as you see it and showing the wisdom of your choice. The feedback to this instruction is the value you have received from going through the decision-making/problem-solving process, and the experience that can be immediately applied to your social work practice.

Discussion

Having completed this major project, it is important to discuss some of the skills learned from it.

1. What did you learn about strategic planning in terms of compliance or compromise with values outside those which you profess?

2. To what extent are you willing to compromise on your personal or professional values to begin a program such as this? Where are you unwilling to compromise?

3. What have you learned about the nuts and bolts of working on such a project—research, time management, use of resources, group processes, writing a professional paper?

4. What have you learned about analytic skills in the process of this exercise?

Portfolio Building

1. How do you define and differentiate problem, policy, and program?

2. What is the connection of values to policy?

3. Can you now reformulate a policy?

4. Why should social workers working at any level understand policy?

5. How do you analyze a policy?

6. What more do you need to know about social welfare policies and their uses in the social work profession?

Concluding Remarks

As you have seen, the exercises in our workbook span a wide range of practice skills and tasks. The workbook is not, nor was it intended to be, an all-inclusive compendium. Rather, it relies highly on your instructor for information and choices and on the various problems, social settings, and individual tasks and skills necessary to generalist practice in social work. We hope that the exercises have been helpful to you and that they have helped you to bridge the gap between being a social work student and being a social work practitioner. We also hope that the exercises have given you new creative insights into the simultaneous dimensions of social work practice—particularly relational and cognitive knowledge and skills and congruent issues of policy practice and interpersonal practice. Good luck in your professional career.

Notes

1. See Chapter 2. Remember, major societal values are:

   Judeo-Christian ethic
   Protestant work ethic
   Puritan morality
   Social Darwinism
   Patriarchy
   Individualism
   Democratic egalitarianism
   Capitalism
   American ideal

2. A "function" is a purpose or use. Manifest functions—obvious purposes—are usually written into policies or program guidelines. Latent functions, or hidden uses, are not written and may benefit certain elite groups of society by maintaining values favorable to the status quo. If a program or policy continues even if it seems detrimental to clients, it probably has latent functions.
3. Welfare drug testing Okd (March 26, 1998). Chicago: *Chicago Tribune*, p. 3.
4. Tough "one-strike" drug policy leaving some tenants homeless (April 3, 1998). Richmond, IN: *The Palladium Item*, p. A8.
5. Nursing Home Center Facing $360,000 Fine (1998, April 11). Chicago: *Chicago Tribune*, p. 8.
6. Taken from an idea by David Gil (1976). *Unraveling Social Policy*. Cambridge, MA: Schenkman Publishing Co., pp. 59–61.

FIGURE 9.1.   *The Policy Continuum Revisited*

PROBLEM	*POLICY*	*PROGRAM*
A lot of people think something is a problem	They develop and enact a solution for the problem	They set up methods to carry out the solution (policy).
Each problem has a context and a set of values that may be different from those of policy or program	Each policy has a context and a set of values that may be different from those of problem or program	Each program has a context and a set of values that may be different from those of problem or policy
Example: mothers on welfare	Example: TANF law	Example: Workfare
Context: What social, economic, political factors happened in our past that we consider mothers on welfare a problem?	*Context*: What political, social, economic factors influenced passage of TANF?	*Context*: Why is TANF politically feasible today? What manifest and latent functions does it have for society?
Discrimination against women; need for more jobs for men; end of war. *Values*: What societal value most accurately applies to this problem? *Patriarchy.*	*Republican majority in congress; conservative values against women and workers.* *Values*: What values were incorporated in TANF? *Protestant work ethic, patriarchy.*	*Fewer workers are needed because of computers and robotics. Workers cut into net profit. TANF does not train them for work but will get rid of their expense.*
		Values: Protestant work ethic favored over Judaeo-Christian charity values.

Glossary

Client system A person, group, or organization (or larger system) agreeing to be helped by the worker in alleviating a self-defined problem.

Competence Ability to be effective in one's environment.

Direct services A set of activities aimed at and involving a client system.

Empowerment Making surrounding systems more responsive, addressing the power differential, and assisting clients to exert their personal, political, and economic power.

Indirect services Activities that result in influencing others on behalf of a client system or population-at-risk.

Person as political Any situation that derives from values or policies has an affect on personal lives and in terms of social work practice. What seem to be personal problems are very often the result of political action. Conversely, political processes impact on and alter personal interactions causing oppression and social injustice.

Person in environment In the ecological perspective, the person or client system must be considered within the context of its environment, for human beings are in constant interchange with all elements of their environment.

Population-at-risk The larger aggregate of systems grappling with some common problem situation. From the viewpoint of working with the client system, it is a *parallel population-at-risk* in that it includes *only* those people, groups, or organizations that are within the target system's concern.

Resilience Skills, abilities, knowledge, and insight that accumulates over time as people struggle to surmount adversity and meet challenges.

Target system Those who must be influenced to promote or not impede action on behalf of the client system but who have not agreed to be "helped."